The Making of the Modern World

The Making of the Modern World

An Introductory History

R.T. Robertson

Zed Books Ltd.
London and New Jersey

The Making of the Modern World was first published under the
title *The Contemporary Era* by the University of the
South Pacific Extension Services, PO Box 1168, Suva, Fiji, in
1984. This revised and expanded edition was first published by
Zed Books Ltd., 57 Caledonian Road, London N1 9BU, UK,
and 171 First Avenue, Atlantic Highlands, New Jersey 07716,
USA, in 1986.

Cover designed by Andrew Corbett
Printed and bound in the United Kingdom
at The Bath Press, Avon.

British Library Cataloguing in Publication Data

Robertson, R.T.
  The making of the modern world: an
  introductory history.
  1. History, Modern
  I. Title
  909.8   D299

  ISBN 0-86232-461-0
  ISBN 0-86232-462-9 Pbk

Contents

Figures

FOR JULIAN
AND IN MEMORY OF
PHILIP ALLEY

Foreword

One of the critical needs of history in the late twentieth century, particularly as taught in the Third World, is to escape the political and cultural biases inherited from colonial pasts and the contemporary ideological pressures exerted from the metropolitan core. Too often relationships between and within countries are taken for granted, with the unfortunate result that transformations are rarely accorded the depth and global analysis they require. Invariably history becomes something that can be transcended, confined to the past by a grand sweep of intent, and bearing little relationship with noble visions of order, prosperity and freedom. Perhaps ironically the historian's own self-imposed role as the supposedly unbiased recorder of events bears some responsibility for this sorry state of history. Unable to glimpse their own position within the dialectic they seek to describe, far too many historians have been shy of breaking prescribed bounds, of being deliberately provocative, or questioning the ideological assumptions of their societies. And yet it has never been more imperative that they should do so. The time has surely come when historians must stop playing "the cheerful idiot" (to paraphrase C. Wright Mills) when "to cry for 'the constructive programme' and 'the hopeful note'" is recognized for what it usually is, "an incapacity to face facts as they are even when they are decidedly unpleasant".[1]

Change within any society has rarely been rational. Perhaps for that reason alone, notions of progress have assumed linear dimensions as the march of civilization, particular manifest destinies or models for emulation. Certainly these have been and are important concepts of history which have shaped people's thoughts and actions. Indeed this is one reason why our study has focused on European, Japanese and American imperialisms. But such notions fail to accommodate the setbacks, the disappointments and irrationalities which have so often frustrated the "forward march of progress." And, if we are to be truthful, it is these very failures or unintended consequences that have always proved most troublesome for analysts of the past and social scientists alike, particularly when they conflict with strongly held convictions or ideological positions. What ardent supporter of "free enterprise" and "democracy" wishes to reveal the contradictory reality of capitalism and its drift towards greater and less controllable crises, what fervent nationalist does not seek to hide nationalism's often irrational character by resort to individualism or concepts of demonic forces, and indeed what staunch socialist does not attempt to escape the failures of many socialist states to march resolutely and confidently into the communist future? Who among us has not at some time sought to shrug off the unpleasant in the hope that it is but an aberration, temporary, and best passed over with proper speed? If this has been true of the contemporary apologists for imperialism, Stalinism, and neocolonial modernization, to give but a few examples, then it has been equally true of the many historians who have sought to describe these movements or their various parts. By placing themselves outside of the historical process, by claiming objectivity, they have succeeded only in obscuring their own biases and deep commitments.

The constant process of reaction, adaptation and transformation that has shaped our contemporary era will always remain the core of historical debate and confusion. Yet it is vitally important that this fact be recognized, for undoubtedly it has become one of the major distinguishing features of our time. Developments during the late 19th and 20th centuries —the focus of this study—should at least force upon us the realization that we do live on one globe and that, regardless of political, economic and social differences, we are all linked together through a variety of different mechanisms—whether these be simply vague awarenesses of common experience or more formal class, national or international organizations. Two hundred years ago no such wide mechanisms existed. The first task of any contemporary historian must be to accommodate the growing interrelationships among the world's various parts. There seems no better way of accomplishing this than by according primacy to the role of modern capitalism. From the diverse and contradictory development of industrial capitalism, at first in Western Europe, and from its articulation with less developed modes of production have sprung all subsequent transformations. Here lie the roots of contemporary imperialism, of international and superpower conflict, of nationalist movements, and of the continuing struggle for political and economic decolonization, to name but a few of the major historical concerns we will survey.

Here too lie the roots of the confusion which has bedevilled historical work. Because what is being described is so recent, it has not been easy to perceive the general outline and structure of the process of change. To the Victorians capitalism was synonymous with progress within Europe and North America. Perhaps grudgingly it might have been considered a Japanese phenomenon as well. But it was hardly considered a global process. Today, however, there are few places to which it has not been extended, and, as Tom Nairn has described, that spreading has produced its own confusion.

Capitalism has indeed unified humanity's history and made the world one. But it has done so at the cost of fantastic disequilibria, through near catastrophic antagonisms and a process of socio-political fragmentation (numbering 154 states at the latest count) still far from complete. The momentum of the conflictual phenomena denoted by 'uneven development' has so far proved greater than the other more unitary and rational tendencies of capitalism's growth. They and all their ambiguous progeny have become lodged in the resultant global order.[2]

What we, as students of the contemporary era, have to accommodate then is not just the importance of the growth of capitalism but also its accompanying dialectic of uneven development, for it is within the latter that we can place the power of ideology, imperialism, nationalism and the crucial issues of Third World development.

Indeed these twin concerns have most informed the structure and content of this book, from the initial descriptions of capitalism and imperialism to their subsequent transformations and the various responses those changes evoked—the search for socialist alternatives, the containment or escalation of international rivalry, decolonization and neocolonization, and changing strategies for industrialization. Only twice has it been considered necessary to devote an entire chapter to one country (Japan and the United States) in order to illustrate more fully these concerns. For the remainder of the work a more synthetical approach has been used to examine the major characteristics of the contemporary era and the transformations it has undergone, and to illustrate that change can be studied without assigning to it any finality or transcending nature. It is also hoped that this work will demonstrate the relevance and importance of historical study for accommodating the present and enabling the evaluation of future strategies.

Many people contributed variously to the writing of this book from the time of its inception in discussions with my colleague Brij Lal. Sabbatical leave from the University of the South Pacific during 1983 enabled me to gather material and ideas from people and institutions in Japan, China, Thailand, the Netherlands and Britain, and of these special mention should be made of the Chinese People's Association (CPAFFC), the Institute of Social Studies and the University of Sussex. My colleagues Alan Robson and William Sutherland, helpful and generous in their comments and time spent assisting me, also need special mention, as do those who helped prepare the original manuscript and bore the brunt of pressures of time—Marie, Urmila and Christine.

Notes

1. Quoted in J.W. Dower (ed.),*Origins of the Modern Japanese State, Selected Writings of E.H. Norman*, Pantheon, New York, 1975, p. 56.
2. T. Nairn, *The Break-Up of Britain, Crisis and Neo-Nationalism*, Verso, London, 1981, p. 356.

List of Abbreviations

ACP	Africa Caribbean Pacific
ASEAN	Association of South East Asian Nations
CER	Closer Economic Relations
CIA	Central Intelligence Agency
COMECAN	Council for Mutual Economic Aid
ECLA	United Nations Economic Commission for Latin America
ECOWAS	Economic Community of West African States
EEC	European Economic Community
ESAPTA	Eastern-Southern Africa Preferential Trade Area
GATT	General Agreement on Tariffs and Trade
GNP	Gross National Product
GSP	Generalized System of Preferences
IDA	International Development Agency
ILO	International Labour Organization
IMF	International Monetary Fund
LDCs	Less Developed Countries
NATO	North Atlantic Treaty Organization
NEP	New Economic Policy
NICs	Newly Industralized Countries
NIEO	New International Economic Order
NSC	National Security Council
OECD	Organization for Economic Cooperation and Development
OEEC	Organization for European Economic Cooperation
OPEC	Organizaton of Petroleum Exporting Countries
SADCC	Southern African Development Coordination Conference
SCAP	Supreme Commander of the Allied Powers
SDRs	Special Drawing Rights
SEZ	Special Export Zone
SPARTECA	South Pacific Regional Trade and Economic Cooperation Agreement
SPD	Social Democrat Party
TNCs	Transnational Corporations
UN	United Nations
UNCTAD	United Nations Conference on Trade and Development
USA (US)	United States of America
USSR	Union of Soviet Socialist Republics

1. Contemporary History

Perspectives

In 1889, one hundred years after the French Revolution had swept away the vestiges of feudalism, a new monument was erected in Paris. It was a huge industrial structure, a phallic summation of the wealth and power industrial technology seemed to promise. For the millions who made the journey to its top, a new perspective of their city awaited them. From the Eiffel Tower they could see Paris laid out in a way that today's air travellers take for granted. In the late nineteenth century, however, this was a new revolutionary and mass experience.[1] The world had not grown smaller; rather technology allowed more of it to be accommodated wtihin a man's field of vision than before. Perhaps more importantly, the Tower demonstrated that the French nation could count itself among the possessors of that new and potentially limitless technology.

Industrialization in the nineteenth century transformed the social and political structures of Europe and provided its states with an all encompassing power that only a century before would have seemed unimaginable. Clearly a new age had dawned for mankind, or so many middle class Europeans believed. With Europe's expansion unchallengeable and the applications of science unlimited, the future of the world seemed bright and assured. Arnold Toynbee reflected:

> The celebrations of Queen Victoria's Diamond Jubilee in 1897 called to mind the history of the preceding sixty years and this retrospect opened up a view of the whole of history which looked clear and simple. Between 1837 and 1897 the West had completed the establishment of its ascendancy over the rest of the world . . . Apparently history had reached its denouement in the political unification of Italy and Germany in 1871 if 'history' was synonymous, as in 1897 many people assumed it was, with the alarums and excursions of the Western Civilization's turbulent past that, within living memory, had been left behind.[2]

This optimism and belief that the power Europe had gathered for herself was a manifestation of the superiority of Western Civilization, imbued her traders, missionaries, soldiers and politicians with a sense of historical mission. Jules Harmand, the *commissaire-général* in Tonkin (French Indochina), wrote in 1910 that superiority imposed strict obligations.

> The basic legitimation of conquest over native peoples is the conviction of our superiority, not merely our mechanical, economic, and military superiority, but our moral superiority. Our dignity rests on that quality, and it underlies our right to direct the rest of humanity. Material power is nothing but a means to that end. [3]

A brave new world was in the making and nothing could be allowed to thwart its evolution, not even the objections of traditionally self-sufficient peoples who in ignorance saw little to distinguish Europe's civilizing destiny in any meaningful way from exploitative imperialist expansion.

When, for example, the British decided in the 1840s to extend forcibly the sale of opium to the Chinese in order to redress in their favour the balance of trade between the two countries and to secure new markets for their industrial commodities, the American John Adams justified British aggression in the following way.

> The moral obligation of commercial intercourse between nations is founded entirely . . . upon the Christian precept to love your neighbour as yourself . . . But China, not being a Christian nation, its inhabitants do not consider themselves bound by the Christian precept...[Therefore] the fundamental principle of the Chinese nation is anticommercial . . . It admits no obligation to hold commercial intercourse with others . . . It is time that this enormous outrage upon the rights of human nature, and upon the first principles of the rights of nations should cease. [4]

Progress demanded that those who claimed to possess a higher state of development should have automatic access to all parts of the world and a right to the resources that access revealed. China's reluctance to trade, therefore, was an unacceptable affront to the march of civilization.

Europeans displayed the same self-righteousness and confidence thirty years later when Britain took control of the Pacific islands of Fiji. "Fijian history, as recounted by native tradition", they declared, "may be said to have begun with the advent of the white race." [5] Empire brought civilization to the backward peoples of the world. With the vast resources increasingly at its command, the British Empire seemed capable of absorbing vast tracts of the world and ensuring their positive transformation into mirror images of the motherland. Who could doubt that on such a noble Empire the sun would never set? "God has not been preparing the English-speaking and Teutonic peoples for a thousand years for nothing", wrote US Senator Albert Beveridge in 1903. "No! He has made us the master organizers of the world to establish system where chaos reigns. He has made us adept in government that we may administer government among savage and servile peoples." [6]

The European conception of contemporary history and its faith in a new millennium did not long survive the opening of the twentieth century. Bitter intracore rivalry for imperialist goals and the onslaught of two world wars destroyed forever Europe's belief in her infallibility. As the century wore on the promise of industry had also to be substantially qualified. Its polluting destructiveness and inability to resolve problems of poverty amidst plenty did not make for a brave new world. Nearly ninety years after the Paris World Fair had celebrated the dynamics of capital, the Club of Rome published a gloomy forecast of catastrophe. Having already accepted that industry could be used to contrive such atrocities as Auschwitz, Hiroshima and My Lai, Westerners were informed that their hitherto unchallenged belief in industry's potential for unlimited growth was without foundation.

Nor was this all. After 1945 the hegemony once enjoyed by Europe had fallen firmly to the United States of America, but this change brought little of the peace or stability anticipated. American fears of Soviet and socialist challenges precipitated a series of confrontations and wars and revived the time-worn statements of Western righteousness. US Secretary of State, John Foster Dulles, declared in 1953 that his country's aggressive foreign policy reflected a new moral duty. "Any nation", he argued in the manner of John Adams and Jules Harmand, "which bases its institutions on Christian principles cannot but be a dynamic nation."[7] The high cost of sustaining American hegemony, together with the impact of increased Japanese and European economic competition, bore heavily on the over-committed US economy and precipitated the first major world recession in forty years. By the 1970s, therefore, the brief reassertion of Western confidence was largely over. The high hopes held for the development of countries emerging from the yoke of empire had, by this time, also mostly evaporated. Political independence had not automatically produced peaceful prosperity, nor compliance with metropolitan policies. Instead an increasingly demanding Third World had emerged which seemed able, at least in the instance of the OPEC countries, to threaten the economic security of all oil-dependent countries.

With the past certainties gone, historians began to reconsider their own role in evaluating contemporary events. Affected by the gloom of the Oikoumêne in crisis during the 1970s, Arnold Toynbee wrote:

> Our view of the relations of past events to each other, of their relative importance, and of their significance, changes constantly in consequence of the constant change of the fugitive present. The same past viewed in the same country by the same person, first in 1897 and then in 1973, presents two different pictures; and no doubt the self-same past will look still more different when viewed in China in 2073 and even more different again when viewed in Nigeria in 2173.[8]

All histories and social analyses are the result of an interaction between the researcher and his material. They cannot escape the inevitable inclusion of personal biases, class perspectives and dominant contemporary preoccupations. One has only to examine the insular histories of Europe and the United States, even of many independent countries in Africa, Asia and the Pacific Basin, to discover nationalistic or imperialistic purpose. Histories are a reflection of how people at a certain place and point in time view their past or the past of other peoples, an illustration of what Toynbee termed "the constant change of the fugitive present". Geoffrey

Barraclough argued in the mid-1960s that there would always be a major difference in approach between the historian who takes a stand in 1715, for instance, and proceeds to work through events as they occur in order to discover their logic, and the contemporary historian whose starting point is really at the end of the period under study. The differences in perspective which so mark the work of contemporary historians and analysts are due not to their lack of distance from the events under investigation but to their primary concern to explain the origins of the present framework. "Contemporary history", Barraclough maintained, "begins when the problems which are actual in the world today first take visible shape." [9] The notion that history is an objective and scientific study "for its own sake" has no place in contemporary history.

Nationalism

At the global level the difficulties confronting contemporary historians are a measure of the growing complexity of international relationships. First, the historian faces a multiplicity of varied and changing circumstances which defies simple generalization. Even the usage of terms such as the First, Second or Third Worlds must be qualified by cognizance of the vast differences within each hypothetical set of countries which automatically restricts their individual adherence to any group norm. Second, contemporary historians must acknowledge that increased global economic integration has considerably narrowed the gap between national and international studies. It is not just the case that the two fields can no longer be accepted as separate, but that international and national events are so interlinked that it is impossible to distinguish clearly the origins of one from the other. This is particularly obvious when dealing with the Third World, the one-time colonial periphery of a core of metropolitan nations. "Change in the Third World", Ian Roxborough wrote in 1979, "is primarily the consequence of the externalization of West European capital through the formation of a world market and through various forms of imperialism and colonialism." [10] Where exogenous factors have reshaped internal structures, it is difficult to analyse national developments without reference to the international setting in which they took place. Modes of production and structures are both internally and externally articulated (interrelated). We may refer generally to the historical processes involved, but less easily in respect of particular instances.

The effects of global integration have not always been acknowledged by historians. Too often they have consciously or unconsciously accepted notions of Western superiority and bestowed upon contemporary developments geographic and cultural biases that reflected their own preoccupations rather than reality. For instance, numerous studies of modern nationalism have, on the basis of chronology and Western experience, implied the development of a natural and indigenous force which was exported to the world by means of European ideology, culture and values.

Awakened initially by the French Revolution, nationalism forced the unification of Italy and Germany and the disintegration of Austria-Hungary, and eventually drove colonial inhabitants to seek independence from the metropolitan countries which dominated them. Not unnaturally the very Eurocentricity of this interpretation has produced a prolonged debate on the origins of nationalism, much of which fails to acknowledge that contemporary nationalism emerged as a response, varied though it may have been, to the transformation effected by capitalism. Feelings of loyalty to a nation on the basis of geography, language and culture were not new; they were as prominent in the pre-industrial development of Japan, Thailand and China as they were in Britain and France. What was new in the contemporary era were the uses to which such feelings could be put as a direct result of the consolidation or penetration of the new mode of production. In many respects nationalism came to represent an emotional equivalent of industrialization's economic integration, generating mass support for a state's modernization policies or imperialist plans, or justifying the independence of a new state whose existence was simply the accident of imperial history.

The failure of many historians to locate nationalism within the transformations effected by the growth and spread of industrial capitalism has, as Tom Nairn recently described, resulted in many odd distortions.

> Most approaches to the question are vitiated from the start by a country-by-country attitude. Of course, it is the ideology of world nationalism itself which induces us along this road, by suggesting that human society consists essentially of several hundred different and discrete 'nations', each of which has its own postage stamps and national soul. The secret of the forest is the trees, so to speak. Fortunately this is just the usual mangled half-truth of common sense. [11]

If nationalism was really a natural product of native peculiarities and a necessary stage of development, there still remained the difficulty of accommodating its less progressive or rational examples, the most well known being Nazi Germany. Were these to be regarded simply as demonic exceptions to the nationalism rule or alternatively as the forerunners of future capitalist institutions? [12] Or should we, as Nairn recommends, regard nationalism as a response to the dialectic of uneven development, a Janus-like process that has propelled nations (more particularly their dominant classes) both to resist and accommodate change by means of the rhetoric of nationalism. In the Third World this often initially entailed

> the conscious formation of a militant, inter-class community rendered strongly (if not mythically) aware of its own separate identity vis-à-vis the outside forces of domination . . . Mobilization had to be in terms of what was there; and the whole point of the dilemma was that there was nothing there—none of the economic and political institutions of modernity now so needed. All that there *was* was the people and peculiarities of the region; its inherited ethnos, speech, folklore, skin colour, and so on . . . The new middle class intelligentsia of nationalism had to invite the masses into history and the invitation card had to be written in a language they understood. [13]

Nationalism, therefore, was and is the manifestation of a changing set of inputs, often both endogenous and exogenous in origin, and their varied articulation. As such it cannot be examined in isolation from wider global transformations nor confined simply to the logic of insular national or linearly progressive developments. It is an ongoing process of reaction and adaptation firmly located within the development process. In India, for example, a middle class—itself largely the product of colonial transformation—gradually developed an independence movement which combined the grievances of the peasantry with new nationalist sentiment. But its successful attainment of independence did not mean that the concept of a nation was well developed. India, like many other newly independent countries, had to reorient nationalism away from its predominant anti-imperialist stance and emphasize nation-building in order to prevent class, religious or tribal divisions from frustrating national unity. Success has been elusive, partly as a result of the very transformation effected by its own development policies. Because the nature of these policies has been shaped by the historical process of imperialist domination and by the continued imperatives of capitalism, India has been unable to prevent the continued disorganization of her economy and the inevitable distortions and inequalities which breed internal unrest in a number of different forms.

Distorted social formation and economic relations within many countries that were subordinated to the interests of a metropolitan core have produced various ethnic, racial or tribal micronationalisms which reflect the uneven character of the transformation experienced. Dissatisfaction among minorities is representative of their perceived failure to attain the prosperity or equality expected. To the extent that they regard their own development as inferior to those parts of the economy integrated with metropolitan capital, their protests are in effect cries for equality. In this way ethnic and racial nationalism often assumes the characteristics of a class struggle, its adherents regarding themselves as members of a distinct "out-class".[14] The more deprived they feel, the more the culturally assimilating tendencies of nation-building appear to threaten them, with their own annihilation as the final injustice. In desperation, therefore, many cling tenaciously to the only certainties remaining to them—their past and their culture. The struggle of minorities, whether Sikhs in India, Aboriginals and Maoris in Australasia, or Amerindians in North America, is in many respects similar to that of the Third World in the global economy. Participants in both know only too well that the nationalism (or development strategy) which succeeds provides its own justification; that which fails is doomed to incorporation and servitude.

Defining Contemporary History

In the last decade Alan Bullock subtitled his edited history of the twentieth century "A Promethean Age" because he believed the widening gap between promise and reality revealed a frustrated revolution in expectations. [15] Indeed in 1956 the Chinese Communist Party had raised the same point when it declared that the major problem facing China was the contradiction "between the demand of the people for rapid economic and cultural development and the existing state of our economy and culture which fell short of the needs of the people". [16] In acknowledging the existence of contradictions within the process of development, analysts and historians brought us closer to accommodating the diversity of change within the contemporary era. But without a down-to-earth theory of social change, these contradictions were often dismissed as isolated occurrences or irrelevant when compared with the grander sweep of history. In a manner similar to the late 19th century European historians, development theorists in the 1950s and 1960s described periods of take-off when countries would shake off the shackles of past economic patterns and emerge as fully-fledged industrial and capitalist nations. "The new manifest destiny", wrote Harry Magdoff in 1971, "the manifest destiny of our times is the responsibility to teach the heathens the art of economics, so that these poor peoples can also become healthy, wealthy and wise." [17] Once more, it seemed, history could be transcended, this time by the adoption of modernization policies.

At no time, of course, can people escape the relationships of past and present and simply transcend history. Long before imperialists and revolutionaries in the twentieth century espoused such a view in order to generate support, Karl Marx in an often quoted paragraph described their actual impotence as supreme creators.

> Men make their own history, but they do not make it just as they please; they do not make it under circumstances chosen by themselves, but under circumstances directly encountered, given and transmitted from the past. The tradition of all dead generations weighs like a nightmare on the brain of the living. And just when they seem engaged in revolutionizing themselves and things, in creating something that has never yet existed, precisely in such periods of revolutionary crisis they anxiously conjure up the spirits of the past to their service and borrow from them names, battle cries and costumes in order to present the new scene of world history in this time-honoured disguise and this borrowed language. [18]

Past traditions and relations have defined the possibilities for change. They have also contributed to the nonlinear and uneven developments that form the basis for Bullock's frustrated revolution in expectations, and provide a further example of the Janus-character of modern transformation that we encountered earlier in Nairn's description of nationalism.

The contemporary historian must, therefore, avoid assigning to changes a completeness or finality which they can never enjoy. However, he or she can argue, as Barraclough did, that it is possible to delineate major turning points by defining what was new and different about them. In arguing that 1890 should be taken as marking a divide between modern and contemporary history, Barraclough admitted that there existed no sharp dividing line between one period and another, but still maintained:

> When we seek to identify the forces which set the new trends in motion, the factors which stand out are the industrial and social revolutions in the later years of the nineteenth century and the "new imperialism" which was so clearly associated with it . . . [I]t is only by distinguishing what was new and revolutionary in them—in other words, by emphasizing the differences between the "first" and "second" industrial revolutions and between the "old" and "new" imperialism—that we can expect to measure the full consequence of their impact. [19]

Yet behind these structural changes lay a more gradual but equally revolutionary transformation. This fact, Tom Kemp maintains, must never be distant from the concerns of the contemporary historian.

> As some historians have observed, Europe, or rather its most advanced regions, became the core countries in a world economic system in which other areas made up the periphery. The starting point of change, however, is to be found, not in the expansion of trade and the opening up of new markets, but rather in the transformation of social relations in the leading European countries. This transformation, which had been going on for some time, had begun to assume a more decisive form in the course of the sixteenth century. The change, which can be briefly summed up as the rise of capitalism, provided the means and the impetus for overseas expansion and prepared the way for the transformation of production and the transition from an agrarian to an industrial society. [20]

It is impossible to understand the logic of contemporary developments without first examining closely the transformation which occurred during the 19th century, which radically altered the nature of industry and imperialism, and without relating such transformation to the general development of capitalism.

The forces which were so revolutionary were not of course events. One cannot for instance maintain that the invention of the spinning jenny revolutionized the textile industry. Its application may have had profound effects but was only possible because of a prior change in the division of labour. We can learn more, therefore, from examining the forces which altered the mode of production than in the detailed examination of one event. The emphasis rests on the process of change, not on isolated and seemingly startling events. By means of such analysis we also avoid the kind of distorted perspective that in the past assigned pre-eminence to one or more of the major powers. The tendency "to dwell on those aspects of the history of the period which have their roots in the old world", Barraclough argued, only makes understanding change more difficult.

> We shall find more clues, for example, in Nkrumah's autobiography than in Eden's memoirs, more points of contact in the world of Mao or Nehru than in that of Coolidge and Baldwin; and it is important to remember that, while

Mussolini and Hitler were prancing and posturing at the centre of the European stage, changes were going on in the wide world which contributed more fundamentally than they did to the shape of things to come.[21]

Only by devising a framework for analysis which accommodates both the diversity of social structures and their relationships, and the transformations to which they have been subjected, can contemporary historians begin to free themselves from the distortions and political biases that in the past have so often limited the value of their work.

In this short history we have selected a number of topics that specifically illustrate the constant process of transformation. These are not presented as definitive accounts; indeed time and space has forced us to keep our discussion at an extremely general level. Nevertheless, we believe that the framework provided should enable undergraduate students to tackle detailed examinations of individual countries with more confidence and with more understanding of the interplay of contemporary forces. The study begins with a short account of industrialization, in particular the transition to and impact of a new mode of production. The consolidation and expansion of capitalism at the global level and the transformations this in turn generated are examined further within the context of imperialism. By the beginning of the present century, the transition to capitalism had provided European countries with a pressing need to expand globally and to transform for their own purposes the colonies they so acquired. Integration necessitated economic, social and political transformation. More than anything else this characteristic of change has distinguished the contemporary era from previous ones, and, while for a time it bestowed upon Europeans a sense of supreme power and confidence which was often thought of as a historical mission, it also guaranteed the rise of new forces that would destabilize and in turn transform their cherished world order.

Indeed, capital's need to remain competitive produced changes in the structure and technology of industry which served to widen the impact of imperialism and intensify social and economic transformation in the countries that were integrated with the expanding metropolitan-based world economy. At the same time, however, the process of transformation was accelerated further by competition between the industrialized powers themselves. Increasingly prepared to take advantage of their new ability to mobilize national (and colonial) resources for aggressive purposes, the European states twice sought competitive advantage over their rivals by resorting to war. These were not isolated or restricted affairs; the extent and nature of European activities ensured that they rapidly became global in character and impact. The importance of intracore conflict is examined in Chapter 4.

The development of socialism, both as a reaction to the transformation effected by expanding capitalist relations and as a response to imperialism has been accorded a chapter of its own. Socialism was not unique to the contemporary era, but like nationalism developed certain characteristics that were a direct result of the transformation societies underwent in the nineteenth century. The emergence of socialist states opposed to the dominance of capitalist relations, at first only Russia but after 1945 including also the countries of Eastern Europe, China, North Korea, Vietnam and Cuba, provided a new challenge that profoundly affected intracore and core-periphery relations. At first the states of the industrialized core feared that Soviet propaganda might revolutionize unrest among their own proletariat; indeed such fears were partly responsible for the swing to the right in many European countries during the interwar years. But it was not until after the Second World War that socialism—particularly its Russian Stalinist form—presented a threat of a different kind to the capitalist core by attracting the attention of many Third World countries and liberation movements.

The core's response to socialist and Third World developments was conditioned also by changes within the core itself. In this study two of these changes have been singled out for special attention, first, the nature of Japanese industrialization and its impact on intracore relations, and second, the American attainment of global hegemony at the close of the Second World War and its attempts to consolidate a new world order. At the same time, however, the position of the Third World within that order began to change. The inability of the European powers to sustain their old empires, pressure from the United States to reduce Europe's privileged access to its periphery, the growth of indigenous nationalist movements seeking independence, and the spread of socialist ideologies increasingly transformed relations between the core nations and their once compliant colonies. In Chapter Eight we examine the nature of those relations and their impact on social formation in the Third World itself, the two factors which have most determined the character of development since decolonization. These relations and the impact of further transformation within the First and Second Worlds since the late 1960s are the subject of the final chapter.

The single most important feature of the contemporary era has been the consolidation and expansion of the world capitalist system. No states and no peoples have remained unaffected by this remarkable transformation. At different times and in different places the mechanisms and nature of global integration have varied, shaped as much by the changing character of international capital as by reactions to it. Integration (and the transformations effected) has not been an even process. The contradictions it has generated have aroused frustrations and disappointments in a number of different forms and under a number of different labels. Yet their manifestations as various imperialisms, nationalisms, or socialisms should serve to remind the contemporary historian of the all-pervasive and inescapable character of modern integration. No country can stand alone. No peoples can remove themselves from their past or seek to deny the reality of present world circumstances. Undoubtedly the struggle for equality proceeds apace with transformations and will remain the major preoccupation of the world in the decades to come. But at no time can the effects of integration and transformations within the world order be simply pushed aside and history transcended.

Notes

1. Robert Hughes, *The Shock of the New, Art and the Century of Change*, BBC, London, 1980, pp. 10-14.
2. Arnold Toynbee, *Mankind and Mother Earth*, Oxford University Press, 1976, p. vii.
3. Jules Harmond, *Domination et Colonisation*, Paris, 1910 quoted in H. Alavi and T. Shanin (eds.), *The Sociology of 'Developing Societies'*, Macmillan, London, 1982, p. 74.
4. Cited in Harry Magdoff, *The Age of Imperialism, The Economics of US Foreign Policy*, Monthly Review Press (MRP), New York, 1969, p. 174.
5. *The Colony of Fiji*, Suva, 1924, p. 8.
6. A.Beveridge, *The Russian Advance*, New York, 1903, quoted in Alavi and Shanin, p. 74.
7. Dulles, "Faith of Our Fathers", 1954, quoted in J.K. Galbraith, *The Age of Uncertainty*, Andre Deutsch, London, 1977, p. 238.
8. Toynbee, p. 589.
9. Geoffrey Barraclough, *An Introduction to Contemporary History*, Penguin, Harmondsworth, 1967, pp. 15, 20.
10. Ian Roxborough, *Theories of Underdevelopment*, Macmillan, London, 1979, p. 42.
11. T.Nairn, p. 332.
12. Ibid., p. 350.
13. Ibid., p. 340.
14. Donna Awatere, "Alliances with Pacific Island People, White Women, the Trade Union Movement and the Left", *Broadsheet*, October 1982, pp. 24-9.
15. Alan Bullock, "A Promethean Age", in A. Bullock (ed.), *The Twentieth Century*, Thames and Hudson, London, 1971, pp. 26-7.
16. "Resolution on Certain Questions in the History of Our Party since the Founding of the People's Republic of China", 6th Plenary Session of the 11th Central Committee of the Communist Party of China (CPC), 27 June 1981, in *Resolution on CPC History, 1949-1981*, Beijing, 1981, p. 23.
17. H. Magdoff, "Economic Myths and Imperialism", in *Imperialism: From the Colonial Age to the Present, Essays by Harry Magdoff*, MRP, New York, 1978, p. 151.
18. Karl Marx, *The Eighteenth Brumaire of Louis Bonaparte*, Progress Publishers, Moscow, 1953, p. 10.
19. Barraclough, p. 25.
20. Tom Kemp, *Industrialization in the Non-Western World*, Longman, London, 1983, p. 2.
21. Barraclough, p. 36.

2. Industrialization

Phenomenon or Process?

The process of industrialization[1] has been examined with renewed interest in recent decades as many newly independent Third World countries have sought to replicate the Western experience. At first it was assumed by many analysts that the mere fulfilment of certain prerequisites would permit self-sustained takeoff into a new era of prosperity and growth. First, it was necessary for nations to transform rural relations in such a way as to allow agriculture to accumulate capital for industrial investment and to enable the development of a strong internal market capable of consuming industry's products. This latter task was dependent upon the ability of labour to consume, in other words it was tied to the standard of living. Second, it was necessary to ensure the dominance of the new mode of production. Wherever possible industry should be urban-based and oriented towards large-scale factory and machine production. Third, if internal markets or the availability of resources did not permit rapid industrial expansion, industrialization could proceed by shifting to export production, the assumption being that given the existence of a range of countries with similar standards of living, one could expect the development of a single world economy in which trade between countries was based on equal exchange.

The failure of Third World countries to take off into self-sustained growth sparked off a major controversy. What had gone wrong? Apologists for the major industrialized countries argued that Third World people lacked the necessary entrepreneurial skills to develop a successful industrial base or that their governments had failed to transform adequately agrarian relations and establish a viable expanding internal market which industry could service. In these various arguments (which we shall examine in more detail in Chapter 8), one basic assumption predominated—that the development of the Western industrial nations provided a model which the rest of the world could follow and profit from. After all, industrialization was a simple and natural phenomenon that could be easily replicated at any place or point of time. History, it was assumed, had proved this. Japan,

North America, and Europe had at various stages profited from the initial example of Great Britain.

A number of points need to be made clear if industrialization is to be viewed from a historical perspective. First, its occurrence in Britain and Europe was the result of a unique historical transformation, a process of economic development that was tied in, an extremely complex manner, with a constellation of internal and external social and political forces. Second, it is too often overlooked that the very success of industrialization in Western Europe determined different processes of change in the wider world. Industrialization, whether in the First, Second, or Third Worlds is a process of economic development with far-reaching social and political consequences. It is not a static or linearly progressive phenomenon. In many respects its nature is shaped by internal structural changes and these are, as many early analysts noted, very important in defining its limitations or directions. But it is equally shaped by external influences which countries in the process of industrializing have little influence over. In order to understand industrialization and the implications its characteristics have posed for the contemporary era, we need briefly to account for the transition to this new mode of production and its subsequent transformations, particularly during the nineteenth century.

The Transition to Capitalism

Accustomed to a rapid rate of change we are perhaps too easily deceived into regarding the past as static, with the result that we often fail to appreciate the extent to which all societies have been constantly subjected to forces requiring change and adaptation. This is not a problem unknown outside the Third World of course, but it is exaggerated there largely because many of its societies had no written records prior to their integration and because many historians insist upon referring to "precontact" periods as something that occurred before history began. In the South Pacific, for instance, the contemporary use of the word "traditional" has also tended to condition us into accepting past structures and systems as something fixed and unchanging. Writing of traditional land tenure systems, Ron Crocombe has remarked:

> . . . many do not realize that what they believe to be their ancient heritage is in fact a colonial legacy . . . What is called customary or traditional tenure in the Pacific today is a diverse mixture of varying degrees of colonial law, policy and practice, with many varying elements of customary practices as they were in the late nineteenth century, after many significant changes had been wrought . . . in the post-contact but pre-colonial era. [2]

At first through European involvement in Asian trade and later by the establishment of colonial forms of enclave production, South Pacific island communities were gradually and unevenly brought into the periphery of metropolitan economic activities. This was a new and often dramatic

13

experience for the South Pacific peoples, but it should not be supposed that until that time their societies had been stagnant. For centuries Pacific communities had been evolving differing systems to accommodate a wide variety of environmental and demographic pressures. In the west, the decentralized and kin-based Melanesian societies developed a mode of production which reflected the abundance of land and resources available to them. In the east, the more rigid social structures of Polynesian societies reflected their greater vulnerability and dependence on smaller islands and atolls. In both, demographic and environmental pressures could and did produce dramatic upheavals that required social and economic readjustments and change. [3]

In Fiji for instance, despite the existence of differing class relations between its eastern and western portions, control over land in general provided the material basis for chiefly power. Fiji's class society however was by no means static. As the power of chiefs increased, what had previously been extracted as gifts and services in the form of mutual aid gradually took the form of levies, taxes and forced labour. As the number of chiefs and non-producers (priests, warriors etc) increased, class contradictions also multiplied with the result that the ruling classes were forced to intensify exploitation of their own peoples in order to resolve labour, land and subsistence shortages. Relief was sought by means of war and by fostering new and stronger ideologies that legitimized their dominance. The result was the evolution of larger class societies. [4]

In these respects European and Asian societies were similar. But they were also less isolated and scattered, and far more vulnerable to external pressures that could drastically transform social and economic structures. European society, for instance, disintegrated into a collection of relatively self-sufficient units after the break-up of the extensive Roman Empire. Such units afforded protection to the population in the absence of Roman authority and during the onslaught of marauding tribes which had swept initially into Europe from Central Asia. These units were eventually to form the basis for a varied feudal society. Agrarian in character, they fell under the control of a hierarchy of nobles and warriors who defended the peasantry and in return extracted their surplus production. By the time the threat of invasion diminished, the feudal lords had consolidated their power by claiming ownership of the land they controlled and by exploiting the existence of servile peasant labour.

In Asia generally, the state, although also affected by the massive migration of tribes, did not disintegrate as Roman authority had, and by and large retained ultimate control over a somewhat less servile peasantry. In many respects the Asian peasant enjoyed greater security than his European counterpart. He was still exploited, but the inability of a feudal class of nobles to claim or sustain a claim to land ownership made him less susceptible to separation from his means of production. In India the mansabdari system of tax farming enabled the state to maintain itself and its military. But by means of rotating positions it also prevented officials from establishing a feudal-type base from which it feared they might challenge the crown. With few links between communities and their ruling classes, therefore, peasant society tended to remain organic. Artisans resided within the agrarian community and produced its requirements in return for what amounted to a salary paid in kind.

The uses to which the feudal nobility of Europe put their power tended to create a less organic society. Artisans did not live among and work for the peasantry. In fact they had little relationship with the land. Production was specialized and paid for with money. As Europe became more secure and communications between feudal principalities revived, the production of commodities for the nobility shifted to small towns from which merchants also engaged in trade. Increasingly a vicious triangle of conflict emerged between the merchant seeking independence from feudal obligations, the nobility wishing to retain its privileges, and the state, desirous of obtaining maximum control at the expense of all rivals.

Since the expansion of trade tended to improve their financial position, the nobility encouraged the growth of towns. As a source of wealth, they hoped it would enable them to withstand the growing power of the state. But the rise of markets served also to increase the wealth of merchants and caused a greater reliance on production for the market and on monetary relations which the nobility could only satisfy by squeezing their peasantry further. Peasant reactions, therefore, added a new dimension to the contradictions raised by feudalism, and in the conflicts which followed, the predominance of the nobility was slowly broken. Sometimes the state assisted the nobility, but in the end it too was unable to resist the changes brought about by new class relations. Invariably its efforts to centralize authority served only to provide the rising merchant bourgeoisie and middle classes with a weapon which, once seized, could be used to hasten the demise of feudalism. The 1789 French Revolution is perhaps the most dramatic example. Sometimes the state indirectly supported the bourgeoisie by encouraging greater national integration and by adopting policies which accorded to their interests. In Britain, for instance, bourgeois control of the state was effected by relatively peaceful means during the seventeenth century.

Feudalism therefore declined, not rapidly, not even consistently, but over a long period of transition the dominance of the nobility was eclipsed by a new bourgeois class which had benefited most from the transformation of labour into a commodity. In Asia, where the state retained its power, few classes were able to assert themselves or effect such a change in the mode of production. The nobility remained dependent on the state for what privileges they enjoyed, the peasantry also depended on the state to check abuses and maintain their land rights, while the bourgeoisie—limited to production for the nobility because of the organic nature of peasant society—was unable even to transform towns into rival centres of authority. Because of the lack of expansion in relations based on money and of land ownership that enabled the alienation of the peasantry from the land, the nascent bourgeoisie in parts of Africa and Asia (in the latter particularly Japan and India) were unable to assert themselves. Deprived of a dependent market, they were restricted to supplying the limited needs of the state and its officials or to seeking opportunities in the unrelated but growing international trade.

Japan provides a useful, if untypical, example of the restrictive influence of strong central authority on class development. When the Tokugawa shogunate consolidated its rule over Japan in the early seventeenth century it restricted the activities of aristocratic samurai classes by barring them from commerce and agriculture. At the same time their feudal lords were forced to accommodate new expenses which arose out of an institutionalized hostage (Alternate Attendance) system. The Tokugawa required all feudal lords (daimyo) to leave their families in the capital, Edo (later Tokyo), and to make annual visits themselves. The hostage system and the huge costs it involved prevented the daimyo from challenging Tokugawa authority, but it also necessitated increased taxation which fell heavily on the peasantry and forced many daimyo to make up for short-falls by borrowing from a bourgeois class which naturally grew as a result. As in Europe the development of a money economy pressured the samurai and daimyo to exploit their peasantry further, but since the former's power in Japan was not based on land ownership but on rice revenue, the resultant commercialization of agriculture did not dispossess the peasantry of their land or benefit the feudal aristocracy. Increased taxation and the development of new forms of agricultural production weakened feudal organization and in the normal course of events should have provided the new bourgeois class an invaluable base from which to expand. But in 1638 the Tokugawa, again for security reasons, had introduced a series of Exclusion Edicts which barred all Japanese from participating in international trade. Thus the rising merchant class found an important avenue for expansion blocked, and was forced to depend upon the limited luxury demands of the aristocracy and upon internal trade. Both were by no means unimportant. Japan was certainly more urbanized in the eighteenth century than Europe, but to little effect. Until the nineteenth century the Tokugawa feudal system remained strong enough to stifle all independent class initiative and expansion. [5]

In Europe, as we have seen, this was not the case. The transition from feudalism to capitalism came about because it was possible to transform labour's organization for production and because the bourgeois classes were not so restricted. During the long period of change, a primitive form of capital accumulation (internally generated by means of enclosure of land, the confiscation of church estates, and externally by tribute or plunder) stimulated a market in land and increased the availability of capital, leading inevitably to the dispossession of the peasantry and their incorporation into the market. [6] "It is not the production of commodities as such", notes Ian Roxborough, "which defines the capitalist mode of production . . . but rather the existence of labour-power as a commodity." [7] The development of merchant capitalism, therefore, consolidated a social system based on property and the sale of labour. By utilizing surplus extraction as a means to accumulate capital for investment, the merchant laid the foundations on which industrial capitalism could be built.

Mercantilism alone could not complete the transition to a new mode of production. As middle men, merchants operated between the consumer and producer only; even in instances where the latter came under merchant control, production remained predominantly decentralized and small in scale. Only when the capitalist intervened to alter production in order to become more competitive and to satisfy a perceived or potential growth in his market, did a significant change occur. As we noted earlier such a change was dependent upon a number of other developments. For there to be a growing demand there had to be people increasingly dependent on the market for the goods they required. They had also to be able to pay for what they required; in other words they had to be working for wages. In Europe, particularly in Britain, the dispossessed peasantry provided both a ready supply of cheap labour and a potentially large market for consumer products, a market moreover which was complemented by the possibilities inherent in commodity exportation to the American colonies.

Land enclosure and the commercialization of agriculture, therefore, produced an alienated class that had little alternative but to sell its labour. These developments, together with the capital generated from increased merchant activity, provided the incentive and means to invest in new systems of production and laid the basis for what Tom Kemp has described as the "dynamic of industrial capital".

> Once the capitalist mode of production had taken root, principally in parts of Britain and northwest Europe, during the sixteenth century and afterwards, competitive market forces compelled individual entrepreneurs to plough back part of their profits into expanding and improving plant and equipment, and extracting more surplus from the dependent labour force of wage earners. At the same time they were subject to market forces on the demand side; they had to follow changes in tastes and purchasing power, improve existing products, seek out new ones and continue the drive to reduce costs of production through new efficient organization and cost reducing methods including new technologies. This was the dynamic of industrial capital which made it superior to all preceding and contemporary modes of production. It was this superiority in developing the productive forces of human labour which made possible revolutionary changes in one section of the economy after another, propelling it onto a path of ascending growth while giving a new shape to society as a whole. [8]

The long and successful rise of the merchant class in Britain also ensured a collusion of interest with the state, such that the new class of industrial capitalists who emerged triumphant in the nineteenth century were able to act with some degree of autonomy. In the remainder of Europe, however, the transformation was less complete. In France, for example, the dissolution of feudal relations consolidated the position of the peasant farmer instead of dispossessing him of his land. During the nineteenth century the continued existence of this conservative and independent rural force imposed severe restraints on the bourgeoisie vis-à-vis the state and weakened autocentric development.

Nevertheless, in both Europe and Britain a class of capitalists existed both able and prepared to meet the challenge of an expanded internal market by altering the actual process of production. Whereas previously craftsmen had been involved in the production of a complete item, they were now to be given only one small part of the process. Dividing labour into separate component parts had the advantage of reducing the necessity for skilled labour. It also raised rates of production, thereby reducing the cost of production per unit.

Changing the organization of production began first in Britain. It was not a rapid transformation and initially applied only to a few commodities, namely cotton and textiles. If merchants had wished to do no more than increase production, they had only to employ more weavers and spinners or make them work harder. But such actions risked increasing prices and would certainly have reduced the quality of the goods produced; given the highly competitive nature of mercantile activity, they might also have proved suicidal. What the merchants required, therefore, was an increase in sales at the same time as a reduction in costs. The only way to produce more cheaply, to become more competitive and profitable, was to break crafts down into a series of repetitive operations. Once this new division of labour had been effected, a whole range of possibilities opened to the capitalist which had to be taken if he was to remain competitive. Once a worker's role in the productive process had been reduced to a repetitive simple task, he or she could be easily replaced by a machine.

It is important to note the order. New technology did not initiate the industrial revolution, rather it enhanced a process begun by the new division of labour. Technology ensured that the momentum generated was maintained, that production would continue to rise and costs fall. Imperialism also spurred the application of new technology. Overseas markets allowed production to be raised to a higher level than could be absorbed by the internal market. Mass production, therefore, both satisfied market growth and reduced production costs, giving industrialists a further edge over their competitors. Colonies, moreover, enabled the acquisition of cheaper and newer sources of raw materials, thereby serving the same purpose. As we shall see in the next chapter, colonies also provided an additional means to accumulate capital but their main role remained to supply raw materials and act as outlets for manufactured goods. Productive forces within colonies were rarely developed if they conflicted with their purpose.

Contradictions

The exploitative core-periphery relationship that became a feature of industrial capitalism was intensified by the spread of industrialization and the expansion of global economic integration. As industrializing countries sought to break free from the restrictiveness of their home markets and sought to overcome greater external competition, they took for themselves more and more colonies, not just because colonies offered new markets or sources of raw materials, but because their acquisition also prevented rivals benefiting from them. We have already noted that this form of imperialism created a dependency that denied subjected countries the opportunities to industrialize themselves. By bequeathing a form of economic development and social formation which limited and distorted growth, colonialism raised a barrier to their equal integration into the expanding world economy. In the long run this was to distort and hinder economic development and on occasion produce violent reactions against core domination. At the time, however, colonialism served to satisfy capital's immediate needs for expansion and continued profitability.

"Impelled by the logic of the economic system to accumulate capital", industrialists had constantly to seek new ways to maintain or increase their profitability. [9] An expansion in the internal market certainly offered one solution, but, as competition increased, capitalists tended to react by cutting wages in order to lower costs, thereby reducing the possibility of internal market expansion. Although the reality of such action was obscured during the early nineteenth century by the impact of new methods of transportation in breaking down rural isolation and increasing the size of the market available to industry, it had a profound and immediate effect on the working classes themselves. Invariably the state was forced to intervene to reduce dangerous class conflict by providing workers greater protection. Of course urbanization itself raised new social complexities which necessitated increased state involvement in social policy. Capitalists could only attempt to reduce the impact of such involvement on their own interests. In the long run that meant adopting or readopting a range of mechanisms to ensure industry's continued profitability. Certainly the option remained to shift production to where capital faced fewer restraints but by and large this was not a practical alternative in the 19th century given the periphery's inability to provide the necessary infrastructure in which industry could operate.

As the century progressed, the problem of maintaining profitability became more acute. The newly industrializing countries of Europe, in particular, suffered the additional handicap of incomplete economic transformation. The consolidation of the small peasantry in France, for instance, and their precarious existence on smaller and fragmented plots of land, retarded economic growth. It also raised food prices and forced both peasants and capitalists to rely heavily on the state to protect agriculture and industries from international competition. Prolonging the peasantry's existence, whether in France, Germany, Japan or India, merely disrupted proletarianization and limited the market available for industrial commodities. The problem also exists today, most clearly illustrated by the EEC's Common Agricultural Policy and Japan's rural subsidy programmes. Without a complete transformation of agrarian relations, capitalist development would remain tortuous and uneven.

The application of new technology to industry, therefore, provided capital an attractive new means to remain competitive and profitable. While permitting the employment of fewer workers, new technology also enabled industry to overcome some of the restrictions imposed by the contradictions of internal development. But more importantly it opened the way

19

for a major expansion in the activities of industrial capital. Occasionally new technological developments had a negative effect by encouraging antiquated methods of production. Manual and electric sewing machines were notable examples of new technology enabling the continuance of decentralized small-scale production. [10] But such production had little in common with the cottage industries of the past and the decentralized clothing industry did much to boost the mass production and standardization of commodities.

Technological innovations and their applications permitted a tremendous expansion in the size and activity of industry. As the cotton and textile industries grew, they stimulated ship building, the extension of port facilities, and the application of new methods of transportation. The development of railways also had important effects, enabling new regions to be absorbed into the market, permitting factories to be sited away from sources of power, and stimulating the iron, steel and engineering industries. Expanded ocean shipping facilities improved contact with overseas markets and cheapened the transportation of raw materials and manufactured commodities. They also extended the potential offered by colonies, enabling their greater penetration and integration into the world economy.

The application of technology and the expansion of capitalism provided fresh opportunities for maintaining or improving competitiveness and profitability. But their impact was also limited or conditioned by the nature of the capitalist transformation in each of the industrialized countries. In many European nations the severe fragmentation of economies hindered the development of extensive networks of credit facilities such as Britain possessed. If industry was to finance the changes needed to remain competitive and to expand, it had to look to the state for assistance. This was particularly the case with the development of the railway, vital if internal markets were to expand. State rail construction, therefore, stimulated industry but at the same time promoted the interests of the state. Railways served to connect distant regions with the capital, to intensify centralization and nation-building, and to assist in the maintenance of state defence requirements.

Because of the distortion of social formation and the disarticulation of modes of production in many newer industrializing countries, greater state inputs were required. In Japan and Germany the state promoted industrialization to effect the necessary capital accumulation and to offset damaging foreign competition. To overcome the advantages Britain enjoyed as a result of her earlier industrialization, industrial organization tended to be more corporate and oriented towards a greater scale of production. Such competitive reactions reinforced industry's dependence on the state for both capital and assistance in obtaining markets outside their restrictive home boundaries. Ironically the nation state became more sharply defined in economic terms by the introduction of tariffs, currency systems, and commercial laws and practices at the same time as different components of the world economy were being drawn together. This did not imply the application of nor indeed the acceptance of planned state development.

Rather it demonstrated differences in historical development between the various industrializing countries which in an atmosphere of increased competition and national rivalry necessitated the involvement of the state in a protectionist and promotional role. In the more secure island state of Britain the same kind of state intervention was not required. Britain's network of private credit facilities was well developed and her early industrial lead gave capitalists an international advantage that was in no need of enhancement. Free trade and policies of laissez-faire, therefore, served the interests of Britain's dominant economy.

Nevertheless, in both Britain and Europe, the state was forced to curtail aspects of the free operation of market forces wherever their impact on society became too anarchic or debilitating. With more and more people grouped together in cities, dependent for their existence on low wages, it was less easy for the state to ignore social problems than it had been when populations were rural and widely scattered. The new cities were not necessarily more tyrannical or poverty-stricken than the countryside. Indeed wages in urban industry were pegged at agrarian levels and the poor treatment of factory workers merely reflected the contempt once reserved for rural labourers. What was different, however, was the collection of vast numbers of poor dependent workers within an urban setting and the potential this phenomenon created for mass unrest on an unprecedented scale. Industrialization, therefore, brought existing problems into the public arena and forced the state to become increasingly involved in social policy on the grounds that it was in the long term interests of the bourgeoisie, and indeed of the middle classes, to ensure a healthy and contented working population. [11]

Industrialization, together with the greater dependence of the work force, created practical problems which the state had no alternative but to address. Unemployment, for instance, could no longer be passed off as simply a problem of idleness or poverty. In preindustrial societies the balance between supply and demand had always been affected by external factors such as famines, plagues and wars. But in industrial societies these were of lesser importance than fluctuating economic activity. In Britain by the middle of the nineteenth century it became all too apparent that the country's old Poor Laws could no longer cope with large scale industrial unemployment. The confidence which had earlier marked the adherents of laissez-faire rapidly disappeared with the economic crisis of the 1880s, a confidence which was equally shattered by the growing articulation of the working classes and the new unionism of unskilled workers. While the growth of socialism and New Liberalism made the case for greater state intervention in social problems more popular than before, the social research of investigators like Booth and Rowntree revealed not only the extent of poverty but also encouraged the notion that unemployment was a social problem which could be cured scientifically in the same manner as a disease. [12]

State intervention during the nineteenth century, therefore, derived largely from circumstance, not preference. It reflected, however, a far-sighted recognition that complete reliance on the free-play of market forces would ultimately work against the interests of industrial capital. Even in Germany, where the Bismarckian state played off the middle classes against the proletariat in order to maintain political dominance, there was never any intention of creating an independent industrial state sector. In Japan, also, state intervention sought only to create a bourgeoisie strong enough to maintain industrial development. The Japanese state created the necessary infrastructure, abolished restrictive feudal relations, and developed industries it considered would best promote a modern and strong nation. But it did not seek to monopolize industrial development, and eventually sold off its industries to officials and merchants who supported its nation-building philosophy.

Transformation

During the last decades of the nineteenth century capitalism underwent further changes as competition between a growing number of industrial nations increased and as the world experienced its first widespread and devastating depression. Intracore rivalry and economic recession intensified the movement away from free markets and free trade as states increasingly intervened to protect home markets as bases from which their industries could conquer foreign markets and develop new techniques of mass production. [13] Mass production became very important in the newly industrialized countries as a way of spreading costs over a large volume of outputs. It also encouraged businesses to seek control over both supplies of raw materials and markets, to which end large corporations were formed from the merger of industrial and bank capital. The formation of cartels, trusts and holding companies, particularly in the newer industrialized countries of Europe and North America, intensified monopolization and the exploitative character of imperialism. At the same time, however, it made financially possible the further application of science and technology to industrial production, a process often referred to as the second industrial revolution.

The development of new techniques for the cheap mass production of steel, the utilization of electricity and the application of diesel and petrol engines were important in the promise they held for future expansion. The commodities this revolution made possible—notably cars, telephones, radios, phonographs, light bulbs, synthetic fibres to name but a few—were to have a powerful impact on societies in the twentieth century. But until methods of production could substantially reduce their cost or society itself became more affluent, they were not immediately of benefit to an industry suffering from competition and recession.

The world depression of 1873-96 reflected the major structural changes facing capitalism, which, together with the inability of internal markets to absorb sufficient products to maintain profitability, drove states into adopting greater protectionist solutions. Some states found it necessary to respond to pressure from an expanding working class which after the

1870s began increasingly to organize itself to effect a greater distribution of wealth. The introduction of state-endorsed wage agreements, national pension and unemployment schemes also bore witness to the influence of state officials who held that a less poverty-stricken working class would reduce the tendency towards underconsumption. But raising standards of living, however slightly, ran counter to the immediate desire of capitalists to reduce costs, particularly labour costs. With state backing, they redoubled their efforts to find new outlets for their commodities and searched more aggressively for newer and cheaper sources of raw materials.

Increased intracore rivalry, the growth of large powerful state-supported cartels, and the growing dependence of industry on imports from the periphery, determined that colonial competition also intensified. Issues of national pride and beliefs in colonizing missions played a part in imperialist expansion as we shall see in the following chapter, but the intense and increasingly dangerous level to which states were prepared to support expansion suggests that far more was at stake, in fact the very survival of national industry and its bourgeoisie. In Britain the age and relatively small size of industrial concerns began to reduce their competitiveness with the newer and larger cartels of Europe and the United States which increasingly specialized in the production of heavy industrial commodities. As a result Britain came more and more to rely upon her colonial possessions, particularly India, to make up for trade deficits and upon the flow of income from overseas investments.[14] Colonies, more completely than ever integrated into the world economy, came increasingly to be dominated by the advanced economies and subjected to external pressures which, in distorting internal social formation, finally removed all hope of their duplicating the West's historical experience of industrial transformation.

The Mass Society

The transition to a capitalist mode of production in Europe and North America was without doubt the single most important transformation to affect mankind in modern times. In the chapters which follow we will examine some of the major consequences of that transition and the impact of subsequent transformations of the world economy. Because of the sheer diversity of responses both to the transition and to the externalization of West European capital, it is extremely difficult to make generalizations which have universal application. This problem notwithstanding, we shall conclude our introductory chapter on industrialization by making some brief general comments on the nature of the mass society which emerged as a result of the dominance of a new mode of production. The word mass implies integration; certainly the changes effected by industrial capitalism, unlike other modes of production, left few peoples untouched. For a start the transformation of the world economy and the practical applications of science and technology accelerated population growth. The newly industrialized countries of Europe were the first affected. Their share of the world's population rose from an estimated 18.3 per cent in 1650 to 25.2 per cent in 1933. Britain's population alone increased 955 per cent between 1600 and 1951, while between 1871 and 1911 Europe's total population rose by 45 per cent. [15] (Europe's population rose from 190 million in 1800 to 300 million in 1870 and to 460 million in 1914. These figures do not include the 200 million Europeans who emigrated to North America and Australasia within the same period.) The debilitating effects of social and economic change were gradually experienced by more and more countries as they were integrated into an expanding world economy. Inevitably high rates of population growth became the global norm. In time Europe and North America, advantaged by their positions of universal economic and political dominance, were able to bring economic restraints to bear successfully on population growth. In the periphery, however, the distortion of internal social and economic structures due to imperialism made similar responses less attainable.

Populations have not only expanded, they have also become increasingly urbanized. Towns have become cities; as agrarian relations have changed and as transport facilities improved, cities have sprawled out into suburbs or joined neighbouring cities to form large conurbations. In the majority of cases the new urban populations have come from the countryside, forced to move because of changes in agricultural production and land ownership or attracted by the perceived advantages of urban employment. In Europe the rural population fell from 70 per cent in 1850 to 51 per cent in 1900, and to 39 per cent by 1950. In North America during the same years the rural populace declined from 65 per cent to 38 per cent and to 13 per cent. Nearly everywhere the pattern has been the same, although the rate of urbanization in different countries depended on the extent and nature of industrialization and the degree to which it has been possible to transform agrarian relations in order to facilitate the new mode of production. Britain, for instance, had already reduced her rural population to 22 per cent by 1850. It was to decline further in the years which followed—to 9 per cent in 1900 and to 5 per cent by 1950. [16] Japan, which industrialized much later and did not immediately utilize the peasantry for industrial labour, experienced a different rate of urbanization. In 1870 her population was still overwhelmingly rural, 82 per cent. It was to fall to 63 per cent by 1910, however, and to 33 per cent fifty years later. In India, on the other hand, imperialism effected a totally different pattern of change. Forced to deindustrialize for the sake of British development, her rural population increased from 61 per cent in 1891 to 73 per cent in 1921. [17] Even as late as 1960 it amounted to as much as 74 per cent of her total population, in 1980 62.2 per cent.

Along with urbanization came the anonymous standardized mass society which mirrored industry's emphasis on mass production and consumption. The growth of huge worker populations, affluent middle classes and narrowing concentrations of bourgeoisie together helped give rise to new expressions of class discontent and increased possibilities for mass action. Urban tensions among Europe's industrial proletariat at the end of the

Figure 2.1   URBANIZATION

As nations industrialized their populations became
increasingly urbanized; the rate of urbanization depending
on the extent and nature of industrialization and of
the transformation of agrarian relations.

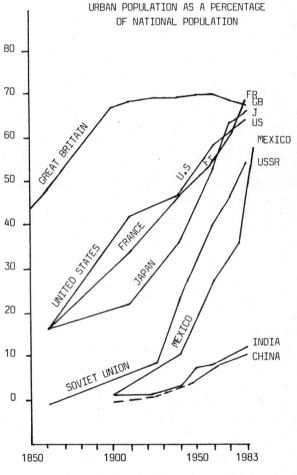

URBAN POPULATION AS A PERCENTAGE
OF NATIONAL POPULATION

Sources : R. Jones (ed.), <u>Essays in World
Urbanization</u>, Philip and Son, London, 1975;
<u>World Population Sheet</u>, Population Reference
Bureau Inc, Washington, 1983.

nineteenth century, for instance, produced mass worker combinations prepared to use industrial strife as a weapon for higher wages and improved living conditions. In reacting to this discontent, the state was forced to intervene more widely in social affairs and to regulate more closely the lives of its peoples. Of course there were limitations to the kind of assistance it was prepared to provide. In Britain the Minority Report of the Royal Commission on the Poor Laws and the Relief of Distress through Unemployment, which preceded the 1911 National Insurance Act, had argued for a radical and urgent overhaul of welfare services and massive state involvement. Most governments in Britain and Western Europe, however, neither saw the urgency, nor had the will, to become so heavily involved. By the early twentieth century they were prepared only to introduce "temporary expedients" such as labour exchanges and unemployment insurance.[18] Insurance, for instance, had the advantage of demonstrating state concern without forcing governments to depart from the entrenched ideals of self-help and self-reliance.

Urbanization also provided industry with a more captive market to exploit and shape for its own purpose. The equalizing effect of mass consumption would have important social ramifications in the twentieth century, particularly in respect of reducing class perceptions and, in the case of the United States, promoting a national consciousness that seemingly denied the existence of social and economic inequalities. With standardization and its accompanying regulation came vastly expanded bureaucracies to collect records and statistics and to enforce laws and controls. While purporting to effect higher literacy and maturity, mass education combined with the development of new media and political organizations to permit greater mass mobilization for a variety of political and economic motives.

In the transition from one mode of production to another, the way in which societies are related to the world system has created distortions which continually frustrate transformation. Under these circumstances, instruments of mass control or persuasion have become vital for deflecting class conflict and for perpetuating distorted development. The last decades of the nineteenth century were no exception. As the industrialized states struggled to minimize internal unrest and satisfy the expansionist demands of capital, they were driven by the logic of the dominant economic system into courses of action which were to reap havoc during the coming century. In an age of the masses it was inevitable that there should also be mass warfare and mass destruction on an unprecedented scale.

Notes

1. In writing this chapter I have drawn extensively on Tom Kemp, *Industrialization in Nineteenth Century Europe*, Longman, London, 1969, and *Historical Patterns of Industrialization*, Longman, London, 1978, as well as Anupam Sen,

The State, Industrialization and Class Formations in India, A neo-Marxist perspective on colonialism, underdevelopment and development, Routledge and Kegan Paul, London, 1982.

2. R.G. Crocombe, *Land Tenure and Agricultural Development in the Pacific Islands*, Food and Technology Center, Extension Bulletin 187, Taipei, 1983, pp. 3-4.

3. For an example of the processes of transformation that affect Pacific communities see P. Kirch and D. Yen, *Tikopia: The Prehistory and Ecology of a Polynesian Outlier*, Bulletin 238, Bishop Museum, Honolulu, 1983.

4. W. Sutherland, "The State and Capitalist Development in Fiji", Ph.D Thesis, University of Canterbury, 1984, p. 31.

5. Jon Halliday, *A Political History of Japanese Capitalism*, MRP, New York, 1975, pp. 4-14.

6. Roxborough, pp. 7-11.

7. Ibid., p. 49.

8. T. Kemp, *Industrialization in the Non-Western World*, pp. 3-4.

9. Roxborough, p. 5.

10. Kemp, *Historical Patterns*, pp. 88-96.

11. Ibid., p. 96.

12. J.A. Garraty, *Unemployment in History, Economic Thought and Public Policy*, New York, 1978, pp. 123-7; see also M.E. Rose, *The Relief of Poverty*, London, 1972.

13. Kemp, *Historical Patterns*, p. 101.

14. Ibid., pp. 105-6.

15. Ibid., pp. 194-5.

16. Carlo M. Cipolla, *The Economic History of World Population*, Penguin, Harmondsworth, 1970, p. 30.

17. Sen, p. 196.

18. Rose, p. 49.

3. Imperialism

Transformation

During the late nineteenth century imperialists justified the territorial and commercial expansion of their nations on the grounds of progress and the forward march of civilization. They believed Europe's supremacy to be God-given, her empires a natural and progressive phase of historical development that would spread the benefits of Western civilization to the backward peoples of the world. Kipling called it "the White Man's Burden", and few Europeans doubted that the cessation of benevolent and strong rule (in Macaulay's words) "would not be the signal for universal anarchy and ruin".[1] During the twentieth century, however, partly as a result of Third World nationalism and independence, such views were no longer tenable. Instead imperialism was equated with exploitation and domination for purposes which did not accord with the high motives expressed by the imperialists themselves. Partly because of the emotions and ideological concepts that have been attached to the term imperialism, some historians have declared its use unscientific. Others have argued that the term has no specific contemporary meaning, that imperialism is not a new phenomenon.[2] Afterall, the Mongols and Manzhus created empires in central and eastern Asia after the thirteenth century, the Mughals established themselves in India, the Muslims in the southern and eastern Mediterranean, and the Khmers in Annam and Burma. It has not been uncommon for indigenous peoples to be ruled by alien minorities.

Similarly, imperialism has been equated with colonialism, although such an equation requires the invention of new terminology to overcome the kind of contradictions that have arisen during the post-colonial era. For example, the persistence of relations of dependence between metropolitan nations and their former colonies has necessitated coining terms like neocolonialism. Obviously imperialism did not begin and end with colonies, and neocolonialism is simply a term to account for the persistence of nothing less than imperialism itself.

If we are to come to terms with imperialism we have to make the same kind of distinction applied earlier to nationalism, simply that there exists a qualitative difference between the imperialism of the contemporary era and past imperialisms. That difference, as Harry Magdoff once explained, centres precisely on the degree of social and economic transformation effected by imperialist activities. [3] Most early forms of imperialism did little more than extract tribute from the territories conquered or influenced. The Mughals and Manzhus, for instance, did not seek to transform the societies they conquered or dominated, rather they sought to preserve existing social and economic structures. The activities of European imperialists after the fifteenth century were similarly limited. The Portuguese and Spanish mined gold and silver, and collected tropical products like sugar and spices. Their own level of development was such that they had no need to establish markets for home industries or find the latter new sources of raw materials. No motive for expansion existed beyond the accumulation of capital, and this objective could on occasion be satisfied simply by plunder or piracy. [4] As long as imperialism served no purpose other than the extraction of wealth and did not promote the growth of productive forces, it remained a form of looting, with limited impact on social and economic structures. This does not mean that early imperialisms had no debilitating impact. One has only to note the effect of the Mongols on the peoples of Xi Xia or the Spanish on the Aztecs and Incas to realize that imperialism had severe consequences for those subjected to foreign domination. But the nature of their domination was such that it was not possible to effect a continuous expansion in the extraction of wealth. That could only occur if and when imperialists set out deliberately to transform the economic base of the countries they subjected.

During the 17th century, however, the rise of merchant capital in Europe began to effect an important change in the nature of imperialism. Although still based on the direct appropriation of surplus, merchant capitalism expanded the imperialist activities of the European nations. Europeans gradually came to control a major share of the traditional intra-Asian trade, which allowed them to partly offset the initial costs of buying commodities in demand in Europe. But supplies were not always regular, particularly of sugar and spices, and the cost of maintaining monopoly control high. To meet expanding home demand, new plantation colonies were established in the Americas based on the importation of African slaves. Trade gave colonies a new purpose, but since mercantile activity involved little direct influence over methods of production or markets, the mercantilist transformation, while important, was still limited.

Only in the late eighteenth century did the nature of imperialism radically alter. As industrial capitalism expanded, initially in Britain, it transformed relations of production and created demands for new materials and markets for the products of industry. Since the home country could not provide for both adequately, it began increasingly to establish new foreign relationships specifically for those purposes. Colonies were taken for the raw materials they contained or were thought to contain, and their economies developed in ways which served the core or its subimperialists. Hence New Zealand and Australia specialized in the export of wool and meat, and Fiji in sugar, as the southern United States much earlier had begun supplying Britain with raw cotton. Colonies and settler communities also acted as extensions of the metropolitan power's own internal market, absorbing manufactured products from the home country. Given that settler societies were off-shoots of the core, their requirements were not markedly different. However, the same was not true of non-settler colonies or spheres of influence. Their traditionally self-sufficient societies had first to be transformed before they could become profitable markets for products which previously had not been required or had been produced internally. In 1895 Lord Salisbury argued:

> If we [Britain] mean to hold our own against the efforts of all the civilised powers of the world to strangle our commerce by their prohibitive finance, we must be prepared to take the requisite measures to open new markets for ourselves among the half-civilised or uncivilised nations of the globe. . .[5]

Such transformation was both deliberate and necessary. Modern imperialism, therefore, was vastly different from earlier forms of imperialism. For the industrial core, periphery exploitation alone was inadequate; the periphery had also to satisfy capital's competitive and expansionist demands. Imperialism accommodated those needs, promoting the search for cheaper sources of raw materials, providing opportunities for new markets and investments, and creating the potential for future expansion and profit.

The Logic of Capitalist Expansion

Although these remained the dominant motives for contemporary imperialism, the methods by which they could be satisfied constantly changed. The very processes of transformation that contemporary imperialism produced ensured that relationships or reactions to them were never uniform or static. Consequently colonial powers had constantly to adapt the nature of their control in order to maintain advantage and the successful pursuance of imperialist designs. Also, the emergence of new industrialized nations in the late nineteenth century—each intent on seeking the same imperial advantage that Britain had for so long enjoyed—further necessitated changes in the exercise of imperialist control. Informal methods of domination could no longer guarantee the maintenance of successful core-periphery relations, particularly as increased intracore competition resulted in larger portions of the world being carved up between the industrialized nations.

In many respects Britain was the most seriously affected by these changes. Because of her early industrial lead, she had emphasized the exploitation of foreign markets rather than her own internal market. Throughout much of the nineteenth century her economy had boomed as a result, and a vast informal empire had been created. Occasionally reliance on native middlemen proved inadequate and direct methods of obtaining raw materials had to be implemented; but the impetus for formal expansion came more from the very orientation of her economy, as Bernard Porter explains.

> Throughout the second half of the nineteenth century Britain had been manufac-
> turing far more textile goods than she could consume herself, and from materials
> she could not grow herself; and she had been leaving much of the food she ate
> to other nations to supply. If it ever happened that her trade with other nations
> had been cut off, she could not have survived except at terrible cost. World trade
> was not just a luxury to her, an exchange of the morsels left over at the end
> of the day when her own people had been catered for. In a very real sense she
> lived by it.[6]

By the 1880s conflicts with native peoples arising from increased penetration and settler-trader greed had already forced an extension of Britain's
formal empire. In the decades which followed, however, the rise of West
European and American industry and commerce forced Britain to secure
her empire by annexing more and more countries simply for strategic
reasons. Without such security she was doomed.

There was another reason for the new British focus on empire. Unlike
her trade relations with Europe or North America, those with her formal
empire produced a healthy surplus, absorbing 33.7 per cent of Britain's
exports in the 1890s and supplying 22.3 per cent of her imports. At a time
when Britains's lead in manufacturing and trade was being severely reduced
by West European and US competition, the dependence of her new and
underdeveloped colonies assisted Britain to offset her growing trade deficit.
(British imports exceeded exports by 50 per cent during the 1890s.)[7]

The rush for colonies affected all industrialized nations by the end of
the nineteenth century. As imperialist actions gathered their own
momentum and politicians came to regard colonies as a prerequisite for
big power status, many areas were claimed simply on the grounds that they
offered a future potential for assisting industrial expansion at home
(Rosebery in 1893 called it "pegging out claims for the future"[8]), or that
their acquisition denied a rival the same potential. Cecil Rhodes spoke in
England at the end of the 1890s of this change:

> The people have found out that England is small, and her trade is large, and
> they have also found out that other people are taking their share of the world,
> and enforcing hostile tariffs. The people of England are finding out that "trade
> follows the flag", and they have all become Imperialists . . . When I began this
> business of annexation, both sides were most timid. They would ask one to stop
> at Kimberley, then they asked one to stop at Khama's country . . . Now, sir,
> they won't stop anywhere; they have found out that the world is not quite big
> enough for British trade and the British flag; and that the operation of even
> conquering the planets is only something which has yet to be known.[9]

In many instances, also, the successful retention and management of one
colony demanded similar control over neighbouring regions. Thus, in seeking to maintain her lucrative trade with India, Britain also found it necessary
to secure her trading routes by assuming control over strategically placed
countries along the way, most notably Egypt and South Africa.

Although European nations in 1800 had exercised control over 35 per

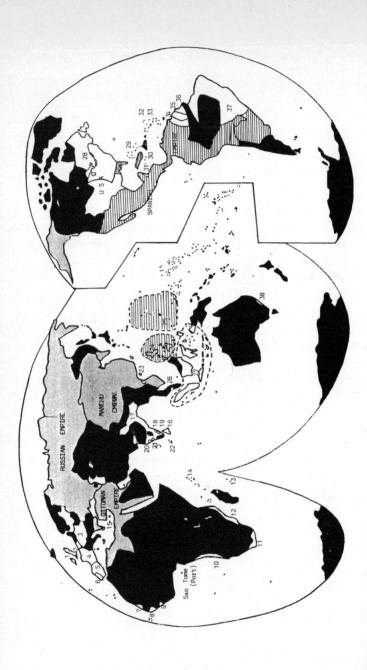

Figure 3.1   EMPIRES AND COLONIAL EXPANSION 1815

1. United Kingdom and Ireland
2. Netherlands
3. German Confederation
4. France
5. Spain
6. Portugal
7. Senegal (France)
8. Portuguese Guiana
9. Sierra Leone (Britain)
10. Angola (Portugal)
11. Cape Colony (Britain)
12. Portuguese East Africa
13. Mauritius (Britain)
14. Seychelles (Britain)
15. Malta (Britain)
16. Ceylon (Britain)
17. India (Britain)
18. Madras (Britain)
19. Pondicherry (France)
20. Bombay (Britain)
21. Goa (Portugal)
22. Maldives (Britain)
23. Macao (Portugal)
24. Philippines (Spain)

25. Marianas, Carolines and Marshall Islands (Spain)
26. Penang (Britain)
27. Dutch East Indies [incl. Portuguese Timor]
28. Canada (Britain)
29. Bahamas (Britain)
30. Jamaica
31. British Honduras
32. Virgin Is (Britain) Barbuda (Britain) Antiqua (Britain) St Martin, Guadeloupe and Martinique (France)
33. St Lucia, St Vincent, Barbados, Grenada, Tobago Trinidad (Britain)
34. British Guiana
35. Dutch Guiana
36. Portuguese Guiana (France after 1917)
37. Brazil (Portugal)
38. New South Wales (Britain)

Figure 3.2   EMPIRES AND COLONIAL EXPANSION 1914

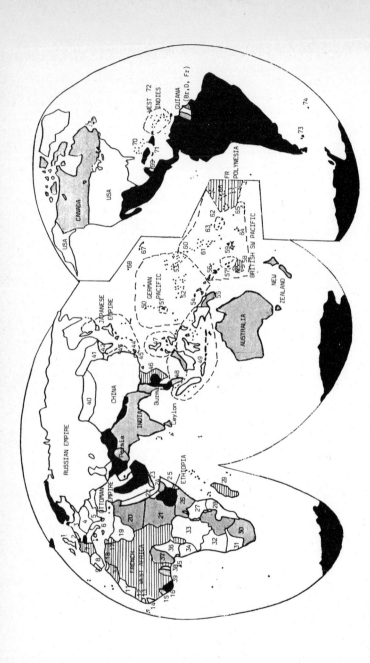

1. United Kingdom (Br) and Ireland
2. Netherlands (N)
3. Germany (G)
4. Austria-Hungary
5. Balkan States (Serbia, Montenegro, Rumania, Albania, Greece)
6. Italy (It)
7. France (Fr)
8. Spain (Sp)
9. Portugal (P)
10. Morocco (Fr)
11. Rio de Oro (Sp)
12. Senegal (Fr)
13. Gambia (Br)
14. Portuguese Guinea
15. Sierra Leone (Br)
16. Liberia
17. Tunis (Fr)
18. Algeria (Fr)
19. Libya (It)
20. Egypt (Br)

21. Sudan (Br)
22. Eritrea (It)
23. Aden (Br)
24. British Somaliland/ French Somaliland
25. Italian Somaliland
26. Uganda/Br East Africa
27. German East Africa
28. Mozambique (P)
29. Madagascar (Fr)
30. South Africa (Br)
31. German S-W Africa
32. Angola (P)
33. Belgium Congo
34. French Congo
35. Spanish Guinea
36. Cameroon (G)
37. Togo (G)
38. Nigeria (Br)
39. Gold Coast (Br)
40. Mongolia
41. Manchuria

42. Korea (Jap)
43. Shanghai
44. Taiwan (Jap)
45. Guangzhou, Macao (P), Hong Kong (Br)
46. French Indochina
47. Philippines (US)
48. Malaya, Sarawak, Sabah, Brunei (Br) Dutch East Indies
49. Marianas (G)
50. Guam (US)
51. Carolines (G)
52. Marshalls (G)
53. German New Guinea
54. Papua (Br)
55. Solomons (Br)
56. New Hebrides (Br-Fr)
57. New Caledonia (Fr)
58. Fiji (Br)
59. Gilbert Is (Br)
60. Ellis Is (Br)
61.
62. Somoa (G and US)

63. Tokelau (NZ)
64. Niue (NZ)
65. Cook Is (NZ)
66. Society Is, Tahiti, Marquesas, Tuamotu (Fr)
67. Hawaii (US)
68. Midway Is (US)
69. Br Honduras
70. Bahamas (Br)
71. Jamaica (Br) Puerto Rico (US)
72. Virgin Is (US-Br) Barbuda (Br) Antiqua (Br) Guadeloupe (Fr) Dominica (Br) Martinique (Fr) St Lucia (Br) St Vincent (Br) Barbados (Br) Grenada (Br) Trinidad and Tobago (Br)
73. Falkland Is (Br)
74. South Georgia (Br)

35

cent of the globe's land surface, intracore competition raised this proportion to 67 per cent by 1878. Structural changes in industrial capitalism towards the end of the 19th century—the application of new technology and the growth of large national monopolies—combined with the spread of industrialization to intensify competition further and produce an almost desperate rush to expand at the expense of colonial rivals. New technology, particularly improved means of communication, together with the availability of greater resources from giant cartels, certainly enabled the periphery to be penetrated more thoroughly. By 1914, therefore, 85 per cent of global land had fallen to European control. [10]

Some historians have sought to explain the expansion of imperialist activity by reference to European diplomatic rivalries. The formation of a new German nation in 1871 upset the traditional balance of power and provoked new conflicts between European nations. While the emergence of a unified Germany undoubtedly altered the status quo, it did not in itself precipitate the mad rush for colonies. By the mid 19th century industrialization had already effected important changes in Western Europe, not the least being the role of the state in promoting development. Since many governments in the more recently industrialized nations viewed colonies as essential for acquiring greater power and prestige, they came eventually to regard colonial possessions as prerequisites for greatness itself. As intracore rivalry intensified, new displays of might became necessary to impress or upstage rivals, and colonies were found useful as a way of demonstrating claims to equality with other industrial nations. This was particularly true after 1900, as we shall see in the following chapter, when the maintenance of prosperity and the social order it supported came to depend more and more on foreign markets and investment opportunities.

Imperialist activities also helped relieve the social tensions industrialization created at home by providing opportunities for the export of surplus population. While schemes for systematic colonization, such as Wakefield's in Australia and New Zealand in the early and mid-nineteenth century, were not always successful and often ran counter to government policies, they did popularize the idea of colonies in the home country itself. Certainly colonial adventures quickly became important in providing much needed external distractions, particularly as the growth of new political parties and the advent of mass electorates forced politicans to appeal more and more to the masses for support. Hence German foreign secretary Kiderlen-Wächter's intervention in the Moroccan crisis in 1911 on the grounds that action would "change the views of many disaffected voters" and produce "a significant effect upon the outcome of the pending Reichstag elections". [11]

Imperial campaigns, therefore, particularly successful ones which upstaged rivals, were carefully exploited by politicians to demonstrate that they were indeed working in the interests of the whole nation. Of course new media forms, notably mass circulation newspapers and magazines provided additional opportunities to influence their electorates. Accounts of the exploits of soldiers, explorers and missionaries became the regular diet of subscribers and helped spread the belief that imperialism was part of Europe's God-given "civilizing" mission.

Nevertheless, only in the respect that imperialism no longer existed solely for extractive exploitation but necessitated the deliberate transformation of societies to meet the expansive demands of industrial capital, was there a mission. Popular justification for imperialism, however, was never so frank. The Japanese in the 1930s defended expansion into Asia and the Pacific by claiming a divine mission for liberation and justice. Nationalist Okawa Shumei wrote:

> It is my belief that Heaven had decided on Japan as its choice for the champion of the East. Has not this been the purpose of our three thousand long years of preparation? It must be said that this is a truly grand and magnificent mission. [12]

Although myths of civilizing or liberating missions enabled popular support to be generated, the real intent could never be suppressed for long. Japan, like Germany, wished to be regarded as an equal of the metropolitan powers.

> It is just that since the Powers have suppressed the circulation of Japanese material and merchandize abroad, we are looking for some place overseas where Japanese capital, Japanese skills, and Japanese labour can have free play, free from the oppression of the white race. [13]

While the economic motive for imperialism has always remained dominant, at times it has been obscured by and even subordinated to other considerations. "National prestige, military ambition, 'retaliation', pure power politics, the various 'civilizing missions'", Arghiri Emmanuel has written, "often provided sufficient motivations for this or that costly and irrational colonialist operation". Nevertheless, "all this belongs in turn to an ideological superstructure that would not have existed if international imperialism itself had not been there already, with its need for economic expansion". [14]

Colonialism, therefore, could and often did develop a momentum of its own, but it remained the imperatives of capitalism which determined the nature of imperialism. The expansive demands of industrial capital, reflected in national rivalries, remained the driving force of imperialism and most defined its outcome. The Russian Bolshevik Lenin was among the first to recognize the relationship between structural changes in capitalism and the more competitive nature of "new" imperialism in the late nineteenth century. Like the British economist J.A. Hobson before him, Lenin maintained that imperialism had become necessary because of fundamental weaknesses in the capitalist system. When production increased at a rate greater than internal markets could consume, prices fell and reduced the profitability of investments. Industrialists, therefore, were forced to seek new avenues of investment beyond their internal markets. The resulting export of capital, Lenin claimed, was the determining feature of the "Highest Stage" of capitalism. [15]

Lenin's argument has been the subject of much debate. Some economists like Dan Nabudere have argued that the new importance of capital exports was largely the product of increases in technological investment and the growing concentration of capital. Declining profitability meant that new sources for generating profits had to be found. The shift in emphasis from the export of goods to the export of capital was by no means sudden, but it did reflect the structural change from competitive to monopoly capitalism which was already making itself felt through the growth of offensive tariff systems, the gradual demise of colonial free trade and of course increased competition for markets. [16]

Because of the length of the transition under view, and its differing impact on core nations, the mechanisms of change have been variously interpreted. Arghiri Emmanuel has maintained that the rise in exports indicated only that there were more countries than ever engaged in expansion. To extract and process new and larger quantities of raw materials and to control wider markets required new and substantial capital investments. Capital was exported not because home markets were no longer profitable avenues for investment, but because exports provided a new margin for profit, while also permitting future additional investment opportunities and a means to restrict the growth of competitors. [17] Indeed, most foreign investments went to already industrialized or industrializing countries (for example from Britain to the United States or from France to Russia) where returns were guaranteed by the existence of substantial or at least favourable internal markets capable of sustaining future industrial expansion. Not surprisingly the new colonies did not receive huge injections of capital. Not only could they not offer the same potential but they had been incorporated into the world economy for substantially different purposes. Further, Paul Sweezy has noted that although foreign investments increased markedly between 1870 and 1914, the increase itself was not always achieved by means of fresh injections of capital. Investments could easily be maintained or expanded simply by ploughing back profits or by accumulating interest. In fact, as we noted earlier, industrialized countries like Britain, far from sustaining economic growth by exporting capital, actually needed to import capital invested overseas in order to cover their own large and growing trade deficits. [18]

Imperialism, therefore, did not represent capitalism's failure to sustain adequate consumption. Certainly underconsumption was a feature of industrialized societies in the late nineteenth century, but capitalists responded to it not just by exporting capital but by seeking new and protected outlets for their goods. Hence the imperatives remained—to secure from competition cheaper or newer sources of raw materials and to obtain new outlets for manufactured products. Accordingly the world was carved up between the industrialized nations and deliberately transformed into markets for their industrial produce. Precisely for this reason colonies could not be permitted to become the mirror image of the imperialist nations, as colonial industrialization would conflict with the primacy of industrial interests in the metropolitan base. All the actions of the imperialist powers were dictated by this imperative, with the inevitable result that the development of colonies took paths vastly different from those once taken by the industrialized countries themselves.

Colonial Forms

Implementation of the imperial design varied considerably, depending on the circumstances encountered within colonies and, of course, on the intensity of the imperial drive itself as competition increased. Nevertheless, three basic forms of colonial activity after the mid-eighteenth century are discernible.[19] The first and more obviously different form was that imposed on weak and sparsely populated communities for the purpose of settling large numbers of Europeans. In North America and Australasia indigenous peoples were pushed aside (and occasionally exterminated) wherever they threatened or impeded settler ambitions. Yet the development of settler colonies did not always prove satisfactory from the point of view of industry in the home countries. Settler demands for self-governing institutions and for indigenous industrialization eventually resulted in colonies competing with the core or acting as its partners. American withdrawal from the British Empire in 1776, for instance, represented a movement for political and economic independence that was later adopted less aggressively by Canada, Australia and New Zealand with varying degrees of success. In the main, developments within settler colonies quickly revealed that they could not easily be exploited as sources of cheap raw materials or as dumping grounds for manufactured goods.

Countries with larger native populations or whose physical conditions were not immediately attractive to Europeans provided a second but varied form of colonial activity. Instead of exporting larger numbers of colonists to effect the production of raw materials for the core, metropolitan capitalists elected to make use of native labour. To obtain native labour, business interests had either to enter into agreements with local rulers or to pressure their own states into assuming control of the machinery of government itself. In the early nineteenth century, when Britain's hegemony had still to be challenged and when the demands of industry were more limited, indirect control by means of indigenous alliances was usually very effective. The indirect rule system of colonial administration was well represented by that of northern Nigeria in Lugard's time and was widely followed elsewhere. Even where Britain annexed regions to demonstrate formally her control, she invariably retained the earlier mechanisms of collaboration because they offered the cheapest and most convenient means to rule and penetrate.

However, native populations did not always prove adequate to meet the needs of metropolitan capital. In the South Pacific, for instance, island populations were too small and widely scattered. Attempts to make up for plantation labour deficiencies by kidnapping men from distant islands were never a successful alternative to normal methods of labour recruitment, and in any case soon earned the condemnation of the powerful missionary societies operating in the region. As long as native communities remained self-sufficient, they could never be transformed into reliable dependent wage labour for the expanding colonial economies. The solution which soon came to be widely accepted, even by various humanitarian bodies, and which had the advantage of immediate application, was to import labourers from other colonies where social and economic transformation had already produced a surplus of dependent labour. [20] Once in the new colony they would produce the raw materials required and, importantly, because of their complete alienation, would remain cheap reliable wage labourers and dependent consumers of imported subsistence food.

Fiji provides a useful example. During the early and mid-nineteenth century the increased presence of European settlers and merchants gradually destabilized traditional forms of government and upset the balance of power within the island groups. Just as in the settler colonies, resident Europeans tended to act as an independent force generating the colonial phenomenon. Their greed and the persistence with which they pursued their ambitions had a debilitating effect on the Fijian peoples and, as far as the British Colonial Office was concerned, threatened an independent form of economic growth which sooner or later would fall victim to its own lawlessness. Hence, Britain intervened in Fiji in 1874, for the same reasons she had acquired Aotearoa (New Zealand) in 1840. The British Government, faced with the inevitability of Europeans incorporating yet another region, did not wish to save the native from the destructiveness of Western development as is often suggested, although this was always a powerful and emotive argument that could be used publicly with effect to justify intervention. Certainly the colonial policies of the British were often humanitarian in origin, and nominally oriented towards the preservation of indigenous populations in the face of settler aggression. But they were always latently shaped by Britain's desire to ensure that development proceeded along lines which were favourable to her, and not necessarily to the active colonists, and which, importantly, would not precipitate heavy financial, even military, commitments in the future.

Once in control, therefore, Britain moved swiftly to avoid the further destabilization of native government by reforming and consolidating what has since become known as the "traditional" Fijian social system. Thus her colonial administrators could claim to be protectors of the native peoples; certainly by rewarding compliant dominant elites they gained valuable allies and avoided the kind of unrest that had earlier plagued New Zealand's administration. Enlisting Fijian chiefs as collaborators in the government of their own people served also to make their exclusion from decision-making outside the "traditional" sphere more palatable. Colonial affairs were now deemed to be separate from native affairs although in reality Fijians were being increasingly exploited by the colonial state as cheap wage labour and as peasant producers. Hence Britain could import Indians to work on the expanding settler sugar plantations without reference to Fijian opinion and justify such action on the grounds that if the colony was to pay its own way and not disrupt the new relations established with the Fijians, there was no alternative to the use of foreign labour.

By restricting the sale of native land and by encouraging the Australian Colonial Sugar Refinery to monopolize sugar production, the colonial government was eventually able to steal a march over the independent-minded colonists. Lacking the opportunities once offered by a susceptible Fiji, many settlers left and the threatened influx of Europeans never materialized. With European settler activities restricted, Fijians locked firmly into "traditional" affairs under the guidance of a loyal and dependent chiefly class, and the growing Indian community isolated both by law and by the nature of their work, colonial rule was secure. Social and economic segregation, therefore, ensured that the colonial government retained control of the country's central policies and that development proceeded in ways which allowed the continued exercise of that control. Not unnaturally such divisions had profound political consequences for the future. At the time, however, Britain could be satisfied that once more she had created a system of colonial organization which gave the appearance of recognizing and securing separate communal social and economic interests while enabling their isolated transformation into integral parts of the dominant colonial economy.

Collaboration, together with policies of political and social segregation, provided imperialists with a cheap but effective means to rule large parts of the world. Not all colonies were like Fiji. Larger native populations and differing political systems meant that there could be no one standard method of colonial rule. The extent and nature of European economic activity were equally important determining factors, as of course was the size of settler communities. Where large numbers of minority settlers existed, as in Kenya or Rhodesia, native collaboration was less necessary to effect colonial rule. [21] This was certainly not the case in countries which had both large populations and highly developed, strong systems of government. These countries reveal a third, and once more irregular form of imperialist activity. Again collaborationist techniques were used, but given the positions of weakness from which Europeans often began, opportunism was clearly its central feature. In Asia and in parts of Africa and the Middle East, European merchants set out to woo local elites in the hope that they could pressure their governments into granting greater trading opportunities. If these failed, efforts could be made to destabilize existing ruling classes or to coerce them by means of gunboat diplomacy. The methods utilized in order to win control over foreign economies clearly altered as the character of capitalism itself was transformed in the late 19th century. Geoffrey Barraclough wrote of the French penetration of Morocco after 1900:

> Trade was no longer the issue; it was, in the American idiom, "peanuts". What mattered now was property rights, mineral rights, mining rights, but above all else financial control, for loans meant the right to control the wherewithal to repay the loans, which usually was customs duties, and this meant foreign . . . control of the customs finances, and perhaps also the right to insist on new

taxation to provide the means to service the loans. And if, as was only to be expected, new taxation produced unrest and even revolt, that also would create a pretext for intervention which could only be welcome. [22]

The risks were always high, not the least being the competition penetration generated from rival powers. But of course the profits or benefits to be accrued from such actions made gambles worth taking. On occasion however—as in the case of Japan and China—Western imperialism generated greater competition than expected and brought about its own nemesis.

In fact the ruling Qing (Manzhu) dynasty in China was far more vulnerable than the foreign merchants and industrialists had assumed. By pressuring China's government for further and further concessions they seriously weakened its prestige at a time when the successful attainment of their policies depended upon its survival. European trade had always been under severe restrictions. Until the nineteenth century foreign merchants were only permitted to operate in the southern Chinese ports of Macao and Guangzhou (Canton), and most were unable to reduce the high trade deficit in their favour. Given the large European demand for tea, porcelain and silks, it was a problem they could not afford to ignore, especially since they had to pay for these products with silver. By the turn of the century, however, the British had found a way to reduce the impact of the trade deficit at China's expense. While the introduction of Indian-grown opium did little to improve relations with the Chinese government, it eventually provided the merchants and opium smugglers an excellent opportunity to extend their trading activities when the Manzhus attempted to end the illegal trade. What became known as the First Opium War (1834-1842) resulted in British naval and military forces stopping the campaign against opium and forcing the Chinese to open more ports to merchant activity. There were five treaty ports under the 1842 agreement but during the remainder of the century European, Russian, American and Japanese imperialists were able to extend this number to 11 by 1860 and to 45 by 1899.

The presence of new centres for foreign trade and the introduction of foreign-owned and foreign-controlled factories had a disastrous effect on China's traditional economy. Vast numbers of boatmen, porters and coolies were thrown out of work in Southern China as Guangzhou lost its earlier dominance as a trading centre and as the use of steamboats and machines increased. Opium sales had expanded greatly with the freedoms now enjoyed by foreign merchants, with the result that Europeans were able to pay for much of the produce they bought from China with the silver exchanged for opium. This loss in revenue combined with the huge indemnities forced on China as a result of the wars and the withdrawal of silver to pay for imported luxury goods (now increasingly sought after by the Confucian scholar-gentry class) to precipitate a major monetary crisis which was felt throughout all of China. As the value of silver increased with its scarcity, peasants were forced to pay more in taxes and rents since their copper coinage lost its value in relation to silver. Increasingly large numbers of peasants fell into debt and were forced to sell their land and migrate or simply become exploited wage labourers. New methods of production, particularly in the treaty port enclaves, also destroyed the traditional handicraft industries on which many peasants depended to supplement their incomes.

This gradual transformation of the Chinese economy, while serving the interests of foreign capital by making China increasingly dependent on larger colonial and world markets, did little to help the collaborating Qing dynasty. Its prestige fell with every concession made to foreign interests. Accordingly, as government corruption mounted and natural disasters combined with foreign economic penetration to worsen the position of the peasantry and wage labour, large-scale peasant revolts erupted throughout the provinces during the mid-nineteenth century. The largest of these, the Taiping Tianguo (1845-1864), came close to toppling the Manzhu regime. As foreign competition intensified penetration at the end of the century, it became increasingly obvious to foreign interests that the Manzhus had little effective control over their large empire. Normally Europeans would have singled out new elites to collaborate with but it was by no means certain that other classes could exercise any more authority than the Manzhus. Nor could Europeans assume direct control and divide China among themselves as they had earlier divided Africa. The new presence of Japan in China as an expanding imperialist power restricted any value that could be gained from European and American cooperation. Instead the foreign powers had to be satisfied with grabbing what new concessions and zones of influence around mineral and railway operations they could, and hope that by intensifying exploitation of the country they would compensate for the lack of more secure arrangements.

In fact they did extremely well. By the time the Manzhu central government collapsed in 1911, they already controlled the country's postal services, taxes and customs, and because of China's heavy debts, its financial structure as well. By siding with the new gentry and military factions which superceded the Qing they were, for a time, able to maintain their interests, but not provide a hedge against the unsettling changes their own activities generated. Germany's defeat in the First World War permitted Japan a more extensive base from which to intervene directly in China's affairs and to challenge the interests of the remaining European nations. The disintegration of government into rival warlord factions further destabilized China and gave rise to new political forces derived from the growing middle and working classes, themselves the products of economic transformation. Under the banner of nationalism and reform, these classes eventually combined with the downtrodden peasantry to overthrow both their foreign and indigenous exploiters and in 1949 to withdraw China from the world economy it had been forcibly integrated with.

Intervention in Japan was even less successful, despite the early hopes raised by collaboration with the Tokugawa Shogunate. The United States was the first imperialist nation to push for the penetration of Japan. By the middle of the 19th century it was beginning to establish itself as a

Pacific power, expanding its frontiers along the Pacific coast and casting greedy eyes at the opportunities opening up for trade in China. Japan, it decided, provided an ideal refuelling point en route to Shangahi. Accordingly, in 1853 its navy began to pressure the Shogunate to establish diplomatic contacts and within five years Japan had been forced to sign unequal economic treaties with the United States, Holland, Russia, Britain and France.

As in China, European economic activities created severe inflation and resulted in the debasement of the Japanese currency. This had serious political ramifications, not the least being the acceleration of peasant revolts. More importantly, however, was the effect of capitulation on the prestige of the Bakufu, the Tokugawa Shogunate. Anti-Bakufu feeling was strongest in the southern hans or fiefs (notably Satsuma, Choshu, and Hizen) which were less integrated with the central government and had traditionally retained a degree of political autonomy. Their southern position also permitted them greater contact with the West. Hence, they were more aware of the threat posed by foreign penetration, either by way of the Opium War example in China or by the retaliation they experienced when they attempted to expel foreigners from Kagoshima in 1863 and from the Shimonoseki Straits in 1864. Eventually Satsuma and Choshu allied and by means of limited civil war and court intrigue were able to overthrow the Bakufu in 1868 and proclaim a new Meiji government.

The organized resistance of the Japanese ruling class helped prevent Japan from being turned into a colony. They were also assisted by the fortunate preoccupations of the major powers in the mid-century—Britain, France and Russia with the Crimean War; France with Mexico and Prussia; and the United States with civil war. In any case the main East Asian imperialist thrust was in China, and Japan was clearly of subordinate interest to the powers. Nevertheless, as Jon Halliday records, while "Japan was not jarred right off track by external pressures as were most countries subjected to classic colonialism" and was able to continue structurally along her own course, "the pace and timing of [her] economic development were fundamentally altered by the irruption of the West".[23]

The new Meiji government of lower samurai and intellectuals moved quickly to use the state to transform the economy in order to strengthen Japan as an independent country capable of dealing with future foreign threats and to consolidate its own position as the new ruling bloc. As we shall see in Chapter 6, the social and economic policies pursued by the Meiji government resulted in the creation of a national-capitalist economy based on Confucian ethics. For the Meiji revolutionaries China remained a useful lesson of the impotence of nominal independence, and they were under no illusion that economic subservience and political independence were compatible. It was a lesson few collaborating governments learned however. As anti-foreign reactions increased with the growth of imperialist activities, most collaborating governments found that they had lost the support of their own people. Without popular support of course they could not effectively serve the interests of imperialists. Isolated and ineffectual, they invariably collapsed as new internally-generated forces gathered their own momentum and imperialists sought other means to protect their interests. Such was the case in Egypt in 1882 under the British, in Indochina under the French in the 1880s, and in Japanese-controlled northern China during the 1930s.

The incorporation of these densely populated countries into formal empires did not end the use of collaboration as a mechanism for control, unless force was increasingly resorted to. In most cases, the imperial power was only too pleased to patronize traditional or new elites as their cooperation permitted easier penetration. The former were much preferred because they were less likely to revolt or demand modern secular institutions. Content to pursue primarily traditional interests, they gave support to the colonial government in return for continued privileges. This, as historian Ronald Robinson has explained, gave colonial governments the same sort of opportunities they enjoyed in the weaker and less populated colonies.

> [Imperial] rulers had wide scope for action without clashing head on with the leaders in indigenous, social, religious and political establishments; and so many collaborative bargains took the form of tacit agreement for mutual non-interference and mutual support between colonial government and indigenous society. In India this indigenous political focus was provincial; in Africa, it was normally local or tribal. The minuscule nature of traditional unity and their undifferentiated character usually made such bargains effective. Collaborators, on their side, were concerned to exploit the wealth, prestige and influence to be derived from association with colonial government, to increase their traditional following or improve their modern opportunities. For these reasons collaboration, as colonial rulers well understood, could be a dangerous game. It involved dealing some of their best cards to potentially overmighty subjects. If one set of collaborators grew too powerful as a result, patronage had to be withdrawn and given to another. [24]

Collaboration also served to provide a buffer between the colonial government and the peasantry and tribal peoples. Social segregation, as we saw earlier, prevented the development of a unity of interest among indigenous peoples, which once actuated, as it was to be increasingly during the twentieth century, made the maintenance of colonial rule if not impossible at least prohibitively expensive.

These, then, were the mechanisms which sustained colonial rule, and which so often strained against their own tendency to create forces that denied the imperial purpose. European settlers fought against dependency, indigenous elites wished to create their own base for exploitation, and new classes formed from colonial development strove to consolidate their special position. The facade of colonial missions and civilizing ideals could not hold forever against these forces. Nevertheless, the flexibility and endurance of colonial institutions attested to the strength of the imperial drive. Long after colonialism succumbed to the forces of nationalism, the imperialist demand for dependency remained, upheld by the new classes that inherited the colonial machinery and by the economic structures on which it had been based.

India

India, Britain's mightiest colony, where implementation of government by law became enshrined as the greatest of colonial purposes, provides a classic example of imperialism's social and economic impact. Forced to focus on international trade because of the self-sufficiency of its own peasant society, India's expanding indigenous merchant class had by 1700 established a thriving trade with Europe in silks and textiles worth an annual £800,000 in silver, which Europe financed largely by the plunder of South America and by the sale of African slaves in the West Indies. [25] Indo-European trade increased phenomenally during the eighteenth century and by 1800 Britain alone was importing £26 million of goods. From this trade a nascent Indian bourgeoisie slowly emerged, effecting changes in the division of labour and often causing village industry to decline.

However, several factors worked against the successful transformation of relations of production. The economic strength of the Indian bourgeoisie was based on international trade, not on an expanding internal market. The restrictions this imposed for economic development reflected also the bourgeoisie's vulnerability in relation to the traditionally powerful Indian state. The latter's ownership of land, in particular, provided the peasantry with a security against alienation that made the creation of dependent wage labour difficult and frustrated the expansion of the bourgeoisie. At the same time, however, the bourgeoisie's weakness forced them to remain heavily dependent on the state for the retention of what privileges they enjoyed; a weakness that was to be increasingly exploited by the growing body of resident British (and French) traders desirous of ending their own dependence on Indian middlemen. The British, unable to pay for all their imports by means of the African and American links, were anxious to turn the balance of trade in their favour. Since India had little practical use for European commodities, the British could not rely upon increasing the volume of exports to India for this purpose. Accordingly, opportunities to redress the balance by other means were eagerly sought. Hence, when the Mughal Empire began to decay during the early 18th century, the British East India Company in Bengal quickly secured the support of rival provincial factions and assumed the role of the state itself. By collecting the land revenue which normally went to the state, the Company was able to finance its trade deficit and, after 1760, slowly drain India and its bourgeoisie of their wealth. [26]

As a mercantile concern, the East India Company was satisfied with simply controlling the export of Indian commodities. The rapidly expanding industrial bourgeoisie of Britain, however, were not. They demanded both markets for their products in India and the elimination of competition from Indian industries. During the late eighteenth century they pressured the Company through the British Parliament to export their industrial products to India and imposed prohibitive duties to keep Indian manufactures out of Britain. Once the Company was brought into line, land reform effected to stabilize support, and rule by civil service established, the process of transforming India began in earnest. Denied markets, Indian manufacturing quickly slumped and its rising bourgeoisie was ruined. By 1850 deindustrialization had reduced India to the status of an importer of manufactured goods. The finished goods she had once exported were now imported, particularly cotton cloth which accounted for nearly one-quarter of all Britain's foreign cotton trade by the mid-19th Century. India still exported more than she imported, but mostly raw materials. Moreover, only 30 per cent of her imports were British in origin. The resulting surplus, estimated at £5 billion between 1757 and 1815 alone, was siphoned off to Britain to pay for her own imports from India.[27]

Indian wealth, therefore, assisted capital accumulation in Britain and enabled further penetration of the subcontinent. To consolidate their control, particularly in the countryside, the British introduced new land tenure systems to create a loyal landlord class. While these changes served to alienate the peasantry from the land, they did not promote agricultural reform. The new landlords (zamindari) were simply a parasitic class, content to live off rents and squander the agricultural surplus on non-productive consumption. Certainly they could never have used the surplus to expand local industry, since the British discouraged competition with their own imported manufactures. Further, the militarily-useful expansion of the Indian railway network served also to encourage the production of industrial raw materials instead of subsistence grains. These changes, when combined with the effects of high land revenue assessment, the diversion of surplus trade for British service costs, the financing of military expeditions to secure India's borders and Britain's other territorial interests, and the imposition of high home charges and remittances, completed the subordination and transformation of India. But for the peasantry, expanding under conditions of peace, yet forced from the land through debt, usury and the concentration of large property holdings, there were no urban industries to absorb them. They had no alternative but to remain in the countryside, landless and abandoned to poverty.

During the nineteenth century British trade with India rapidly increased, particularly in the exportation of raw materials required by British industry (cotton, coal, rice, jute, tea, indigo and rubber) and in the importation of manufactured produce. From this commercial activity an indigenous bourgeoisie reemerged but under conditions more restrictive than before. Since Britain opposed investment in industries which might jeopardize her own export markets, this new bourgeoisie had few opportunities to expand. They were denied access to capital and prevented from making use of new industrial technology. Nevertheless they survived, but only by tapping the native Indian market for cotton products. As a base for future expansion it was pitifully limited. Weak and small in size the Indian bourgeoisie offered no challenge to British dominance.

Under the Mughals, exploitation had not necessitated vast social and economic change. The British, however, could not avoid transforming the country if her capitalists were to profit from its exploitation. To minimize the risks, the British formed alliances with local princes and rulers, Hindu and Muslim leaders, and with the new landed classes. But the nature of change was such that these traditional elites were unable to prevent discontent from erupting into revolt in 1857. In responding to the Indian Mutiny, the British Government assumed direct control of the colony and placed greater emphasis on the rule by law. This too had unforeseen consequences, particularly in respect of the Indian civil service. Under the British the traditional literati class was reshaped by English education, and, while still conditioned by traditional deference to the state, it became increasingly conscious of itself as a new middle class. The British were not immediately concerned however, for although they began to press for greater involvement in internal political affairs (notably through the Indian National Congress after 1885) and joined with the bourgeoisie in demanding a revision of industrial policies, the middle classes' major preoccupations remained self-oriented. Only when they concentrated less on the educational and employment restrictions they faced and began to tap the discontent of the peasantry, as Gandhi was to do after 1916, did the British have cause for alarm. By that time, of course, the First World War had intervened to create new opportunities for India's middle classes and bourgeoisie, and to demonstrate Britain's weakness as a major industrial power. Yet by 1914 Britain's subjection of India was long completed and what had been accomplished could not easily be undone. Britain had cause to be satisfied with her imperial achievements. India had provided a model, a demonstration of imperial intent that was the envy of and inspiration for industrial capital elsewhere.

Notes

1. Macaulay, quoted in Bernard Porter, *The Lion's Share, A Short History of British Imperialism, 1850-1970*, Longman, London, 1975, p. 43.
2. See Magdoff, "Economic Myths", pp. 148-64.
3. Ibid., "Imperialism: A Historical Survey", in Alavi and Shanin, pp. 11-27.
4. Ibid., p. 19.
5. Porter, p. 132.
6. Ibid., pp. 139-40.
7. Ibid., pp. 120-1.
8. Ibid., p. 133.
9. Rhodes, quoted in Alavi and Shanin, p. 72.
10. Magdoff, "Imperialism", p. 19.
11. G. Barraclough, *From Agadir to Armageddon, Anatomy of a Crisis*, Weidenfeld and Nicholson, London, 1982, p. 37.
12. Okawa Shumei, in R. Tsunoda, et. al., *Sources of the Japanese Tradition*, Columbia University Press, New York 1958, pp. 288-9; see also Michio Morishima, *Why has Japan 'Succeeded'? Western Technology and the Japanese Ethos*, Cambridge University Press, 1982, pp. 141-50.
13. Hashimoto Kingoro, "The Need for Emigration and Expansion", in Tsunoda, pp. 796-8.

14. Arghiri Emmanuel, "White-Settler Colonialism and the Myth of Investment Imperialism", in Alavi and Shanin, p. 90.
15. Ibid., H. Magdoff, "Imperialism without Colonies", pp. 147-8; V.I. Lenin, *Imperialism, The Highest Stage of Capitalism*, Foreign Languages Press, Beijing, 1975.
16. D. Nabudere, *The Political Economy of Imperialism, its theoretical and polemical treatment from Mercantilist to Multilateral Imperialism*, Zed Press, London, 1978, pp. 112-14.
17. Emmanuel, pp. 98-9.
18. Paul Sweezy, "Center, Periphery, and the Crisis of the System", in Alavi and Shanin, pp. 210-33.
19. Emmanuel, p. 91.
20. The case of imported Indian labour for Fiji plantation development is explored in Brij V. Lal, "Girmitiyas, The Origins of the Fiji Indians", *Journal of Pacific History*, Canberra, 1983; and in Vijay Naidu, *The Violence of Indenture*, World University Service and University of the South Pacific, Suva, 1980.
21. Ronald Robinson, "Non-European Foundations of European Imperialism: sketch for a theory of collaboration", in R. Owen and B. Sutcliffe (eds.), *Studies in the Theory of Imperialism*, Longman, London, 1972, pp. 122, 134.
22. G. Barraclough, *Agadir*, p. 75.
23. Halliday, pp. 15-22.
24. Robinson, pp. 133-4.
25. Sen, pp. 38-9.
26. Ibid., pp. 52-3.
27. Ibid.

4. Crisis: Intracore Rivalry and Conflict

Lingering Eurocentricity

The beginning of the 20th century saw the industrialized nations of the world—Britain, France, the United States, Germany, Japan and to a lesser extent Russia—in possession of the most power and wealth ever accumulated in the world's history. Their new might was derived from industrialization which, under the impetus of capitalism, had already pushed them into courses of action from which they found it difficult to escape. Industrial capitalism fostered competition between new and large national cartels as each sought an edge over their rivals and greater profitability. In the hunt for cheaper or newer sources of raw materials and markets for their manufactured produce, what has since become known as the Third World was rapidly incorporated into the economies of the industrialized nations.

Already by 1900 the global economy had taken definite shape as relations between the core and an expanding periphery were consolidated. The core gloried in its new expansionism, and saw little threat to its overwhelming industrial hegemony from the newly incorporated regions. It was more inclined to take seriously its own internal divisions. The growth of newer industrialized countries challenged Britain's early dominance, resulting in bitter competition after the 1870s. Intracore rivalry was not in the long-term interests of international capital, but in the increasingly nationalistic atmosphere generated by imperialism and the need to secure industrial gains, there were few capitalists prepared to question the rationality of intense national rivalry. As a result the first half of the 20th century witnessed the devastating culmination of imperialist struggles in Europe itself.

There are three reasons why metropolitan rivalry centred largely on Europe. The first lay in Europe's mistaken notion of its own superiority. Of course industrialization, not European civilization, had laid the basis for its power, but such was the mythology—promoted widely to make imperialism acceptable to all classes—that even Europe's leaders believed it to be the determining factor. Europe was naturally ordained to lead the world. Eurocentric beliefs remained deeply ingrained in its peoples long after events suggested that a more realistic perspective was overdue. For instance the rise of Japan as an industrializing imperialist power should have destroyed Europe's myth of its innate right to rule; instead Europeans convinced themselves that Japan confirmed their superiority. A backward people had accepted and profited from Western civilization. Given time the whole world would be similarly transformed.

European self-confidence was hard to shake. The loss of markets to the United States, Japan and India during the First World War, even the demonstrated weaknesses of European economies compared with other industrialized nations in the interwar years, failed to produce a dramatic reappraisal.[1] Few economists appreciated the consequences of the world's economic restructuring and tended to equate slumps and depressions with natural laws. Politicians, who mostly understood even less, followed suit; indeed, economic imbalances caused Europeans to cling more firmly to what had once provided them with greater certainty.

A second cause of Eurocentricity lay in the preoccupations of the non-European industrialized powers—Russia, the United States, and Japan. With the exception of their earlier colonial rivalry in East Asia, they remained worlds unto themselves after 1919. The new Union of Soviet Socialist Republics focused on repairing the damage of war and on creating a self-sufficient socialist economy. The United States concentrated on internal integration and on consolidating its hegemony over Latin America. Although both countries were already the largest producers of manufactured commodities by the late 1930s, their share of the world's exports was sufficiently small to prevent a new awareness of their importance within the global economy. Japan, also, was content to expand her industrial base in ways which did not result in increased economic relations with other industrialized nations. In fact her expansion into East Asia was designed precisely to reduce dependency on international trade.

These tendencies towards self-absorption were intensified by the Great Depression of the 1930s. Industrial capital within the United States became more inward-looking, re-emphasizing American reluctance to assume a greater public role in international relations between the industrialized countries. Japanese expansion into China escalated, while the Soviet Union, already shaken by intraparty strife, warily refused to be drawn into new European rivalries. The existence of four strong but temporarily isolated spheres of economic activity, permitted the older European sphere to continue to act, in the face of events, as if it alone determined the course of world history.

A third cause for the primacy given to European events lay in the new focus of imperialist competition at the turn of the century. The rise of an industrialized united Germany with fewer outlets for trade than Britain or France intensified metropolitan rivalry within Europe at the same time as Russia, deprived of the opportunity to expand further into Asia because of her defeat by Japan in 1904, once again sought advantage in Europe. Germany and Russia, either directly or through their allies, also pressed for gains in both Asia Minor, a region already dangerously destabilized

Figure 4.1   WORLD TRADE

Changes in the pattern of world trade after 1850 challenged Britain's early dominance and helped generate greater intracore rivalry and conflict.

(a)

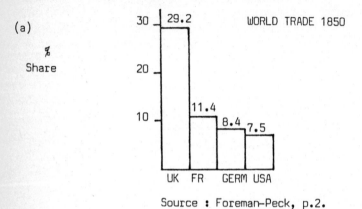

Source : Foreman-Peck, p.2.

(b)   BRITAIN'S DECLINING SHARE OF WORLD TRADE

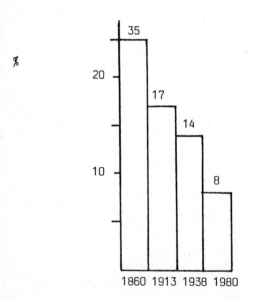

by the collapse of Ottoman authority, and the neighbouring Balkans, where the intrusion of Austro-Hungarian industrial and landed interests had created bitter unrest among the peasantry and a growing urban working class.

The continuing use of nationalism to justify and popularize expansion, particularly among the newly industrialized countries which were more keenly aware of the likelihood of permanent intermediate power status should they fail to industrialize rapidly and aggressively meet all threats to their anticipated future potential, made this new shift in imperialist activities all the more dangerous. Few industrial capitalists, and the socio-political machinery which supported their activities, recognized the dangers this might provoke when disputes arose close to their own borders. Although the growth of cartels had increased the international character of capital, most industrial and financial structures still identified firmly with their nation of origin. Indeed the recession of the late nineteenth century, together with the growth of new industrial competitors, drove capitalists to depend more heavily on the power of the state to provide protection. The state, in turn, found its own operations broadening with those of industry at the same time as the focus of its interests came more and more to concern close neighbours rather than distant colonial posses-sions. The dangers inherent in metropolitan rivalry were to become all too apparent when two world wars erupted. In any case, as industrial and financial capital became more thoroughly transnational, intracore conflict had to be substantially reduced if common state or corporate economic interests were to be served. Indeed, a framework for core unity or collabora-tion became imperative after the First World War as two new external developments began increasingly to challenge the very economic and political activities the metropolitan nations had long considered their natural right.

The first of these external developments, the 1917 Russian Revolution, produced a new socialist Russia intent on opting out of the capitalist economy in order to develop her productive forces without binding foreign assistance. The new USSR claimed that industrial wealth and power was class based, and that a more equitable and peaceful world could evolve only once the international dominance of the industrial bourgeoisie had been terminated. Socialism was not a new force however. The 1848 revolu-tions and the formation of socialist movements in the late nineteenth century had not been without impact on industrialized Europe. Never-theless, its ruling classes had not expected that Russia—long ruled by one of greater Europe's oldest autocratic dynasties—would fall victim through the bitter circumstances of war to communists who preached not only the overthrow of the bourgeoisie but also the radicalization of Europe's working classes. Although world revolution did not materialize, the continued existence of a "maverick" Russia remained a thorn in the side of the capitalist core, particularly once the Russian example provided Third World nations with an alternative that might also threaten core-periphery relations.

The rise of a politically independent Third World was the second major external development which eventually forced metropolitan nations to pay closer attention to their interests in common rather than to their immediate differences. Fed on promises of development if they continued the political and economic models provided by their colonizers, the Third World soon became increasingly sceptical of their value once prosperity failed to materialize. Not only did relationships with industrialized nations come under new scrutiny, but also the role of indigenous leaders who perpetuated such alliances. Third World dissatisfaction after the 1950s and its growing awareness of socialist alternatives, forced the First World to embark on what should rightly be called the third modern phase of imperialism—a subtle, less intrusive campaign to shore up wavering Third World governments and to incorporate dominant internal elites within a new international division of labour. Trade concessions, selective investments, military assistance, generous loans, and aid incentives were specifically designed to tie elites and their governments more firmly to the interests of metropolitan capital. Stronger measures could always be taken if Third World nations threatened to terminate established core relationships. For evidence we need look no further than Korea, Vietnam, Indonesia, Chile, Nicaragua, or Grenada.

The emergence of the Second and Third Worlds did not automatically reduce metropolitan rivalry nor of course did it erode the competitive drive of industrial capital. But it did provide a greater incentive for the representatives of capital to give priority to their collective interests. International warfare as the logical outcome of rivalries fostered by metropolitan states in the interests of capital neither improved relations with the Third World nor reduced the attractiveness of socialist alternatives. New mechanisms were therefore required both to reduce conflicts that might arise from industrial competition and to serve the more transnational character of capital. The League of Nations had been the first step in this direction but it was formed at a time (1919) when awareness of common interests among the still nationally-oriented ruling classes was low and threats to their security, either from socialism or from an independent Third World, were not acute. By 1945 however, a second world war had left Russia the dominant power in Eastern Europe and the battered industrialized nations, now firmly under US hegemony, were only too willing to learn from their mistakes at Versailles. A United Nations Organization (UN) was formed specifically to harmonize the international relations of the First World. Russia was also included but not out of any recognition of the legitimacy of communism. The Americans viewed the United Nations as a mediating agency between the two competing geostrategic systems as they existed at the end of World War Two. However, the US was reluctant to see the UN admit such successful revolutionary regimes as that of communist China, for fear that it might then reflect a changing geostrategic balance. Russia was included in the United Nations Organization because she had been a major partner in the Allied war effort and was clearly the victor in the European sector of military operations. To have excluded her would have been self-defeating. In any case Russia's sheer industrial strength and potential for growth made her the new major rival of what the United States now saw as its own global economic hegemony. Russia, therefore, had to be incorporated into the new global machinery if the peaceful operation of commerce and industry was to be re-established and if her challenge was to be effectively restricted by the procedures of the UN.

The German Excursion

At the beginning of the 20th century, however, these developments could not have been further from the minds of most politicians. There were few substantial external threats to the operation of industrial capital and certainly little popular conception of alternative strategies of development, let alone of how the global economy operated. The metropolitan countries held on to their colonies by utilizing internal collaborators or, where these failed, by sheer military superiority. Threats to the operation or continuance of economic and strategic interests, therefore, tended to derive more from within their own countries or from other rival powers. The former threat, as the following chapter describes, was a continuous problem which reflected the process of proletarianization demanded by expanding industrialization. Low wages and poor living standards, the rise of working class consciousness, and the growth of new organizations seeking to improve the position of the proletariat, served to pressure the state into expanding its involvement in social welfare. Such concessions did not imply that there were structural weaknesses inherent in capitalism. Nor, of course, did they commit governments to costly expansionist policies. In fact governments were prepared to make such concessions because many of their leaders saw them as essential for the successful pursuance of imperialist policies. Lord Rosebery, for instance, wrote in 1900 that "An empire such as ours requires as a first condition an Imperial Race—a race vigorous and industrious and intrepid. Health of mind and body exalt a nation in the competition of the universe." [2] Thirteen years later the British Colonial Secretary, Lord Milner, argued:

> How are you going to sustain this vast fabric of the Empire? No single class can sustain it. It needs the strength of the whole people. You must have soundness at the core—health, intelligence, industry; and these cannot be general without a favourable average standard of material well-being. Poverty, degradation, physical degeneracy—these will always be. But can any patriot, above all can any Imperialist, rest content with our present record in these respects? [3]

Social reform suited the imperial purpose, even if that purpose was only to provide healthy and effective cannon fodder.

By and large, unrest within the metropolitan nations at the turn of the century was manageable. New forms of state control, particularly modernized police and military forces, proved adequate to meet any violent confrontation. The expansion of mass educational facilities and mass media forms, provided further mechanisms to check discontent by spreading supportive ideologies to the urban masses. Imperialist adventures, therefore, came to serve an important secondary function. By promoting jingoism and patriotic nationalism, the state could rally support from the working population and blunt dangerous obsessions with perceived class interests. This is not to say that the metropolitan ruling classes were complacent about working-class radicalism. Their growing sense of failure to sustain economic prosperity after 1907 made them more sensitive to the threat rising proletarian militancy and international solidarity posed for the established order.

Such internal tension gave intracore rivalry a new edge, particularly once the possibilities for unrestricted expansion were greatly reduced after the turn of the century. Not only had Russian ambitions in East Asia been halted by Japan, but all the powers had had to accept that China could not be carved up as Africa had been in the previous decades. The US "open-door" policy for China simply reflected this new stalemate in imperialist expansion and was not designed to reduce perceived inequalities between the metropolitan nations or to forestall future conflict. For the moment, however, Japan remained content with expansion into Manchuria and Korea and with her new diplomatic relationship with Britain. The United States, likewise, was content to focus on internal expansion and the new periphery of Latin America. Britain and to a lesser extent France were also not dissatisfied. Their interests in Asia were secure and their own extensive overseas territories and interests enabled industrial expansion to continue. But it was a temporary peace only. Barraclough observes:

> In reality, the international situation in 1911 was anarchy—a sort of regulated anarchy, but anarchy nevertheless . . . Stability based on fear, suspicion, and an illusory balance of power, was essentially unstable, at the mercy of any incidental shock or tremor. . . The complex, interlocking network of secret treaties and agreements which regulated the relations of the powers, and which was supposed to ensure a balance, meant that any change in the status quo at any point was bound to have repercussions along the whole line, and, needless to say, it did. [4]

For Germany and Russia the halt in colonial expansion was less acceptable. Although Russia possessed a huge Central Asian empire, the nature of her autocratic government and its failure to transform rural relations severely restricted industrial development. At the beginning of the twentieth century her industrial production was almost as great as France's but her potential for internal growth remained hampered by the overwhelming predominance of an impoverished peasantry. Social unrest, in part fostered by industrial transformation, provided a further unsettling challenge to the Tsarist regime. Following the Japanese defeat and the 1905 Revolution, a new imperialist initiative was desperately required to restore the government's credibility and to provide an additional base for industrial expansion.

Unlike Russia, Germany had no large land mass on which to focus development. Her late unification under Prussia in 1871 and more recent industrialization had also prevented her from acquiring an extensive empire like Britain and France. Although new overseas territories such as New Guinea, Samoa, the Cameroons, Togoland, Tanganyika and South-West Africa were obtained during the 1880s and 1890s under conditions of greater competition, they remained largely for purposes of prestige and did little to satisfy the immediate requirements of German capital. Germany, consequently, was forced to seek advantage by other means—notably by rapidly adopting new technology and by placing a greater emphasis on heavy industry in order to break into markets where the British, slower in making the transition, were less able to compete. German competition, therefore, focused more on Europe and its adjacent periphery than on the acquisition of colonial possessions. Nevertheless, the construction of a powerful German navy during and after the 1890s did present a new imperialist challenge, particularly to Britain which regarded its own naval superiority as essential for the maintenance of British security and prosperity. Germany's naval building programme was designed to allow her to fulfil a new historical mission as a major world power, and the challenge it presented to Britain's world-wide predominance precipitated a costly naval arms race after 1906.[5]

German security and ambitions for European hegemony also necessitated maintaining the balance of military and political power in central and eastern Europe, particularly after 1907 when the Anglo-Russian Entente revived German fears of encirclement. Hence her support for the unwieldy empire of Austria-Hungary. Of course Germany also wished to stabilize Austria-Hungary in order to offset any future possibility of the latter's incorporation into Germany. Prussia had no wish to see her own control over the newly unified German states weakened by Austrian entry, nor the seemingly insurmountable problems of minorities which haunted the old Habsburg Empire being introduced into a Greater Germany. The 1879 Dual Alliance between the two countries, therefore, served to keep the status quo while at the same time providing Austria-Hungary with German support for her own expansionist ambitions in the south-east where the dissolution of the Ottoman Empire had freed the Balkans from Turkish control. If the small Balkan states that had emerged in the wake of the Ottoman withdrawal had proved compliant, Austria-Hungary might not have so urgently and ruthlessly sought to establish her own hegemony in the region. But it was not the case and Austria-Hungary quickly took action to prevent Slav nationalism from further infecting her own minorities and also to ensure the continued flow of primary produce, particularly from Serbia, on which she depended. As far as Germany was concerned Austro-Hungarian expansion served to promote her own interests, especially if it impeded Russian ambitions.

The incorporation of the Balkans as a colonial appendage of Austria-Hungary certainly ran counter to Russian interests. Not only had Russia to satisfy the feelings of her own Slav peoples incensed at Austria-Hungary's aggression, but she had also to secure control of the Bosphorus

Straits between the Black and Aegean Seas if she was to anticipate any future expansion in the region herself. Control was necessary to provide a much needed outlet for South Russian wheat exports and also to enable access for her naval fleet into the Mediterranean. Because of German commercial and military influence in Turkey, the Balkans remained the only area through which control could be effected.

By the start of the 20th century's second decade, therefore, the expansionist ambitions of the major powers had begun to focus dangerously on the unsettled borders of south-eastern Europe. In time all the supports of imperialism—state endorsed patriotic nationalism and the utilization of mass media and education systems to glorify the prowess of Western civilization—which in the decades before 1914 had been safely used to promote acceptance of distant overseas goals and to divert attention from internal problems, would be mobilized far more dangerously for activities closer to home. In the course of industrial development, particularly in Europe, the state had come to play a greater role in assisting the expansion of industrial capital. Tariff barriers had been erected to consolidate and protect national markets from competitors. States had also taken greater precautions to guard against the expansion of neighbours into their own sometimes disputed territories. Vast armies were created and huge networks of rail laid, not only for purposes of integrating internal markets, but also to enable the rapid deployment of troops into sensitive areas. French industrial loans to Russia after 1910, for instance, were tied to the construction of railways which might carry Russian troops to the German border in the event of war. Similarly, German military strategists created plans for mobilization which involved the timetabling of 11,000 trains.

Nationalism, technology and expansionism when focused on Europe itself created the potential for more devastating conflict. Although the series of alliances and treaties signed between European nations after the 1870s managed to settle or postpone confrontation over a number of colonial interests, they could not end the imperialist thrust itself or the imperative of national aggrandizement. Treaties like the Triple Entente between Britain, France and Russia in 1907 removed once major difficulties only to allow new crises to assume greater importance. They did not alter the system itself. When France completed its subjection of Morocco in 1911 (and was forced to compensate both Britain and Germany for its new monopoly), Italy decided to invade Libya before all North Africa became French territory. But its attack on part of the old Ottoman Empire and subsequent operations in Beirut and the Aegean precipitated a chain reaction within the Empire which rapidly gained its own momentum, the most notable examples being the Balkan states' wars of 1912 and 1913. In a recent study of the 1911 Moroccan crisis, Barraclough demonstrated that while colonial conflicts could usually be localized (bargains struck at the expense of Africans or Asians), the international system did not permit similar localization when conflicts occurred within Europe itself, at least not without unbearable loss of national prestige and honour, and equally unacceptable consequences in the European balance of power.[6]

Regardless of the huge resources now at the command of states, not to mention the effect new military technology (mechanized transport, barbed-wire defences, machine guns, even fighter planes) might have on the nature of warfare, most European states treated the prospect of war between themselves in much the same way they had imperial campaigns. The German industrialist, Walther Rathenau, likened the outbreak of war to a "ringing opening chord for an immortal song of sacrifice, loyalty and heroism",[7] while the Prussian War Minister, General von Falkenhayn, reflected, "Even if we end in ruin, it was beautiful". Across the Channel in Britain, English poet Rupert Brooke wrote, "Honour has come back, as a king, to earth . . . And nobleness walks in our ways again; And we are come into our heritage".[8] War fostered national solidarity, providing welcome relief from growing internal unrest and fears of economic recession, but above all it enabled a demonstration of the glory and power of the modern state. In one foul swoop, Europe's predatory attitude to international relations had rearmed its nations with a new and dangerous historical mission.

Imperialism generates its own momentum. The lessons that colonists had once provided in the periphery of the world economy was brought to the core with fatal suddenness in August 1914. When the Archduke Franz Ferdinand, heir to the Habsburg Empire, was assassinated in late June, Austria-Hungary decided the time had come to rid herself of the non-compliant Serbia. Germany, mindful of the opportunity this presented for strengthening the position of her only reliable ally at a time when she was increasingly conscious of her international isolation, decided that the timing for such a gamble would never be better. Russia would soon be substantially stronger and more difficult to confront, particularly once Anglo-Russian naval cooperation improved. Britain was currently preoccupied with internal threats arising from union discontent and an Irish rebellion, while France had yet to complete a major reorganization of her military forces.[9] Accordingly Germany gave Austria-Hungary her support and warned Russia not to interfere.

The Serbians, faced with the prospect of annihilation, appealed to Russia for support. Russia complied. To have not done so would have meant abandoning her plans for influence in the Balkans to Germany, thereby undoing all her work since 1905 to regain great power status. It would also have meant rejecting her role as the protector of Slav peoples. For a time in 1912 she had succeeded in uniting some of the Balkan states in order to drive out the remnants of Turkish authority. Only Austria-Hungary remained to thwart Russian ambitions. The Balkan League had collapsed, but the fresh crisis of 1914 presented Russia with a new opportunity. Hence she ordered her army to mobilize to impress upon Austria-Hungary the futility of aggression within the Balkans.

The German military now came into action, assuming that if war with Russia was a real possibility, then France as Russia's ally would first have to be knocked out if a war on two fronts was to be avoided, as German war plans had long emphasized. Germany declared war on Russia and requested that the French hand over their northern defences as a guarantee of neutrality. Not unnaturally France refused to comply and Germany declared war on France. One by one the European nations succumbed to a momentum they had neither the will nor the power to resist. When Germany swept into France to accomplish its long-conceived knockout blow, Belgium's neutrality was violated, and Britain, as its guarantor, chose to declare war on a Germany which if allowed to spread would eventually pose a greater threat to her own interests. Since the 1880s Britain had been acutely aware that her share of world trade was declining. Industrial competition, particularly German industrial competition, had also forced Britain to rely more heavily on her empire. She was under no illusion that German hegemony in Europe, when combined with its growing naval and military strength, threatened the future existence of her international economy on which she was totally dependent. In 1914, therefore, Britain went to war to preserve her empire.

The quick war Germany envisaged, and which in the past had proved so successful against Austria (1866) and France (1870), failed to go according to plan. Against all expectations German troops were unable to complete their sweeping movement across northern France, and the very situation which German strategists had sought to avoid—a prolonged war on two fronts—eventuated. As the new military technology quickly took its toll, Britain and France called in reserves from their colonies, and soon the war spread as Germany tried to cut off the lines of supply from their colonies and from the neutral United States. Eventually intensified submarine warfare against merchant shipping, the possiblity of a German alliance with Mexico, and the collapse of the Russian Tsarist government in 1917, brought the United States into the war against the Central Powers and tipped the balance of resources in favour of the Allies.

Transformation

Although 23 million people, including many civilians, died as a result of the 1914-18 imperialist conflict. Germany's ambition to secure the foundations for dominance in Europe, above all to stave off the challenge of Russia and to rival Britain, had failed. No-one in 1914 had been prepared to concede that the cost would be so high. By 1918 few were in doubt, yet the radical transformation that the war revealed was still beyond the comprehension of most contemporaries. Europe no longer exercised the same control over global events as she had for so long taken for granted. She had now to accept that the United States, in coming to the aid of the Allies, had shown that its military and industrial strength was the equal of any European power. Japan, also, had demonstrated that she was answerable only to herself and had taken advantage of European preoccupations to extend her influence in East Asia. Britain, having fought for empire, found herself more dependent than ever on her colonies and dominions for economic survival. Yet, while war produced fresh colonial gains in Africa and the Middle East, it also weakened Britain's grip on her old empire. Her self-governing dominions viewed their participation in the war as confirming their independent national status; translated into economic terms it meant an accelerated growth in indigenous industrialization which weakened periphery dependence on British manufactured goods. Colonies also exhibited dangerous signs of restlessness for the first time. In India, Britain's most treasured possession, war fostered independent industrial expansion and awakened national consciousness on a scale which in time threatened to paralyse and engulf the whole colonial machinery.

The Russian revolution in 1917 provided further cause for alarm. News of the communist withdrawal from the war with Germany was received with horror and disbelief in Britain and France. Russia had thrown down the gauntlet. Henceforth she would not abide by the rules laid down by the European powers. The Allies took up the challenge and in 1918 directed their armies in both the east and west to work with opposition Russian forces to overthrow the new Bolshevik regime. Not only did they underestimate its strength, but they also failed to provide competent military leadership. Eventually their war-weary troops mutinied and had to be withdrawn. By the time Allied intervention in Russia ended, the Western powers had left a legacy of hatred and distrust that made future attempts to improve relations with the Soviet Union difficult. A *Guardian* journalist remarked at the time:

> The Allies are sowing dragon's teeth in Eastern Europe. Some day they will grow into bayonets and will be turned in directions that we least desire. [10]

With military intervention discredited, anti-Bolshevism degenerated into a brief paranoiac Red Scare at the beginning of the 1920s, the mindlessness of which was perhaps rivalled only by American McCarthyism three decades later.

The new Soviet government challenged the basis of the economic system itself. Given the instability of war-torn Europe, the challenge was taken seriously, particularly by the United States which had no immediate objectives within Europe, unlike its allies. Its president, Woodrow Wilson, was quick to counter Lenin's appeal for the overthrow of capitalism in Europe by issuing a call for democratic revolution to win the support of European minorities seeking self-determination. Wilson also argued that European nations should accept that war was no longer the means to achieve national objectives. If the right to national self-determination in the European periphery could be accepted and a new international organization (the League of Nations) created to mediate disputes before they enmeshed the industrial powers in war, then, Wilson suggested, the Great War would become the war that ended all wars.

Renewed Imperialist Thrusts

For most Europeans, however, threats to the continuance of capitalism were more imagined that real. In time, they believed, life would return to the way it had been before the war began. Having fought for nation, they were not about to forego national aims merely at the insistence of Americans. Nevertheless, at the Treaty of Versailles in 1919 they wisely accepted the principle of national borders in Eastern Europe in order to reduce the potential for further conflict. But when it came to dealing with Germany or with the German and Ottoman Empires, imperialist logic again asserted itself and the spoils of war were divided among the victors according to a self-determined order of rank. Thus Italy and Japan as the lesser powers were almost excluded from a share of war spoils. Their treatment by the major powers was not forgotten; for the moment their desire for equal status remained unsatisfied. In this way the Versailles settlement, rather than removing the potential for conflict, ensured its continuance. Within the as yet unrecognized community of imperialist nations, Italy, Japan and Germany were left no means other than aggression to seek redress of grievances or to satisfy aspirations for equal power status, as Tom Nairn comments:

> What were the factors that Germany, Italy and Japan combined together in the trajectories which made them the Axis Powers of 1939-45? All three were societies with a relatively recent experience of 'backwardness'—a deprivational impotence made humiliatingly evident to them by the impact of outside powers. All three reacted to this dilemma with particularly strong, compensatory ideological mechanisms [which] . . . comprise[d] virtually the whole panoply of nationalist beliefs and sentiments. They then rapidly evolved some of the real substance of nation-state power, through break-neck industrialization and State-imposed societal regimentation . . . However in spite of these successes, the latecomers' position remained precarious . . . All three were confronted with the fact, or the immediate likelihood of breakdown . . . Physical or moral defeat, the menace of internal collapse, or (as they saw it) continued and renewed aggression by the central imperial powers, these were the motives that impelled them into a still more intensive form of national mobilization. [11]

The United States, although having proposed a means to settle core rivalries, still saw the world economy in terms of separate spheres dominated by individual industrialized nations. Its refusal to recognize the common interests of the major powers doomed all future initiatives for cooperation. With the USSR preoccupied with internal reconstruction, the USA reverting to unrealistic political isolation, and Japan disillusioned with the results of allied cooperation, the world's industrialized powers fell back into the pattern of international relations which had predominated from the late nineteenth century. Wilson's "community of power", therefore, did not materialize. [12]

Once more the capitalist drive for expansion turned to the state for assistance, despite the increasingly transnational nature of large industrial and financial monopolies and the growing interdependence of industrial economies. Again the fiercely nationalistic phase of imperialism gripped the industrialized world and could not be shaken, and as before, capitalists found themselves bound by the momentum of forces they had created but which they could no longer control. Japan provides a classic example.

At the turn of the century Japan's dominant bourgeoisie, notably the zaibatsu families, had welcomed military action in China and Korea as it widened their base for raw materials and markets. Likewise intervention in China during the First World War created an industrial boom as industry expanded to meet the needs of military growth and incorporated the regions acquired. The ideological superstructure on which this expansion was based, particularly government-fostered nationalism spread through the media and education systems, served also to promote the interests of capital. Once begun, expansion could not easily be halted without ending the nationalist fervour generated at home or the high expectations now held by the military. Consequently when the 1914-18 war ended and new adventures in Asia were not forthcoming, many military officers felt that Japan's interests were being deliberately betrayed by both industry and government. Of particular concern to them was the government's decision to bow to British and American pressure and reduce the size of Japan's navy in relation to the American and British Pacific fleets (the 1922 Washington Naval Treaty).

Like Britain, Japan found that the First World War had made her more reliant on her empire than before. Although her heavy and consumer industries had grown, there had been no corresponding increase in primary and raw material production. Her increased dependence on raw material and food imports could only be paid for by expanding her exports of silk and cotton textiles. During the 1920s and early 1930s, however, the American silk market collapsed and the growth of national tariff barriers closed avenues for Japanese exports and worsened her trade deficit. Because she had failed to rationalize production and to remove industrial dualism, which restricted internal market growth, Japan could only maintain prosperity by focusing on external expansion. Increasingly, therefore, a larger empire came to be seen both by industrialists and the military as a solution to Japan's economic problems and one way of forcing the Western powers to accept Japan as an equal.

The Japanese military was under the direct control of the emperor and not the civilian government. After 1898 its independence was enhanced by military control of the army and naval ministries, a control which it increasingly used to influence successive civilian governments, although not always with success. During the 1920s it became frustrated with the government's apparent weakness before Western assertiveness and its inability to take the initiative. Accordingly, the army decided to act independently. In 1931 it launched an attack on Manchuria and formed the puppet state of Manzhuguo. Since the government-allied zaibatsu initially resisted military-generated expansion, the army created its own loyal zaibatsu to provide the necessary industrial and chemical commodities for war. By means of coups and assassinations both the zaibatsu and government were eventually forced into line and Japan's economy was rapidly placed on a war footing. Nevertheless, it must be stressed that differences between the zaibatsu, military and government were not so much over goals as on the timing or speed of action. Most officials and businessmen, particularly those who referred to themselves as moderates, walked a very thin line between advocating force and supporting peaceful initiatives. Invariably what reconciled them to aggression was the fear that inactivity could only worsen social chaos and class upheaval, and that in the turmoil which would inevitably follow Japan might not only lose the opportunity to fulfil her independent destiny in East Asia but also risk the sundering of her social fabric.

According to Michio Morishima, the new turn which Japanese imperialism took in the 1930s was of a somewhat different nature.

> Against a background of military aggression in China the Japanese governments of the time were achieving the "rich country and strong army" which had been the aim of the Meiji Revolution; and when the dream was at last becoming reality Japan's energies had run beserk to a degree where she could no longer keep them under control. The military was no longer the strong guard of a wealthy country; it was the economy which had to sacrifice itself completely for the sake of providing a strong army. [13]

In Germany, Hitler also demanded the same sacrifice of industry.

> In my view [he argued], it is to put the cart before the horse when today people believe that by business methods they can recover Germany's power-position, instead of realizing that the power-position is also the condition for the improvement of the economic situation . . . There can be no economic life unless behind this economic life there stands the determined political will of the nation absolutely ready to strike—and to strike hard. [14]

In Europe, also, imperialism generated a momentum of its own which eventually proved counter-productive for industrial capital. The Great War, and the economic dislocation it caused, served only to promote greater national insularity as governments sought to secure their internal markets from competition. The imposition of high tariffs prevented greater intra-European trade and international cooperation as the failure of the 1927 World Economic Conference all too clearly demonstrated. Yet prosperity more than ever depended on cooperation. French demands for German reparations in 1923 and her occupation of the Ruhr caused the fragile German economy to collapse. Only American intervention through the Dawes Plan (1924) to guarantee the German economy and later the Young Plan (1929-30) settled the twin problems of German reparations and Allied debts and demonstrated the very real interdependence of industrial economies which national tariff barriers seemingly denied. The United States sustained the German economy by loans which permitted Germany to pay reparations to Britain and France. These in turn allowed Allied debts to be recovered by the United States. The continuance of high American tariffs prevented European nations using exports instead to repay their debts and created a new dependent relationship that few nations were prepared to admit in their economic policies. [15]

The world economy was thus restricted at the very time it needed to expand. Unrealistic trade barriers inhibited industrial growth and reduced the ability of internal markets to absorb either primary or industrial products. Over-production, therefore, caused prices to fall, further affecting the ability of internal markets (and their colonial periphery) to consume. When the American credit-inflated economy finally collapsed in 1929 it brought down the strangled economies of all industrialized nations.

Nevertheless the symbiotic relationship of industrial economies was still denied. In responding to the new economic crisis, states further restricted international trade and raised new tariff barriers in the belief that insulation could prevent complete collapse. Even Britain, long a defender of free trade because of her extensive empire, retreated behind new tariff barriers in 1932. Officials like Colonial Secretary Leopold Amery believed Britain had few options remaining to her. He argued:

> One [option] is to drift on, with the certain result that from a position of ever-increasing relative weakness, Great Britain, on the one side, will eventually have to be absorbed inside the European Economic Union, while the Dominions will gravitate, as subordinate economic dependencies, towards the great American Union. In the long run, that will mean nothing but the break-up of the Empire. The other alternative is that the nations of the Empire should get together effectively in order to make use of their resources. [16]

The introduction of the Imperial Preference System was an attempt by Britain to make better use of her colonies and to reduce the impact of her declining share of world trade, already down from the 25 per cent she had commanded in 1860 and the 17 per cent of 1913 to 14 per cent by 1938.

Britain had cause for alarm. Production in her old staple industries had declined drastically during the 1920s and the switch to new growth areas was painfully slow. Further, the high cost of the First World War had reduced her ability to use foreign investments to make up for trade deficits. By the 1930s, therefore, Britain was facing serious balance of payments difficulties. Under these circumstances, her empire was becoming of increasing importance as a source of imports and as a market for exports. Imports from the empire rose from 25 per cent to 40 per cent between 1910 and 1939, while exports to the empire rose from 36 per cent to 49 per cent. Its underdeveloped parts were likewise assuming a new importance as old markets were lost. British exports to its dependent non-industrial countries increased from 69 per cent in 1909 to 75 per cent in 1929. [17] For many British administrators and politicians the message was clear.

> The key to survival in the coming age of continental superpowers [Bernard Porter observed] lay in creating a worldwide federation of great white self-governing dominions, victualled by a vast estate of non-white and non-self-governing dependencies: the whole unified in security and self-sufficiency against a malevolent world. [18]

While federation did not eventuate, Britain's Imperial Preference System represented a major and defensive move away from the once cherished principles of free trade. In the long run such contraction of the world economy, either into unrealistic national or imperial units, made international conflict more likely. Indeed, as the 1930s were to demonstrate, reduced inter-

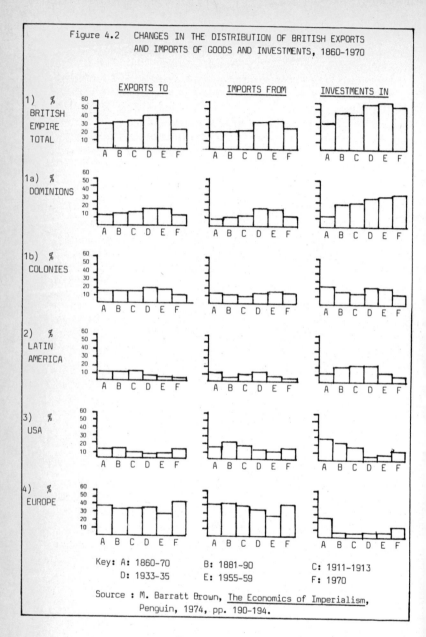

Figure 4.2 CHANGES IN THE DISTRIBUTION OF BRITISH EXPORTS AND IMPORTS OF GOODS AND INVESTMENTS, 1860-1970

Key: A: 1860-70   B: 1881-90   C: 1911-1913
     D: 1933-35   E: 1955-59   F: 1970

Source : M. Barratt Brown, *The Economics of Imperialism*, Penguin, 1974, pp. 190-194.

national trade and massive unemployment forced governments to heal deepening social divisions by resurrecting the very nationalistic mechanisms which had driven them to war in 1914. This time, however, they were more prepared. The Great War had taught them new methods of economic management which could be applied with increasing aggressiveness for purposes of national economic protection. Techniques of resource mobilization, therefore, were administered as if nations were at war.

In countries where economic problems could be conveniently blamed on external factors, for instance in the case of Germany and Italy on Allied treatment following the First World War, commandist economic policies served to rally the nation behind the state and reinforce both the fortress mentality demanded of nation-building and national aggrandizement and the by now familiar predatory attitude towards international relations. The formation of the fascist state, first in Italy under Benito Mussolini in 1922 and in Germany a decade later under Adolf Hitler, represented the culmination of nation-state imperialism. Threatened by socialist-inspired discontent from within, industrial and financial capitalists eagerly supported the new corporative state which promised to suppress union discontent and rebuild industry within a more strongly integrated and dedicated nation. However, as Japanese capitalists also discovered, nation-building nationalism tended to generate a momentum of its own which sooner or later ran counter to capital's long term interests.

The Fascist Phenomenon

To effect the new fascist state Hitler and Mussolini resurrected the companionship soldiers had experienced in the war and offered a purpose and direction other peacetime leaders were unable to duplicate. Hitler spoke of a struggle for survival in which the criteria of fitness was racial superiority. The Germans were the master race; they must struggle for their rightful place in the world. With themselves as charismatic leaders, the fascist rulers promised to restore national honour and make their nations truly great. Fascism, Mussolini argued, would be "the sustainer and creator of a new civilization".[19] Both Hitler and Mussolini were populists, and the mass support they received and continued to foster determined a course of action which neither could deny if they wished to retain credibility. In the end it was the state and not industry which was all important.

Like Japanese nationalists who believed in Japan's divine destiny to "liberate" Asia, the Nazis argued that Germany had an innate right to dominate Europe. In *Mein Kampf* Hitler had maintained that:

> . . . when we speak of new territory in Europe today, we must principally think of Russia and the border states subject to her. Destiny itself seems to wish to point out the way for us here . . . This colossal empire is ripe for dissolution.[20]

Hitler was under no illusion that the balance of world power was shifting. If Germany was to survive it had to expand. In 1941 he declared:

> For me the object is to exploit the advantages of continental hegemony . . . When we are masters of Europe, we will have a dominant position in the world. A hundred and thirty million people in the Reich, ninety in the Ukraine. Add to these the other states of New Europe and we'll be four hundred millions as compared with the 130 million Americans. [21]

Four years later when his Reich lay in ruins, Hitler remained confident that Germany would play an indispensable role in the postwar era.

> With the defeat of the Reich and pending the emergence of the Asiatic, the African and perhaps the South American nationalisms, there will remain in the world only two Great Powers capable of confronting each other—the United States and Soviet Russia . . . [B]oth these Powers will sooner or later find it desirable to seek the support of the sole surviving great nation in Europe, the German people. [22]

Germany needed a periphery to exploit if it was to become a superpower. Hitler did not want a scattered empire such as Britain possessed because he believed it insecure. Her power and prosperity depended too much on Britain's ability to retain her imperial links. Instead Germany would expand her borders eastward. "What India is for England", he declared, "the territories of Russia will be for us". [23]

> Nobody will ever snatch the East from us! . . . We shall soon supply the wheat for all Europe, the coal, the steel, the wood. To exploit the Ukraine—that new Indian Empire—we need only peace in the West . . . [24]

At no time was there a clearer example of German imperialist intent.

The Hitler phenomenon was an imperialist adventure. Installed by industrialists and financiers, Hitler's popularity and effective use of the weapons of propaganda and state power allowed him in time to control his benefactors. All the paraphernalia of imperialism was once more utilized with devastating effect. New technologies like radio became a means to control and direct the popular will—along with contrived mass rallies, careful manipulation of the media and education systems, exploitation of anti-semitic, anti-socialist and anti-Versailles sentiment, the provision of new forms of leadership for war veterans and the depression's youth in paramilitary organizations, and the resurrection of folk myths and concepts of national (racial) superiority to lend historical legitimacy to the Nazi mission—all drove the German people behind the fascist state.

Once Germany's economy had recovered by means of massive public works and rearmament, Hitler's future was assured. But the Greater Germany, on which the whole propaganda of the state was based and to which the expectations of the Germans were directed, remained only partially satisfied by rearmament, by the return of the Saar, and by Hitler's defiant remilitarization of the Rhineland. More successes were required to sustain the propaganda developed. Hence, when opportunities presented themselves, Hitler was compelled to grasp them. In doing so he fuelled expectations further. Expansion became logical and natural. In time even Britain and France were infected by the logic of German expansion, particularly Britain whose imperial preoccupations did not permit an exclusive interest in European affairs.

When local Nazis revolted in Austria, Hitler seized the opportunity to occupy his neighbour and declare the Anschluss in March 1938. Britain, sympathetic to German claims of war injustices and fearing that German grievances might result in a fresh European war, forced the separation of the German-peopled Sudetenland from Czechoslovakia in September 1938, thereby precipitating the break-up of one of the strongest Versailles-created East European states. Having resolved the Czech crisis without resort to war, Britain and France turned their attention to another potential trouble spot—the Polish Corridor which separated the independent city of Danzig (Gdansk) from Germany and which represented another anomaly created by the Versailles Treaty. Since negotiations over the Sudetenland had caused the dissolution of Czechoslovakia, the Poles, not unnaturally, refused to have anything to do with Anglo-French negotiations on the Polish Corridor. Not even a British guarantee to uphold Poland's territorial integrity could allay their suspicions. Hitler knew only too well that the British had no real interest in Poland and gambled that if he intervened Britain would back down to prevent war.

> Close your hearts to pity [he told his generals]. Act brutally. Eighty million people must obtain what is their right. Their existence must be made secure. The strongest man is right. [25]

The gamble failed. The German invasion of Poland on 1 September 1939 brought Britain (and France as her ally) into war with Germany and Hitler was faced with what he had never intended, a full-scale European conflict. Having taken the plunge, however, he could not back down. Each success—Norway, Denmark, the Low Countries and France—took him further. By June 1941 Hitler had achieved German hegemony in Europe. Britain remained unconquered but was too weak to challenge the new and great Germany. In any case Hitler had no intention of conquering Britain or her extensive empire. After the fall of France he appealed to Britain to come to some accommodation with Germany.

> Mr Churchill ought perhaps, for once, to believe me when I prophesy that a great Empire will be destroyed—an Empire which it was never my intention to destroy or harm. [26]

Hitler wished only for a free hand in Europe. As Alan Bullock wrote in his biography of Hitler:

> Any territorial or economic gains which Germany might acquire in the west were secondary to the prime object of the campaign against the Western Powers, to free German energies for the policy from which Hitler had never wavered since he wrote *Mein Kampf*, [27]

the creation of a German Empire in Eastern Europe, west of the Urals.

If Hitler made a mistake, it lay in underestimating the strength of Soviet Russia and the patriotism of her peoples. His invasion of west Russia in

Figure 4.3   THE END OF THE "NEW IMPERIALISM" : 1942, SHOWING THE EXTENT
OF GERMAN, ITALIAN AND JAPANESE IMPERIALIST EXPANSION

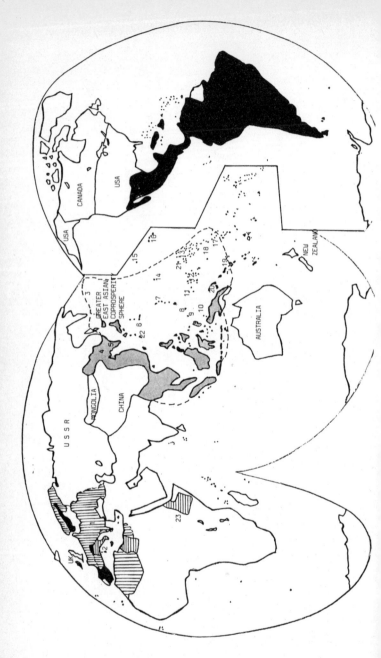

1. German Empire
2. Italian Empire
3. Japanese Empire
4. Manzhuguo
5. Korea

6. Iwojama
7. Marianas
8. Guam
9. Yap
10. Palau

11. Carolines
12. Truk
13. Marshalls
14. Wake Is
15. Midway Is

16. Hawaii
17. Gilbert Is
18. Nauru
19. Solomons
20. Rabaul

21. Kwajalein
22. Okinawa
23. Ethiopia and
    Eritrea (conquered by
    Britain 1941)

June 1941 brought to bear on Germany the very forces he had sought only to rival. Overextended and hopelessly outnumbered, it was simply a matter of time before the second German imperialist adventure within Europe was crushed. By December 1944 Hitler had resolved that "Wars are finally decided by one side or the other recognizing that they cannot be won".[28] But he refused to capitulate. In the end the global human cost of the Second World War exceeded 38 million deaths (20 million in Russia alone) and created a legacy of hatred that forty years later still haunts the world. Yet ironically Hitler precipitated what the First World War and the Great Depression had not. His actions finally convinced the core nations of the value of the very "community of power" Wilson had pleaded for in vain 28 years before. The "New Imperialism" was over and the metropolitan rivalries which had so characterized capitalism's growth were superseded by new forms of imperialist expansion based on core cooperation and American hegemony.

Notes

1. W.H. McNeill, "Peace and War—The Complex Web", *International Relations*, in A. Bullock, p. 45.
2. Porter, p. 130.
3. Ibid., pp. 130-1.
4. Barraclough, *Agadir*, p. 111.
5. James Joll, *Europe Since 1870, An International History*, Penguin, Harmondsworth, 1976, p. 92.
6. Barraclough, *Agadir*, p. 154.
7. Joll, p. 193.
8. Ibid., p. 194.
9. Ibid., p. 180-6.
10. P. Knightley, *The First Casualty*, Harcourt Brace Jovanovich, New York, 1975, p. 154.
11. T. Nairn, p. 346.
12. Barraclough, *Contemporary History*, p. 104.
13. Morishima, p. 131.
14. Alan Bullock, *Hitler, a Study in Tyranny*, Penguin, Harmondsworth, 1962, pp. 197-8.
15. Andrew Shonfield, "The Changing Balance of Economic Power", in Bullock, *The Twentieth Century*, pp. 329-30.
16. Porter, pp. 265-6.
17. Ibid., pp. 260-3.
18. Ibid., p. 266.
19. Bullock, *Hitler*, p. 344.
20. Ibid., p. 318.
21. Ibid., p. 657.
22. Alan Bullock, "Europe since Hitler", *International Affairs*, 47 (January 1971), p. 9.
23. Bullock, *Hitler*, p. 656.
24. Ibid., p. 657.
25. Joll, p. 377.

26. Bullock, *Hitler*, p. 592.
27. Ibid., p. 594.
28. Ibid., p. 762.

5. The Socialist Challenge

The Spectre of Communism

During the late 19th and early 20th centuries, Germany and Japan challeng-ed the hegemony of the major powers in order to attain what they perceiv-ed to be their right—political and industrial equality. Later Third World countries were also to question the "equality" they had gained with political independence. Struggles within the industrial core or between the core and its colonial periphery revealed a constant of imperialism, that relations of dependence denied equality. Class struggles within nations revealed the same constant. Although the working classes of the industrialized core were gradually enfranchised, they still lacked equality with other classes as long as they remained economically dependent on the owners of capital. The challenge of socialism sprang from this contradiction.

Industrial capitalism transformed the societies of all countries in which it operated, regardless of the manner of its operation. Certainly the level of development of productive forces within individual countries, whether China or Britain, India or Germany, varied considerably. But within each country, the process of transformation raised contradictions which stimulated or made possible socialist responses. In the core, socialist challenges were more easily met because of the sheer resources available to the well-established and class-aligned states. In the periphery, however, social change did not result from indigenous industrialization but from imperialism. The state was more vulnerable, controlled either directly by foreigners or by classes whose traditional hold over their societies was being eroded by the same process of transformation. Socialist challenges, therefore, particularly during periods of crisis, were less easily checked, and the resources available to the state less developed.

Socialism has meant different things to different people at different times. At the beginning of the 19th century the term was applied to a set of beliefs which denied the value of laissez-faire economic policies and which demanded planned economic development to reduce social and economic contradictions. Its adherents spoke variously of reform or revolution; those stressing the latter implied that reform was impossible until the then ruling classes were overthrown. Some socialists believed that revolution might be possible once control of the political machinery was gained by means of the electoral system. Others sought to use the weight of proletarian unions to strike against capitalists or the state in order to force radical change. Regardless of the methods they chose to attain their goals, all socialists possessed visions of a brave new world in which the injustices and exploitation of their contemporary era would no longer exist and where the products of industry would be used for the benefit of all mankind, regardless of class, race or religion.

Communists, likewise, predicted a new era. In 1875 Karl Marx wrote:

> In a higher phase of communist society, after the enslaving subordination of the individual to the division of labour, and with it also the antithesis between mental and manual labour, has vanished; after labour has become not only a means of life but itself life's prime want; after the productive forces have also increased with the all-round development of the individual, and all the springs of co-operative wealth flow more abundantly—only then can the narrow horizon of the bourgeois right be crossed in its entirety and society inscribe on its banners: 'From each according to his ability, to each according to his needs!'[1]

This was no pleasant dream or visionary escape from the harshness of the new industrial environment. Marx and his fellow communists believed that contradictions in the capitalist system would create the necessary conditions for a transition to communism. They pointed to the transformation society had already undergone and perceived a pattern which ordained a better future.

During the European Middle Ages the bourgeoisie had emerged as a powerful class to challenge the ruling feudal classes. At various times their challenges succeeded and they were able to capture control of the state, as Marx and Frederick Engels described in 1848 in the first of their major communist publications.

> At a certain stage in the development of these means of production and of exchange the conditions under which feudal society produced and exchanged, the feudal organization of agriculture and manufacturing industry, in one word, the feudal relations of property became no longer compatible with the already developed [bourgeois] productive forces; they became so many fetters. They had to be burst asunder; they were burst asunder.[2]

Marx and Engels claimed that what the bourgeoisie were able to achieve in relation to feudal classes would in turn be achieved by the new industrial proletariat.

> . . . with the development of industry the proletariat not only increases in number; it becomes concentrated in greater masses, its strength grows, and it feels that strength more. The various interests and conditions of life within the ranks of the proletariat are more and more equalized, in proportion as machinery obliterates all distinctions of labour, and nearly everywhere reduces wages to the same low level . . . Thereupon the workers begin to form combinations against the bourgeoisie . . . [the class struggle resulting] in the ever-expanding union of the workers . . . up to the point where . . . the violent overthrowal of the bourgeoisie lays the foundation for the sway of the proletariat.[3]

Just as the bourgeoisie had overthrown the feudal classes, so the proletariat would eventually overthrow the bourgeoisie. Industrial transformation, the authors of the *Communist Manifesto* claimed, would produce its own nemesis.

> The essential condition for the existence, and for the sway of the bourgeois class, is the formation and augmentation of capital; the condition for capital is wage-labour. Wage-labour rests exclusively on competition between the labourers. The advance of industry [however] . . . replaces the isolation of the labourers, due to competition, by their revolutionary combination, due to association. The development of modern industry, therefore, cuts from under its feet the very foundation on which the bourgeoisie produces and appropriates products. What the bourgeoisie, therefore, produces above all, are its own grave-diggers. Its fall and the victory of the proletariat are equally inevitable. [4]

The new communist society which would emerge from the collapse of capitalism, Marx believed, would be a classless society. Without stratification based on property, its states and parties would play a different role, guiding the development of a collection of self-governing associations of citizens. Without also the predominance of market relations, goods would be distributed on the basis of need. Work, Marx believed, should not be for subsistence but should enable individual self-realization. Of course a communist society could not come into existence overnight. It could be accomplished only if there existed a high level of productive forces, if social needs could be self-regulated, and if there existed a sufficient level of communist-consciousness among its peoples.

Obviously a transition stage was inevitable, the socialist state, which would act as a dictatorship for the new proletariat. This socialist state would lay the final foundations for the emergence of a communist society, transferring individual into social property, and perpetuating market relations until work became the prime want and goods could be distributed on the basis of need. Until such a social form of organization evolved, material incentives would remain necessary to ensure the growth of productive activity. Under socialism, therefore, Marx's maxim would become "From each according to his ability, to each according to his work." [5]

Despite their acceptance of the inevitability of transition, few communists in the late 19th or early 20th centuries could agree on either the process for forming a socialist state or its final shape. French socialist Pierre-Joseph Proudhon opposed any suggestion of large political parties and strong centralized states. Mutual economic cooperation was essential, but preferably between decentralized groups of self-reliant peasants and skilled artisans. German Ferdinand Lassalle, on the other hand, was all in favour of a strong self-contained national state and argued that the sheer numerical size of the proletariat made the achievement of power possible through the ballot box. The Russian Michael Bakunin was not so certain. He thought the working classes were benefiting from economic growth and would be reluctant to reject the existing society. Under such circumstances

Marx's assertion that "the emancipation of the working classes must be the work of the working classes themselves" would be difficult to realize. [6]

Despite these disagreements Marx and Engels were undoubtedly correct in beginning their *Communist Manifesto* with the sentence, "A spectre is haunting Europe—the spectre of communism". Most capitalists and leaders of government in the decades following the 1848 revolutions and the 1871 Paris Commune insurrection would have agreed. In fact Bismarck argued in 1884 that social reform was necessary to check the growing danger of social revolution and "to encourage the view among the unpropertied classes of the population . . . that the state is not only a necessary institution but also a beneficent one". [7] The prospect of a non-compliant, restless working class troubled them greatly.

Since the late 18th century the transition to a new mode of production had eroded traditional means of social control. The removal of large numbers of labourers to urban communities divorced them from the influence of restraining rural, religious and social institutions and for the first time brought together an under-privileged and alienated mass of people whose lives were radically reordered by the demands of factory employment. Industry's new divisions of labour, and a growing common dependence on wage labour and market consumption, created a new mass identity that was shaped by collective exploitation and offered a potential for mass unrest never before possible.

> Society as a whole [Marx and Engels declared] is more and more splitting up into two great hostile camps, into two great classes directly facing each other: Bourgeoisie and Proletariat. [8]

As industrialization intensified, the position of the proletariat worsened. Agricultural crises reduced the rural poor to destitution and drove thousands into the cities where they competed for work with an already abundant labour force. Poor harvests combined in Britain with high tariffs on imported grain to raise food prices and make the position of labourers more precarious. Capitalists made full use of this situation. The scarcity of employment allowed them to keep wages low, to make their workers more responsive to monetary incentives and the new demands of industrial employment—its regular, unbroken, daily, repetitive character. Under such circumstances it was not unnatural that violence permeated the new industrial society. Unemployment, insecurity, poor conditions of employment and poverty created tensions that easily erupted into mass violence. The old ruling classes viewed industrial communities with suspicion, as alien phenomena that promised only unrest. To counter its impact they tried first to restrict the power of those who most benefited from its existence—the industrial bourgeoisie.

The history of Europe in the nineteenth century is one of the ascendency of the industrial bourgoisie and of its struggle against old landed and mercantile interests. The revolution of 1789 in France provided a dangerous legacy for political change that the old ruling classes were only too aware of. As a result the ruling classes came eventually to incorporate the new bourgeoisie in order to ensure their own survival. Once power was shared, the former's dominance gradually diminished. In Britain the transformation was effected largely through parliamentary pressure, resulting in the 1832 and 1867 Reform Acts, and the 1846 repeal of corn tariffs. But an alliance of ruling classes and bourgeoisie did not remove the threat of unrest. The activities of Luddites in the provinces, riots in industrial cities, and the growth of national protest movements such as Chartism, together with the revolt of urban masses in European capitals in 1848, served to drive the bourgeoisie closer to landed and mercantile interests in order to meet more effectively the new proletarian challenge.

In Britain some capitalists like W.H. Lever and George Cadbury responded to the problems of the working classes by setting up model villages that would bridge the gulf between rural and urban life. Middle class socialists, particularly John Ruskin, William Morris and the Russian Leo Tolstoy, praised the virtues of pre-industrial life and sought alternatives for the wretched urban masses. The desire to regenerate society by returning to aspects of what seemed a much simpler and harmonious past found expression in a number of ways in new movements and organizations (socialist youth clubs and boy scout movements for example) and was eventually to become an important component of the fascist message in the 1930s. In the late 19th century in Britain another group of middle class intellectuals, the Fabians, argued that all social problems should be tackled scientifically by the state. They declared their intention to effect reform by permeating political and government organizations, and in 1895 set up the London School of Economics to promote the scientific study of society.

Embourgeoisement and Integration

The state, on the one hand pressured by middle class and humanitarian organizations, and on the other wary of the growth of large working class pressure groups, had little choice but to use its power to limit exploitation and improve the conditions of the urban masses. Although reform was made necessary by rapid demographic and social change it was also constrained by it. Nevertheless, by the end of the century it was generally accepted that the state had a duty to act on behalf of its citizens. Expanding urban centres demanded the creation of new administrative bodies, public health measures (hospital facilities, water supply, sewage disposal, etc.) and town planning. There were financial limits of course, but the acceptance of new methods of taxation, particularly progressive income taxation, enabled the provision of new social benefits to the poor, perhaps the most notable early example being Bismarck's social insurance schemes for German workers in the early 1880s.

For a time after the mid-nineteenth century new welfare measures and a growth in industrial activity reduced the pressures on the working classes and helped reduce tension. But they did not prevent the gradual segregation of the working classes and a growing middle class perception of them as an alien community. Indeed it is not without significance that the Salvation Army's campaign to transform the proletariat was entitled "Darkest England". The middle classes set about to tackle the working classes in the same way they were to incorporate colonial elites and to civilize and tame "backward" peoples. Government legislation concerning housing, health, employment and wages enabled greater regulation of the lives of the working classes and created a physical and institutional environment in which undesirable habits could be eradicated. To some extent such legislation sparked off new debates on the philosophy of industrial capitalism and certainly laid the foundation for state welfarism which was eventually the outcome of the bourgeois offensive. But it was not sufficient to temper notions of laissez-faire and individualism by means of legislation; the masses themselves had to be induced to accept the values of their superiors. New centres of civilization were established in the urban working-class outposts, missions which sought to propagate a new moral code and which allowed philanthropic middle classes to visit the poor and influence them by example. The spread of evangelical Christianity, cooperatives, friendly associations, even trade unions, all aided the development of notions of self-help, self-reliance and thrift. By the twentieth century a growing proportion of the working classes had been remoulded to accept "the existing framework of action". Their culture, centred on the music hall and working-men's associations, had become one of "consolation", their activities through trade unions or labour parties decidedly defensive. Increasingly socialism came to be equated only with the abolition of poverty. [9]

Labour was gradually induced to act within bourgeois-controlled political channels. Enfranchisement of artisans and skilled workers in the British Reform Act of 1867 was designed to single out the working class elite for incorporation, and to provide a safety valve for discontent that would make revolution less likely. The development of universal primary education provided an additional means to remould the moral and political codes of the masses. With the further extension of the franchise in Britain in 1884 control and organization of the working classes became even more urgent. Military and police forces and the workhouse system had already been extended to meet violent urban unrest and the breakdown of the old poor laws, but more pervasive and less intrusive methods were required if discontent was to be directed into "positive" channels.

The solution came with mass political parties. New political organizations disciplined the masses from the bottom up and ensured that discontent was expressed through a parliamentary system that was in the interests of the bourgeoisie. By offering the possibility of reform, the new political system derevolutionized socialism. Democratization effectively replaced the now inappropriate traditional restraints once used by the landed and mercantile classes to control rural populations, and in doing so marked the final victory of the bourgeoisie over the old ruling classes.

Working-class political participation swamped the parliamentary control of the ruling classes and had four important consequences. First, democratization replaced parliament as the effective decision-making body with the mass political party. Decisions came to be made within the party caucus and were enacted by executive power. Second, the existence of mass electorates forced politicans to appeal to the masses for support. While elections served to create the illusion of mass participation in politics, they were essentially party popularity polls and as such forced politicians to play constantly to an audience. Undoubtedly there were risks inherent in such a system but they were minimized by the continued control by the bourgeoisie of the media and other avenues of opinion formation. In any case bourgeois monopolization of property permitted powerful economic methods of control to be brought into play whenever democracy threatened bourgeois interests. Third, democratization tended to enlarge the bureaucracy further. Just as the old ruling classes were unable to keep control of the actual reins of power, so the bourgeoisie found that power was being devolved to persons incorporated into the system from outside their class. It became necessary, therefore, to integrate them more fully into the new ruling classes by allowing access to what had once been for the privileged only. Thus educational facilities, clubs, directorships, even residential areas, were shared to incorporate the new power elite and to ensure that it did not deviate from the interests of the ruling classes. [10]

Structural changes within industry and the expansion of administrative functions made embourgeoisement easier. A steady decline in self-employment during the 20th century served to reemphasize the dependence of all wage- and salary-earners. Of equal importance was the dramatic decline in the proportion of manual workers and a corresponding increase in the proportion of technocrats (white collar workers)—30 per cent in the United States for instance between 1890 and 1960. [11] Their embourgeoisement, coupled with the formation of powerful industrial lobbies to pressure political parties, ensured that the ruling elite remained controlled by the bourgeoisie.

The fourth consequence was unforeseen. Popular participation in politics, despite all the checks utilized, tended to subvert ruling class control. In the last chapter we saw how the methods used to engender popular support for imperialism generated their own momentum. Germany and Japan, for instance, both produced regimes which inverted the desired industry-state relationship. Instead of the state promoting imperialism for the purposes of industrial expansion, industry was eventually sacrificed to the popular demand for imperialism. Totalitarian and fascist developments are but one example of the blurring of popular and private interests. Yet while state actions have not always served the interests of capital, they have not resulted in the diminution of capitalist control.

Despite the effects of reformers within and outside of state apparatuses to improve the condition of the working classes, and despite the spread of supportive ideologies through an expanded education system, some class-based associations remained unincorporated and still presented a challenge. The new combinations of unskilled workers after the mid-1880s fell initially into this category. Fired by socialist ideals and determined to confront both employers and government, these new unions and syndicalist combinations wrought industrial havoc at the turn of the century. In less organized societies they might have succeeded in overthrowing the state. But in Europe the state had already grown too powerful and had at its disposal forces which were superior to anything alienated classes could muster. Nevertheless, their activities made the ruling classes increasingly uneasy. The wide anti-state and anti-capital activities of labour organizations and the alarming disunity of bourgeois political parties aggravated ruling class fears of impending economic collapse or revolutionary social change. Certainly they became more aware of the unacceptability of poverty and more determined to remove immediate causes of injustices. The demolition of slums, new housing schemes, pensions, health and unemployment insurance, and improved educational opportunities not only reemphasized the welfarist trend, but also enabled greater mobility into the expanding embourgeoised technocratic class. Democratization further aided the process; the eventual adoption of universal suffrage completed the political incorporation of the masses into a system which did not challenge ruling class interests. In Germany, for instance, the Social Democrat Party (SPD)—founded in 1875 and the largest single party by 1912—soon discovered that its constant need to appeal to voters subordinated its long-term socialist visions to more practical and immediate programmes of reform. In seeking a wider base for support, the SPD was also forced to modify its programmes to suit the middle classes it wished to woo or the bourgeois parties it had on occasion to cooperate with. The revisionist role played by the SPD also came to dominate the actions of the British Labour Party, formed in 1900, and the French Socialist Party after 1914.

Although militant unions were not as easily won over (or suppressed)— huge strikes swept Europe prior to 1914—solidarity among the working classes was prevented. When war broke out, most parliamentary representatives of labour did not oppose it. The few who did were without effect. Nor did unions resort to the general strike to cripple government war policies. Instead the years of imperialist and patriotic pressure on the working classes paid off; like lambs to the slaughter they flocked to the cause of their ruling classes. In the decades which followed it was the same. War became a matter of national honour or of political principle, never a matter of class interest or of economic gain. Union confrontation with employers became formalized and violence less common. In the 1926 British General Strike or the 1951 New Zealand Waterside Workers' Lockout, for example, what was conspicuous was not the unity of working-class interests but the way the state rapidly rallied other classes to oppose and suppress union activity.

The Socialist Party

The failure of unions and working class parties to effect the "inevitable" proletarian revolution and the all too obvious success of capitalist political institutions in deflecting class conflict by reformist tactics and by democratization, created difficulties for those who believed capitalism to be moribund. Some socialists argued that the revolution could actually be effected peacefully by working within the capitalist system. Indeed, by the end of the century, the once proud body of European socialists—the International Workingmen's Association—which had collapsed after the rout of the Paris Communards in 1871 and had not been revived until 1889, was dominated by revisionists like those of the German SPD who believed that reform from within was the most practical way of achieving socialism. It was not long, however, before other socialists who did not share a similar faith in reform, sought to apply the value of party mobilization to the revolutionary cause. The working class might not be able to achieve power spontaneously themselves, but a revolutionary party could act on their behalf to exploit the contradictions inherent in capitalism, and hence become a vanguard for the revolution.

The development of revolutionary socialism within the framework of a party polarized the socialist movement. In Germany the SPD eventually split between socialists arguing for a reformist role and those who believed the collapse of capitalism could be hastened by exploiting spontaneous mass action. Rosa Luxemburg and the Spartacists also believed that a socialist party could only be successful if it actively tried to prevent the embourgeoisement of the working class. A similar split occurred in Russia between the Mensheviks who wanted a mass party allied with progressive liberal elements and the Bolsheviks who stressed the importance of a vanguard role for the socialist party. Other problems were also reflected within this split, not the least being the fear of mass membership dissipating a party's revolutionary fervour. Although these differences were resolved in 1906 by the adoption of the principle of democratic centralism, they had revealed the very real difficulties all socialist parties would face when reacting to a more educated and politicized, although not necessarily discerning, working class.

In Russia these difficulties were more academic because the backward development of her productive forces had delayed bourgeois control of the state and the transformation of agrarian relations. Her masses were more overwhelmingly peasant than Western Europe's and there were few progressive forces for socialists to align with; indeed most revolutionary groups within Russia prior to the 20th century had acted without the benefit of support from a revolutionary class. Only Tsarist industrialization after the 1880s ended their isolation. However, despite her backwardness, Russia's sheer size and population had at various times forced Western European nations to consider her a rival. Although Russian interests in East Asia, Afghanistan, Persia and in Asia minor conflicted with Western and Japanese imperialist policies, political and economic contradictions slowed her emergence as a major industrial power. Feudalism had been abolished in 1861 but the retention of communal systems of tenure and the practice of joint responsibility for taxes and redemption dues did not permit the development of free labour. Fear of peasant revolt and a desire to ensure stability similarly denied the Russian people universal education, with the result that when industrialization began in the 1890s economic and social imbalances were quickly exaggerated.

The state supported industrialization by financing railway development and naval-military expansion. It also raised new protective duties to encourage domestic and foreign capital investment, but did little to change communal tenure or allow peasants either to opt out of communes or consolidate their small and inefficient holdings. The Tsarist regime's slowness in adjusting to what was demanded by social and economic transformation created unrest; after its defeat by Japan (1904-5) land riots swept the country and forced it to revise the old land tenure laws. While this allowed some peasants to consolidate holdings and modernize agricultural production, the majority soon found themselves impoverished by crippling taxes imposed by the state to cover the cost of industry's growing import bill. These problems created further massive unrest, which the government successfully suppressed, but it did little to rectify the problems themselves. The First World War brought the inadequacies of the Tsarist regime to the fore and made it less easy for tight police control to check unrest. Conscripted troops were poorly armed and their movements badly coordinated. Essential services ran down, food became scarce, and inflation rampant. Lacking the administrative capacity to introduce a command economy, Russia's archaic state structures rapidly collapsed. As industrial strikes increased, soldiers deserted, and peasants grabbed land from their masters, the educated and middle classes seized power in March 1917. Poorly organized and lacking distance from the discredited Tsarist regime, the liberal Provisional Government failed to check anarchy and restore order. Having been brought to power by the actions of a radicalized urban industrial workforce and by the militancy of disgruntled and land-hungry peasants, its bourgeois and aristocratic connections doomed it to eventual rejection. In November 1917 the Bolsheviks—careful to woo both the workers' soviets and the peasantry—stepped into the power vacuum and set about achieving the conditions for order which the directionless liberals had failed to create: Russia was immediately withdrawn from the war, and a programme of radical reform embarked upon.

The Soviet Challenge

At first the Western Powers were inclined to regard the Bolshevik revolution as something of a joke. Socialists could hardly govern a country. But Russia's withdrawal from the war and its release of secret Allied documents made the West quickly appreciate the dangers posed by a revived Russian power unwilling to act within the normal capitalist framework. The Bolsheviks also predicted revolution among the working classes of the industrialized nations and promised assistance—thereby providing a new edge to working class discontent in the decades which followed. The new Russian leadership demonstrated a recognition of the international character of capital which even the industrialized countries seemed reluctant to do in their policies. Hence the formation of a Third International (Comintern) in May 1919 to foster an international socialist movement and to exploit the potential for revolution in the destabilized European countries appeared as a new and dangerous threat, particularly to the security of Austria, Hungary and Germany.

Many Bolsheviks believed that Russia could not survive alone in a hostile capitalist world, that an alternative socialist economic order had to be created. Because of the backward nature of her productive forces, Russia would require the support of more advanced socialist states if she was to advance on the road to socialism. The Russian revolution had been the first break in the chain of global capitalism; it was not simply an isolated national phenomenon. Other breaks would naturally follow. Indeed, the three decades from the start of the First World War were to reveal just how fragile the capitalist system was and that the potential for revolution, particularly within Europe, was far more than the figment of socialist imagination.

In the end, Russia's management of the Comintern proved as inept as the industrialized core's use of the League of Nations. Increasingly the objectives of the Comintern were sacrificed to Russian interests. Once the initial hopes for revolution in Europe had dissolved during the 1920s, Russia's leaders became increasingly wary of encouraging foreign revolutionary activities that might undermine Soviet security or aggravate further her precarious isolation. Stalin alternatively asked socialist movements to cooperate with bourgeois nationalist movements (e.g., the Chinese communists with the Guomindang) in the 1920s even when this placed them at a disadvantage, or, during the early 1930s, to shun contacts with all reformist working-class organizations despite the necessity for unity to confront the growing fascist menace. Ultimately Stalin's sacrifice of international socialism for Soviet nationalism not only encouraged the growth of fascism—with disastrous consequences for Russia herself—but also weakened and disillusioned Europe's once progressive socialist parties. Indeed two generations later the scars of socialist disarray had barely healed. Continued Soviet self-interest ensured that old wounds remained festering and the socialist movement divided against itself.

Nevertheless, the challenge presented from the "dangerous" classes by the advent of Soviet-led socialism was considerable and was certainly one factor which caused conservative reactions to intensify during the troubled economic years of the 1930s. Russia provided the first alternative to the little understood free-market model that capitalist nations represented and thus opened a new debate on how societies might be deliberately transformed.

Socialist transformation was not a subject on which many Marxists had expertise; most had concentrated on analysing capitalist relations. Indeed Lenin held a "semi-utopian belief" in the simplicity of economic administration. In 1917 he wrote:

All that is required is that all [citizens] should work equally, do their proper share of work, get equally paid. The accounting and control necessary for this has been simplified by the capitalists to the utmost and reduced to an extraordinarily simple operation, which any literate person can perform, of supervising and accounting. [12]

The administratively inexperienced Bolsheviks had suddenly to address themselves to questions of development. They were to discover that history could not be transcended to produce a new era. Not only had they inherited a nation in which industrialization had been lopsided, leaving the majority of the population engaged in peasant production, but the exigencies of war were to tie their hands further. In fact the first three decades of the Soviet state were not conducive to development at all. The First World War was followed rapidly by civil war as Allied Forces tried in vain to crush the new communist government. These wars, together with the famine which followed, caused over six million deaths. If the disasters of the 1930s and the losses of the Second World War are also included, the young Soviet nation sustained losses well in excess of 30 million people within its first 25 years. The Allied and German invasions of 1918 and 1941, together with the hostile attitude of Western powers in the intervening years, fostered a siege mentality which made Soviet leaders deeply suspicious of Western intentions. The pace of development, therefore, became increasingly tied to security rather than socialist considerations. [13]

Lenin had not envisaged a one-party state, but the onslaught of civil war forced the Communist Party to exercise greater control in order to prevent opposition becoming counter-revolutionary. Bolshevik policies were initially moderate however; land was distributed to the peasantry on an individual basis, soviet (worker council) control of industry encouraged, and a few vital industries nationalized. But as civil war escalated and Allied blockades and occupation affected the economy, the Soviet government was forced to increase its control of large-scale enterprises and resources. The communist economic policies adopted (known as war communism, 1918-1921), which among other things confiscated peasant agricultural surpluses, did not encourage increased production. Peasants reduced planting, hoarded grain and made illegal sales to private traders. "We thought that we could, at a blow and swiftly, abolish market relations", wrote Bukharin in 1925, "yet it turns out that we shall reach socialism through market relations." [14] Once war ended, many controls were relaxed but the lingering fear of Allied intervention continued to distort debates on development strategies, and forced most Soviet leaders to stress the urgency of building up Russia's industrial base in order to secure the nation against future aggression.

Since there no longer existed the kind of economic relations that would have allowed capitalists, landlords or foreign investors to finance development, the state had of necessity to take a leading role in capital formation and industrial promotion. This in itself was not entirely novel. Western European states and Japan had assumed a similar role in the absence of adequate financial and industrial capital. Nor was there much debate over where the state would obtain the capital necessary to finance industrial development. As in Europe the only sector initially capable of generating sufficient surplus was agriculture. Nevertheless, questions did arise over the degree to which agriculture should be sacrificed for the sake of industrial expansion. Bukharin and Zinoviev argued that peasants should be encouraged to increase production and generate a greater surplus for industrial promotion. Increased peasant purchasing power would then enable industry to secure a healthy viable base for its products. Bukharin did not see any problems in allowing market relations to continue if this stimulated agricultural production. Since the socialist state controlled the economy, not capitalists, exploitation would be minimized and the private sector slowly transformed into a socialist one, "moving from a type of economy based on profit to one based on the requirements of the masses". The emphasis, however, should be on slow economic transformation to prevent the growth of inequalities between agriculture and industry and to ensure balanced development in isolation from the world economy: "We shall proceed forward slowly and bit by bit, dragging the peasant cart behind us". [15]

Not all members of the politburo agreed. Leon Trotsky, the architect of Soviet victory in the civil war, was loath to abandon his thesis that Russia could not survive alone in a hostile world. Although possibilities for socialist revolution in Europe became more remote, Trotsky insisted that Russia establish links with other countries, even trade with capitalist nations. He argued that instead of building industry from a solid agrarian-dominated internal base, Russia should expand her industry by exporting grain, as the Tsarist regime had done, in return for much needed industrial machinery. Even foreign investment in Russia should be welcomed if it speeded up the process of development.

It was the question of speed and its consequences which most divided the communist leadership. E. Preobrazhensky emphasized industrial expansion by means of expropriating the surplus of wealthy peasants. Agriculture, he claimed, should be sacrificed for the sake of an industrial sector now deemed as increasingly vital for self-preservation. Lenin's New Economic Policy (NEP), launched in 1921, did not address these problems of strategy. As a temporary measure designed to restore production to pre-war levels and to conciliate a conservative peasantry which had little interest in policies of industrialization and which had suffered much from three years of forced requisitioning, it was relatively successful. Bukharin reflected:

> The adoption of the NEP was a collapse of our illusions. This does not mean that the war communism system was basically wrong for its time . . . war and blockade compelled us to act thus. But we thought then that our peace-time policy would be a continuation of the centralized planning system of that period. [16]

The NEP retained state control of heavy industry, transport, banking and foreign trade but returned the agricultural sector to private hands and decentralized decision-making. In place of requisitions, it imposed a new tax based on a proportion of the surplus. Money was also reintroduced as a medium of exchange.

But the NEP gave no direction for future policy, a point which became increasingly obvious during the late 1920s when grain production fell because of industry's failure to provide sufficient goods for exchange. Bukharin's thesis was not destroyed but the question of what should come first—grain to finance industrial production, or industrial production to encourage independent peasant production of grain—became more central than ever. Given the Party's disposition towards the proletariat and its conclusion that only a strong industrial sector could ensure the survival of an independent socialist Russia, it was not surprising that industry came to receive greater priority than agriculture. If independent peasants refused to cooperate, then agriculture should be collectivized and set targets to fulfil. By this means industrial formation would be satisfied at the same time as the economy socialized.

By introducing the NEP Lenin had hoped to overcome one of the main contradictions of the 1917 Revolution. The Bolsheviks had come to power with the support of urban workers who demanded the socialization of property. But the Party had also relied upon the support of the peasantry whose desire for individual land ownership clearly contradicted that urban ambition. With the decimation of the urban working classes during the civil war, many members of the Party saw in continued peasant demands a new potential for gradual capitalist restoration. Following the death of Lenin in 1924, questions concerning the role of the peasantry and the direction the revolution should take polarized the Party and were reflected in the ensuing power struggle. War and its impact on the workers' soviets inevitably focused greater power in the Party machinery and, hence, on its general secretary Joseph Stalin. Stalin had little faith in the peasantry or in Bukharin's slow economic transformation. By eliminating private property, by creating a highly centralized organizational structure based on commands and directives from the top down, and by expanding the heavy industry sector to facilitate expansion in other sectors, he believed Russia would be able rapidly to increase her economic development.[17] By 1928 Stalin had gained sufficient power to remove those who opposed rapid industrialization and the collectivization of agriculture. In 1929 his first Five Year Plan set out to transform the Soviet economy be coercing peasants to provide sufficient surpluses to allow massive investment in heavy industry. By a single *tour de force* he would accomplish a miracle. "We are on the eve of our transformation from an agrarian to an industrial country", Stalin told a startled 16th Congress.[18]

> . . . The pace must not be slackened . . . To slacken the pace would mean to lag behind and those who lag behind are beaten . . . The history of old . . . Russia . . . she was ceaselessly beaten for her backwardness. You remember the words of the pre-revolutionary poet: "Thou art poor and thou art plentiful, thou art mighty and thou art helpless, Mother Russia!" . . . We are fifty or a hun-

dred years behind the advanced countries. We must make good this lag in ten years. Either we do it or they crush us. [19]

By 1934 75 per cent of all peasants were collectivized and increasing supplies of cheap grain enabled rapid selective industrial growth. A second Five Year Plan consolidated the gains, creating huge new industrial complexes and greater national self-sufficiency. But the cost was high.

Stalin's policies precipitated massive opposition from the coerced peasantry. At times the process of collectivization had to be slowed down. Millions of peasants were transported to other regions to prevent rebellion or to open up new land for development. Others were forced from the land to join the industrial work force. Compulsion did not create efficient reliable workers and many peasants rebelled by walking off collectives or by reducing production. Initial opposition to collectivization resulted in the mass slaughter of cattle which together with increased grain procurements (at the same time as grain production fell) led to a severe famine over parts of Russia. The degree of coercion required to sustain rapid industrialization provoked further opposition from within the Communist Party. Fearing the possibility of an alternative government, Stalin acted quickly. Instruments of coercion designed to enforce economic transformation were turned onto the Party itself with devastating results. [20]

The great purges of the late 1930s, which removed all potential party and military opposition to Stalin, occurred at a time when the deterioration of European relations intensified Russian fears of war and provided "revolution from above" and "self-sufficiency" with renewed justification. It should not be forgotten that although no Allied invasion of Russia took place after 1921, Germany rearmed after 1934, Japan began to expand on the eastern borders of Russia, and in 1935 Germany, Italy and Japan signed a threatening Anti-Comintern Pact. Further, in 1938 the Western powers appeared to encourage German expansion by ceding Czechoslovakia to Germany. To Stalin, internal discontent, when viewed alongside increased external insecurity, could easily threaten the existence of the Soviet state. For this reason also Stalin was prepared to buy time, signing non-aggression pacts with Germany in 1939 and with Japan in 1941. Deutscher, in his biography of Stalin, remarked that the Russians, "wearied by years of strenuous economic construction, attached by an exalted devotion to the results of their labour, made sullen by the hostility . . . of the outside world" were at one with Stalin when he clung to peace. But it was a fragile, short peace, and when the German invasion came in 1941 Stalin discovered that he had grossly underrated Germany's striking power. [21]

Stalin's haste and his centralized selective development strategy created a difficult legacy. In the economy this is evident in the continuing imbalance between capital goods and consumer goods production, one of the initial priorities of Soviet economic planning. Also, Stalin's bureaucratic forms of organization did not produce efficiency and creativity. Problems of underproduction and the maldistribution and misuse of labour, therefore, combined with the exploitation of the peasantry to prevent the equal development of resources and ultimately checked the expansion of Russia's industrial base. The inflow of reparations from Eastern Europe in the late 1940s and the patriotic spirit of Russia's peoples to some extent disguised the seriousness of imbalance and allowed a speedy recovery from the destruction caused by the Second World War. But the onset of the Cold War and its renewed priority to military expenditure, caused the problems of a neglected agricultural sector to resurface. Bureaucratic planning and a continued insistence on low prices for agricultural commodities compared with industrial products, merely aggravated conditions already made severe by war damage and labour shortages. Soviet economic development, conditioned by the twin imperatives of speed and self-sufficiency, created legacies that post-Stalinist governments were to find less easy to ignore. Consequently in 1965 new economic reforms were introduced to overcome a serious downturn in economic growth and a build-up in unsold consumer goods by decentralizing a limited amount of decision-making, by introducing new incentives on the basis of sales or profits, and by introducing minimum wages for farmers, lowering taxation, lifting restrictions on private plots, and extending free social services.

Despite imbalances and the sacrifices demanded by rapid industrialization, Russia had demonstrated the economic viability of an alternative to capitalism. Rural relations had been transformed, massive migration from the land to cities effected, and vast tracts of Central Asia colonized as the country's economy expanded. The pattern of transformation had been remarkably similar to that of Europe's although more concentrated in time and systematic. It differed, however, in not allowing capitalist relations to determine and govern the transformation. The once powerful Russian ruling classes had been replaced by a new elite which set out to use the state, as Engels might have suggested, not in "the interests of freedom but in order to hold down its adversaries".[22] In the transition to communism, the classless state, the old Tsarist service gentry and bureaucracy was replicated in the new power elite and Soviet government. Stalin claimed that under socialism class differences were no longer antagonistic. To the extent that industry did not operate on the basis of capitalist competition for profit and the power elite did not exist to exploit the masses for the benefit of a ruling class Stalin was correct. Yet Stalin exploited the Russian peasantry to expand the industrial base and in the process adulterated many of the principles of the Revolution. Once industrialization had been achieved, however, it was easier for his successors to pay greater attention to problems of the rural sector without sacrificing the gains already made in industry. In fact they had little choice. Industrial expansion depended upon redressing the Stalinist imbalances in the Soviet economy, and correcting the all too obvious organizational problems.

Soviet critics in the late 1950s claimed that the consolidation of the state had produced a new exploitative class of technocrats and party officials. The Stalinist purges of the 1930s had prevented their early dominance, but in the more relaxed post-war years they expanded in similar ways to the

American white-collar labour force as the bureaucracy enlarged and changed technology transformed labour requirements. In many respects Russia's autocratic-bureaucratic tradition, her isolation in a hostile world, the relative weakness of spontaneous social forces, the logic of change from above and a centrally planned economy, together with her initial low level of education, exhaustion after civil war, and the decimation of the proletariat, made the trend towards a hierarchical-bureaucratic system likely. The result was and is "a unihierarchical society" (to use Alec Nove's description), a society which aims at stability and is durable and accepted.[23] As Deutscher notes, many of the revolution's distortions were due to its occurrence in a country whose sheer backwardness necessitated the substitution of social control by bureaucratic control. Soviet leaders were hardly free agents; social and economic circumstances created their own constraints. But the rise of a powerful bureaucracy did not, as we noted earlier, imply that all resultant social inequalities were the product of labour exploitation. The power of the Soviet ruling elite is not based on property and whatever privileges it enjoys are for consumption only. That fact, together with the impact of continued industrialization and mass education on social mobility, has made it impossible for any elite to perpetuate itself as a class.[24]

Regardless of the success or otherwise of socialism within Russia, its new leaders after 1918 were able to realize the industrial potential of the vast continental empire and in doing so challenged the hegemony of capitalist industrial nations. In seeking to establish a socialist world order, they transferred the challenge to a global level and introduced an ideological component which capitalist powers had hitherto only confronted internally. The circumstances under which the Soviet Union had been born and weaned created distortions which did not necessarily make the Soviet model attractive to other peoples and which all too easily could be used for propaganda purposes against Russia. Nevertheless, the formation of a socialist government demonstrated the difficulties any nation would face if it sought to leave the capitalist world order. Its success in retaining economic and political independence, despite internal upheavals and external threats, inspired socialist movements in other industrialized nations, and gave some Third World nationalists a model which indicated the possibility for planned indigenous and independent development and which emphasized the exploitative class basis of relations of dependency as the major cause for backwardness in the periphery of the world economy. Undoubtedly some of its attractiveness as a model was lost during the late 1950s in the wake of the post-Stalinist exposures (thereby forcing many periphery nations to reappraise their adoption of the Soviet model) and with the apparent Western success in sustaining a postwar boom. Yet in a very real sense, the Soviet Union demonstrated where socialism would become most important. Socialism may have been weakened in the core, but within the periphery of the world economy it would become part of the "great compensatory drive to catch up—an ideology of development or industrialization rather than one of post-capitalist society". And, to quote Nairn again, this has meant not only "the worldwide diffusion of socialism, at a tempo far more rapid than that imagined by the founding fathers", but also "that capitalism could not, finally, unify the world wholly in its own image".[25]

Notes

1. Karl Marx, *Critique of the Gotha Programme*, Foreign Languages Press, Beijing, 1972, p. 17.
2. Karl Marx and Frederick Engels, *The Communist Manifesto*, (1848), Nentori Publishing House, Tirana, 1981, p. 33.
3. Ibid., pp. 37-8, 41.
4. Ibid., pp. 41-2.
5. Ron Breth and Ian Ward, *Socialism, the options*, Hargreen, Melbourne, 1982, pp. 17-22.
6. Joll, pp. 52-54.
7. Ibid., p. 28.
8. Marx and Engels, p. 27.
9. G.S. Jones, "Working-Class Culture and Working-Class Politics in London, 1870-1900; Notes on the Remaking of a Working-Class", *Journal of Social History*, Summer 1974, pp. 460-508.
10. Albert Szymanski, *Is the Red Flag Flying? The Political Economy of the Soviet Union*, Zed Press, London, 1979, pp. 27-8.
11. Reinhardt Bendix, "Man, Freedom and the Future-Patterns of Social and Political Change", in Bullock, *The Twentieth Century*, pp. 350-51.
12. Alec Nove, *Political Economy and Soviet Socialism*, Allen and Unwin, London, 1979, pp. 76-7.
13. The following section draws on David McLellan, *Marxism after Marx, An Introduction*, Macmillan, London, 1980, pp. 101-40; Alec Nove, *Stalinism and After*, Allen and Unwin, London, 1975; and Albert Szmanski, op. cit.
14. Nove, *Political Economy*, p. 86.
15. Ibid., pp. 96-7.
16. Ibid., p. 86.
17. Breth and Ward, pp. 115-6.
18. Isaac Deutscher, *Stalin, A Political Biography*, Penguin, Harmondsworth, 1966, p. 321.
19. Ibid., p. 328.
20. P. Short, *The Dragon and the Bear, Inside China and Russia Today*, Hodder and Stoughton, London, 1982, pp. 115, 172. Short claims that as many as 10 million peasants died as a result of forced collectivization, and that 70 per cent of the Soviet Central Committee perished in the 1934-39 purges.
21. Deutscher, pp. 431-2, 450.
22. Engels quoted in H. Kohn, *The Modern World*, Macmillan, New York, 1968, p. 4.
23. Nove, *Political Economy*, pp. 199-201, 216.
24. I. Deutscher, *The Unfinished Revolution, Russia, 1917-1967*, Oxford University Press, 1967, pp. 38, 54-60.
25. Nairn, p. 357.

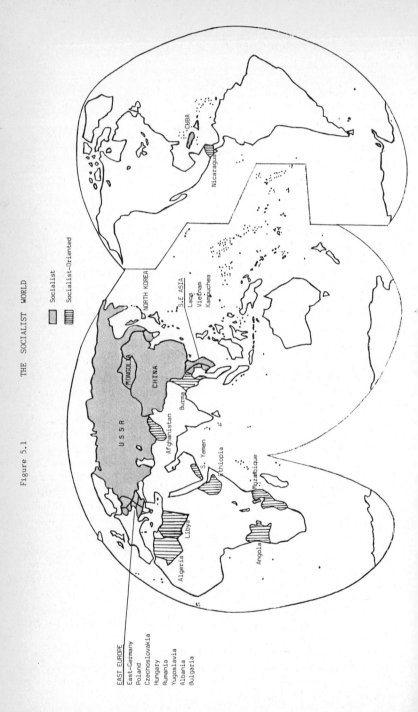

Figure 5.1   THE SOCIALIST WORLD

Socialist

Socialist-Oriented

CUBA

Nicaragua

NORTH KOREA

S.E. ASIA
Laos
Vietnam
Kampuchea

MONGOLIA

CHINA

U S S R

Burma

Afghanistan

S. Yemen

Ethiopia

Mozambique

Angola

Libya

Algeria

EAST EUROPE
East-Germany
Poland
Czechoslovakia
Hungary
Rumania
Yugoslavia
Albania
Bulgaria

6. The Integration of Japan

The Meiji Revolution

In Japan, as in many Asian and African countries, the struggle against metropolitan economic dominance was equated with a struggle against the white races. During the 1930s and early 1940s Japan exploited this equation to her own advantage. By proclaiming the liberation of Asia and the Pacific from the dominance of European and American imperialism, she was able to advance her own imperialist ambitions. In declaring the Greater East Asia Co-Prosperity Sphere, Japan urged East Asia to return "to its original form of independence and co-prosperity by shaking off the yoke of Europe and America," and to develop "in peaceful cooperation and secure livelihood".[1]

Japanese imperialism was a consequence of the nature of her transformation into an industrializing nation during the nineteenth century, itself a reaction to Western penetration into East Asia. Historically, Japan had always reacted strongly to any challenge which carried the danger of domination. As early as the period of the Taika Reforms (645-49) Japan defensively reconstructed her society in order to prevent the penetration of Chinese civilization destabilizing her own institutions. Confucianism was modified to stress loyalty to existing feudal hierarchies, and the position of Emperor placed outside the new centralized arena of politics to remove him from any threat of revolution. A similar reaction occurred at the end of the sixteenth century when Japan encountered the superior technology of Western Europe. Feudal government had already been captured by the strongest of the feudal lords, and after 1603 the military dictatorship of the shogunate (Bakufu government), supported by the new military monopoly of the samurai class, was stabilized under the Tokugawa. By instituting the Alternative Attendance or hostage system (see Chapter 2) and by gradually closing Japan's doors to the West (1614-40) the Bakufu was able to minimize the impact of Europe's culture and technology on its security.

As a foreign policy, isolation maintained the centralized feudal system but did little to meet future threats. By 1853, therefore, the technological gap had grown so large that Japan was powerless to prevent a new imperialist thrust bringing her more thoroughly into the orbit of Western mercantile and industrial activities. As we noted in Chapter 3, the irruption of the West precipitated the collapse of the Tokugawa shogunate and the formation of a new ruling class Meiji government intent on meeting the Western challenge by building a strong wealthy nation. The task was not a simple one given the feudal nature of Japanese society, and for much of the following decades was shaped by her experiences with the Western powers.

Following the establishment of diplomatic relations with the West in the early 1850s, Japan was pressed into signing a number of unequal commercial treaties with the United States, Britain, France, Holland and Russia. Although less drastic than those imposed on China, the unequal treaties restricted the manoeuvrability of the Meiji government and forced Japanese economic development along a restrictive path. Because the treaties deprived Japan of tariff autonomy, industry had of necessity to become highly specialized. Without tariff protection, the development of a wide industrial base was impossible. It was a lesson many industrializing European countries had learned at the end of the nineteenth century, but Japan was powerless to follow their example. The lack of tariff protection necessitated developing an export orientation instead, since specialization did not permit the growth and exploitation of a well-integrated internal market. This, Jon Halliday has argued, had several important effects.

> On the one hand it fostered a climate in which industry, on the grounds of competitivity, based its output on extremely low wages. On the other hand, it stimulated state intervention as the only means to deal with the internationally-induced impediments. The need to specialize and the large-scale intervention of the state accentuated the trend towards monopoly . . . [and] greatly affected the formation of the Japanese combines, the zaibatsu. With the development of heavy industry blocked by Western imperialism, Japan became an exporter of the only two vital industrial raw materials it had—coal and copper. In addition, maintenance of low wages justified by reference to the unequal treaties, and the lack of balance in the economy directly brought about by the treaties, helped to create pressures which played their part in Japanese imperialism. [2]

Although the unequal treaties were due for revision in 1872, 27 years of negotiations lapsed before Japan regained her judicial autonomy and 39 years before tariff autonomy was finally recovered in 1911.

Japan's economy expanded greatly once the treaty restrictions were lifted, but it was not so easy to eradicate their effects: Japan's domestic consumer market remained small, consumer production was still oriented towards export, and heavy industry towards meeting military needs. Japan's experiences with the unequal treaties also formed the background for the ideas relating to peace and the world order which led to the Pacific War. [3]

> What needs to be grasped [Halliday maintained], is the connection between the structure of Japanese industrialization and imperialism—the desire to control sources of raw materials and to secure markets; the relationship between expansion against the West and expansion in agreement with the West; the fusion in

popular consciousness of national prosperity with imperialism; the coincidence of interests between the military and heavy industry.[4]

The Meiji revolutionaries (named after the young emperor who succeeded to the throne in 1868) did not overthrow the feudal structure of Japan. Instead feudalism was "selectively and in piecemeal fashion eased out from above, in a manner which brought about changes in the relations of production but not in the essential locus of power."[5] In 1869 the Meiji government guaranteed universal freedom of choice in occupation and marriage as a first step in removing the feudal privileges of the samurai. Clan domains were abolished three years later and the stipends once paid the daimyo and samurai were diverted to the central government. The 1873 conscription edict, which began the formation of a modern army, also ended the military monopoly of the samurai.

These measures were necessary, the Meiji government argued, if Japan was to modernize sufficiently to prevent further Western encroachments of her sovereignity. Because Japan possessed no substantial bourgeoisie to undertake the development of her productive forces, the state itself was forced to accumulate capital by transforming rural relations sufficiently to enable a larger extraction of the agrarian surplus, and by expropriating the feudal dues of the old ruling classes. This capital was then invested in industries which the state considered best served Japan's defence against foreign domination. Such transformation did not come easily. Paying off its samurai and daimyo, suppressing the discontent generated, establishing the basic infrastructure for development (rail, telegraph, port and banking facilities) and instituting compulsory elementary education nearly bankrupted the government. In order to ease the burden, the stage sold off many new enterprises to merchants and high officials after 1880 and thereby created a new group of wealthy capitalists who would dominate industry thorugh their zaibatsu combines but remain loyal to the Meiji objective of a strong wealthy nation.

Imperialism

The situation facing the Japanese in terms of development strategy was similar to that faced by the Russians during the 1920s. Prosperity was possible if her economic sectors were uniformly developed and a strong internal market created on which to base industrial expansion. But given Japan's desire for security, slow balanced development did not prove attractive. Given also Japan's inability to prevent the penetration of Western manufactured commodities, a wide-based industrial sector was not possible. The formation of the zaibatsu, therefore, represented the government's intention to focus development on selected sectors which could later begin to integrate the rest of the country into a modern economy. The rural sector served only to provide capital for industrial expansion and labour for new industries. Since agricultural production received little attention and the position of the peasantry remained unimproved, Japan soon became dependent on food imports and was unable to exploit her huge rural population as a consumer base for her industries. Given that the rural sector could not sustain industrial investment and expansion, the government and its zaibatsu were forced to solve the problems of imbalanced development by resort to imperialism. This in itself posed no difficulties; after all it was the method by which all Western nations operated, and the Japanese government could easily justify expansion on the grounds that it enabled her to remain independent of the West. Japan, however, could not compete for colonial possessions in East Asia as an equal of the Western powers. Her economy was still weak and backward. Expansion, therefore, was dependent upon heavy borrowing and upon military pressure to ensure that Japanese privileges were not lost to rivals. Hence domestic exploitation increased to make possible the external orientation of her industries. A new ruling class alliance also emerged—between the bureaucracy, the zaibatsu, the landed interests who invested in the new selective growth areas, and the military which secured and protected foreign gains.

Imperialism required more than the alliance of new ruling class forces; it required popular support and dedication, and this could only be obtained by impressing upon Japan's masses a supportive ideology. Universal education provided the means, Confucianism the ideology. What had once been the preserve of the samurai was now spread to the populace as a whole. Confucian values of service and loyalty enabled greater mass acceptance of the sacrifices required for the successful application of imperialist policies. Saburo Ienaga, in his classic study of Japan's involvement in the Second World War, cites a scroll hung on primary school bulletin boards in 1894. It read:

> Battle report, Japanese troops defeat Chinese at P'yongyang and win a great victory. Chinese corpses were piled up as high as a mountain. Oh what a grand triumph. Chinka, Chinka, Chinka, so stupid and they stinka.

From an early age Japanese school children were encouraged to revel in the imperialist activities of their nation. Since there was a war every ten years, it was by no means an isolated instance.

> The national consciousness was markedly affected by those jingoistic booster shots every decade . . . They left a permanent militaristic tint to the standard curriculum . . . [6]

Japanese industrial expansion required substantial mass support and dedication for imperialism if industry's narrow base and lack of indigenous raw materials were to be overcome. It was also necessary since expansion in East Asia created the potential for conflict with the Western Powers. Because of their industrial superiority, Japan had little opportunity to compete successfully on the basis of Open Door policies. Only aggressive military pressure could achieve the necessary foreign advantages to offset her weakness vis-à-vis the European, Russian and American powers.

The nationalism and jingoism that was deliberately promoted to engender popular support for imperialist policies served also to blunt class perceptions. As in Europe, industrialization caused the formation of new working class organizations. but because industry had come to depend upon the easy exploitation of cheap labour in order to compete favourably in foreign markets, it could not be induced to accept that improved working conditions would be in its long-term interests. Given the close bonds that existed between industry and government, it was not unexpected that the state should hold similar views. Union and organized working class activity was invariably met with swift and brutal repression. Nevertheless, the outbreak of riots in Tokyo in 1905, strikes in the major shipyards and arsenals during 1906 and 1907, and uprisings in various mines in 1907 disturbed the ruling class. These were the key sectors of the economy. The Japanese populace had to be conditioned to make sacrifices for the sake of national development. [7]

While education and the promotion of nationalism provided one means of controlling the workforce, the zaibatsu provided another by extending Confucian values to the workplace. Initially there had been little need for such measures. During the 1870s and 1880s the government and zaibatsu had obtained their workers from among the unemployed samurai, particularly their daughters. But as industry expanded the zaibatsu were forced to look beyond the highly nationalistic samurai and to find methods by which the same kind of dedication could be obtained from a wider workforce. The seniority wage structure provided the means, loyalty being rewarded by paying extra wages to employees who stayed longer with a company. This did not mean that all employees were guaranteed lifetime employment, but the bait was there. If they proved their loyalty and remained with the company, they would eventually obtain secure employment. In the meantime hardship should be accepted in the knowledge that there would eventually be rewards. Conversely, disloyalty was discouraged by making it virtually impossible for workers who left a zaibatsu's employment to find work in a similar company. Like the samurai of the past, they were deemed to have failed to provide the loyalty service demanded of them. Hence they became outcastes—ronin—forced to sell their labour like mercenaries to less prestigious, small and medium-sized companies that could never offer the same kind of monetary incentives or security provided by the larger zaibatsu. [8]

The samuraization of the workforce had important effects. Those who made it into the zaibatsu eventually gained considerable economic advantages and opportunities for advancement not available in smaller and non-government-supported companies. Because of the incentives they were able to offer, the zaibatsu obtained the best workers, and by sheer dint of their superior resources remained far in advance of the smaller industries. In many respects the zaibatsu were the new equivalent of the daimyo, demanding loyalty and collective cooperation from their employees in return for substantial housing, educational, sporting, welfare and health support. Because they had been chosen to represent Japan in the achievement of the national aim of building a strong country to compete with the Western powers, the zaibatsu were in turn loyal to the government. Hence the Meiji aim for a rich country and a strong army went hand in hand.

The preferential state treatment received by the zaibatsu and their highly specialized operations produced an economic duality of which the lifetime employment system was both a result and a contributing factor. This gap between the large and small or medium-sized industries, manifested in wages and conditions of service, widened during the early 20th century and created dangerous internal pressures in the future as expectations of a better life failed to materialize. Instead of focusing on the development of a strong, integrated internal economy, Japan pushed ahead with the search for foreign markets and raw materials which would allow the kind of expansion her sacrificed internal markets could not.

Given Japan's growing dependence on external markets and the internal pressures and contradictions that dependency imposed as a result of the speed and direction of her industrialization, it was not surprising that officials were, in the words of one, "always prepared to let the military have their way and in later years at length rather than risk the possibility of civil war or revolution in Japan".[9] Between 1868 and 1945 Japan went to war on ten different occasions. Her early wars (Taiwan 1874, Korea 1876, China 1894, Russia 1904) quickly demonstrated the advantages of aggression: her armed forces were strengthened and the basis of her economy expanded through new sources of raw materials, cheap labour and access to new markets. World War One provided fresh opportunities and Japan declared war on Germany in order to grab the German colonies of East Asia, notably Shandong, the Marianas, Carolines and Marshall Islands, and to pressure the weak Chinese Government into conceding further economic rights in Manchuria and Fujian. Expansion, combined with the absence of European products in Asia for the duration of the war, stimulated Japan's economy and caused a rapid growth in light industry. Heavy industry also became more prominent as military expansion created new demands.

Industrial expansion however served also to emphasize the unbalanced nature of Japan's economy. Failure to modernize agriculture restricted the ability of her internal market to accommodate industrial expansion. At the same time Japan became increasingly dependent on food imports. As industry grew, dependency on imported raw materials aggravated Japan's vulnerability to balance of payments deficits. Offsetting deficits by increasing exports of textiles and silk became more difficult after 1919 with the return of Western competition in East Asia and the erection of tariff barriers in American (and European) markets during and after the 1920s. The unwillingness of Western industrialized nations to permit greater Japanese trade reinforced her determination to establish an imperial base to reduce dependence on the West. That dependence, and the inferiority it assumed, was dramatically demonstrated at the 1921-22 Washington Naval Conference where Japan was forced to cancel plans to extend her navy and accept a Pacific fleet smaller than either Britain's or the United States'.

The Japanese dilemma was partly of her own making. Selective development had created huge internal disparities which served to emphasize her weakness. Exploitation of the peasantry created tensions which could not be met as long as the agricultural sector remained undeveloped and dominated by parasitic landlords. It also prevented the growth of an internal market capable of sustaining economic growth, thereby forcing Japan to look to foreign markets instead. Industrial dualism likewise produced inequalities, weakening the internal market and creating fresh social tensions. Since Japan had not reformed her industry or attempted to reduce internal disparities, she relied solely on expansion to generate prosperity. But the continuation of high production costs, together with the inflationary pressures of war, caused the living standards of many workers and peasants to fall. Prices rose drastically between 1914 and 1918. Rice alone rose 50 per cent between 1917 and 1918 and was the initial spark which set off major demonstrations, strikes and peasant revolts in mid-1918. The Meiji dream for a wealthy nation seemed to have failed. Typically the Japanese ruling class reacted to discontent by suppressing it and by setting out, not to reform internal contradictions, but to transform Korea and Taiwan into major rice producers and suppliers to Japan. Once more the solution to internal problems was to turn to empire.

Unfortunately for Japan's governments, developments during the 1920s (the failure of the Allied-Japanese Siberian expedition against the USSR, the Washington Naval Conference, and the gradual reunification of China under the Guomindang) did not augur well for imperial expansion. Within Japan also poverty grew as disparities widened with the contraction of her domestic economy and with the onset of depression in 1927. Two further blows followed in quick succession. In 1930 the London Naval Conference upset the naval balance established in 1922 by restricting Japan's navy further. In the same year the Smoot-Hawley tariff raised by 23 per cent import duties on Japanese goods entering the United States. Compromise with the West seemed to bring little joy.

The Great Depression hit the rural areas of Japan the hardest and the Japanese army was overwhelmingly of peasant origin. It decided to move against the suffering and misery at home by reverting to the time-proven solution of imperialism. Japan's military and naval forces had been instrumental in securing the basis for industrial expansion. But after the First World War their commanders felt that the government and the zaibatsu, in giving in to Western pressure, had overlooked their value to the nation. Officers in the field eventually came to regard the government as decadent; it had forgotten or betrayed the Meiji ambition for a strong wealthy nation. The semi-independent position of the military allowed over-zealous officers an opportunity to confront the government directly, particularly when developments in China threatened to jeopardize Japanese gains and reduce the possibility for future expansion. In 1928 they assassinated the Manchurian warlord, Zhang Zolin, when he refused to oppose Jiang Kaishek's reunification of China under the Western-supported Guomindang. Despite government requests, the Army Command refused to discipline the officers involved. Regardless of internal divisions over tactics, the army's leaders accepted the need to restore the prestige of its forces and to secure an independent base that would bestow upon Japan equal great power status.

Increasingly the army acted without consulting the government. In September 1931 it invaded Manchuria and by 1934 had extended control over much of Northern China. The army's success fostered a war mood in Japan which was reinforced by the terrorist activities of radical army factions against a wavering government and its zaibatsu. To offset initial zaibatsu resistance, the military created its own loyal companies, but eventually right-wing attacks on government and zaibatsu leaders wore down their opposition. By the time a junior officer coup was squashed in 1936, Japan possessed a quasi-war economy with a new emphasis on heavy industry to meet military needs, and its ideological infrastructure was already extolling war as a viable means for Japan to fulfil her historic destiny.

Despite the increasing role of the military, it should not be supposed that the course Japan took after 1931 was remarkably different from that assumed from the time of the Meiji. Japanese officials—civilian and military—shared the same dream. Like the Soviets, they wished to promote national security; like the Germans and Italians, they wanted to prevent their country from being squeezed into the role of a second- or even third-rate power. Where they differed among themselves was not in respect of the goals of development but, as we saw much earlier, over the speed and methods that could be used for obtaining those goals. Diplomats like Yoshida Shigeru, later one of the founding prime ministers of the post war era, argued that Japan could secure imperial needs without losing the cooperation and goodwill of the Western powers, particularly those involved as imperialists in East Asia. Aggression itself was not the subject of debate, only the extent to which such policies reflected a tendency to go it alone. Inevitably there were moderate politicans like Konoe and Hirota, as well as many businessmen and military leaders, who soon discovered that an independent colonial policy also bestowed upon them advantageous powers and opportunities they might not otherwise have.[10] In any case, the war in China soon developed its own momentum, and it became increasingly difficult for any member of the ruling classes to repudiate the path Japan was now hurtling along.

Japan's invasion of North China in 1931 demonstrated her new determination to challenge the Western imperialist nations which had thwarted her ambitions. Britain and the United States reacted by mobilizing the League of Nations to try and check Japan's aggression.

The Report of the 1932 Lytton Commission made clear the basic complicity among the imperialist powers over events in China. Japan was allowed to advance all the way from Mukden to Indochina over a period of ten years with hardly a finger being lifted by the West. It was only when Japan attacked the colonies of Europe and the United States, and Hawaii, that the Pacific War started.[11]

Military expansion and the effects of economic depression caused Japan's governments to reformulate their Asian policies (the Greater East Asian

Co-Prosperity Sphere) and to protect their new colony of Manzhuguo from Western and Chinese interference. The Chinese threat loomed greater after 1936 when the Communists and Guomindang settled their differences and launched a United Front against Japan. Both Japan's government and military were uncertain what steps they should take to meet this new threat. General Tada in Tokyo saw any extension of conflict in China as "a deviation into a swamp". [12] His field commanders disagreed, and in 1937 began the invasion of China.

Military expansion was accompanied also by a new and aggressive assault on the economic privileges enjoyed by the Western powers. The downturn in economic activity in Europe and North America provided a new opportunity for Japan to cut into Western markets. By devaluing her yen, she succeeded in making her goods more competitive. In India, for example, at the same time as Britain's share of the Indian cotton cloth market fell from 97 per cent in 1913 to 47 per cent in 1935, Japan's share rose from 0.3 per cent to 50 per cent. When the West retaliated with further quotas and tariffs, Japan extended her operations to include parts of Africa, the Middle East and Latin America. Exports in the latter, for instance, rose from 13 million yen to 110 million yen between 1931 and 1936 (from 4.5 per cent of the South American cotton market to 38.6 per cent between 1929 and 1935), again largely at the expense of Britain (whose proportion of the South American market fell from 53 to 46 per cent in the same years) and Italy and the United States (whose combined share fell from 42 to 15 per cent). [13] In Asia, however, Japan had long decided that such equality with the other powers could not be attained by investment imperialism or by trade. A military presence was necessary to secure her interests.

The more Japan sought to overcome her internal contradictions, the more she became committed to empire. Inevitably this brought her into conflict with the major powers whose colonies she coveted. The United States posed the greatest threat to her ambitions, not because of its Asian possessions (it had only the Philippines in South-east Asia), but because Japan was dependent upon the US for supplies of crude oil and scrap iron. America's embargoes on the export of these vital supplies in July 1941 restricted Japan's manoeuvrability, and negotiations with the Americans were pursued in earnest until November 1941 when the United States refused to accept Japan as an equal partner in Asia. The government and military felt they had little choice but to incapacitate the US Pacific fleet (few Japanese believed it possible to defeat the US) long enough to enable South-east Asia to be captured and alternative sources of the vital raw materials secured. [14] Thus was conceived the attack on Pearl Harbour in December 1941 and the simultaneous assault on the Philippines, Malaya, Burma and the Dutch East Indies.

Japan went into South-east Asia with surprising ease. Her troops were superior to any forces encountered and possessed the added advantage of being able to make use of local antagonism towards the European colonial forces which had for so long exploited and suppressed their colonial peoples. Yet despite the militarization of her economy, Japan was unprepared for a long war. Her industrial base was new and its expansion dictated by military requirements not technological progress. Eventually her reliance on shipping to provide the vital raw materials required by the industrial war machine made war difficult to sustain once the American counter-attack began. But as Tada had predicted it was China which most contributed to Japan's defeat, tying down the bulk of her army and preventing its deployment elsewhere. National liberation movements also had a similar effect. Predictably, the American impact was technological. After the fighting in Tarawa in 1943, the Americans deliberately restricted direct fighting against the Japanese and made greater use of her naval forces. [15] When the Americans finally moved in for the kill (to prevent Russia taking advantage of the Japanese collapse in East Asia as much as to save her own forces), their technological superiority was once more demonstrated with overwhelming effect. Ninety-two years after American forces first entered Japan to force her government to open Japan's doors to the West, two atom bombs obliterated Hiroshima and Nagasaki. On 14 August Japan surrendered. Two and a half million of her people (one-third being civilians) were dead, 40 per cent of her urban areas lay destroyed, and industrial production had ground to a halt as a result of fuel and raw material shortages, the collapse of transportation, and the loss of markets. Japan's challenge had failed, but not before the whole face of East and South-east Asia had been changed and the old order of Western political dominance banished forever.

Reintegration

Defeat brought American occupation. Until 1952 Japan was ruled by the Allied General Headquarters under the Supreme Commander of the Allied Powers (SCAP). Partly because of America's desire to strengthen its own position in East Asia vis-à-vis its allies and partly because its allies were not strong enough to resist, the United States did not divide Japan into allied occupation zones. Since defeat had not resulted in the collapse of government, and since SCAP was content to rule Japan through the bureaucracy, the established system of government remained unchanged. Nevertheless the Americans were determined that Japan should never again challenge the Western powers and to this end sought to destroy the materials and to some extent the social basis of her imperialism. Democratization was immediately effected—the franchise extended, education decentralized and reformed, the feudal peerage abolished, and war renounced as an instrument of foreign policy. Organizations which had aided Japanese imperialism—nationalist and militarist groups, the zaibatsu, and armed forces—were ordered to disband. Repressive laws were also repealed. In the purge which followed, some 200,000 business, military and political officials fell. However, in seeking to reduce Japan's economic development to the same level as her Asian neighbours, initially by means of an industrial reparations policy, the Americans were forced to confront their own long-term objectives. If Japan was to be incorporated into a new American-dominated world order there was little to be gained by destroying her economy. Accordingly policies of deindustrialization and the dissolution of the Mitsui, Mitsubishi, Sumitomo and Yasuda zaibatsus were halted.

Pressure from US corporations which held substantial investments in various zaibatsu affiliates was also responsible for the redirection of policy. If Japan was to become a relatively autonomous nation under US hegemony, her industries had to be allowed to expand once more, and for that purpose make use of the new US Asian dependencies as markets. Subservience to American interests would be guaranteed by a continued military presence, and by US control of raw materials (particularly petroleum) and Japanese trading routes. A wealthy Japan would also enable her to become a market for American products, and after 1947, a strong bastion against an escalating socialist challenge in East Asia.

The initial liberalization effected by SCAP after 1945 resulted in the formation of new working-class organizations. Although relatively weak, new trade union combinations—particularly the Sanbetsu—attempted to change the direction of SCAP's economic policies, and organized a number of strikes during 1946 and 1947 for this purpose. SCAP took the challenge seriously and introduced new legislation to limit union activity. The 1949 Dodge programme of retrenchment provided a further opportunity to weaken left-wing influence. Large numbers of workers were laid off and at various educational, media and party political levels retrenchment amounted to a purge of all personnel of left-wing persuasion. A series of measures and reforms were also introduced to permanently weaken the left. Businesses, for instance, were encouraged to establish rival enterprise unions and to reintroduce Confucian management techniques.

The problem of working-class discontent was acute at the end of the war because of food shortages and the collapse of industry. Indeed many conservative officials had urged the Emperor to end the war quickly for fear of impending revolutionary chaos in the wake of the state's failure to maintain control. Postwar purges served to increase the importance of this conservative rump within the government, as of course did the growing dependence upon them of SCAP officials imbued with a "cold war" mentality. [16] As SCAP's director, General MacArthur, remarked, by eliminating

the feudalistic system of land ownership there will emerge in Japan, from a field heretofore fertile to the spread of communism, a new class of small capitalist landowners, which itself will stand firm against efforts to destroy the system of capitalist economy of which it will then form an integral part. [17]

Agrarian reform, therefore, established new internal and external dependent relationships, between the small farmer and the ruling conservative politicians, and between the Japanese rural sector and American agricultural exporters, all in the name of social stability and the preservation of capitalism. Land reform removed the problem of absentee landownership and gave greater security to the tenant farmer. It also enabled a rise in rural living standards and permitted an increase in agricultural productivity. The reforms likewise encouraged urbanization, a necessary transformation if expanding industries were to have sufficient labour. As a result Japan's agricultural population fell from 16 million to 12 million between 1950 and 1960, and to 6.7 million by 1970.

SCAP's land reforms were not radical. By restricting the size of holdings they prevented the consolidation of land into modern and highly productive units. Agriculture's lack of competitiveness, therefore, compelled successive Japanese governments to provide huge subsidies (1.2 per cent of GNP in 1967) to farmers for the rice they produced. While subsidies removed rural discontent, they also enabled the ruling Liberal Democrat Party (LDP) to build up a strong rural base of support. Land reform had not substantially altered tenant relationships, with the result that traditional power bonds were perpetuated. By ensuring that the voting system was deliberately weighted in favour of the rural community, the LDP found a means to retain power after 1955. Votes for subsidies—it was the beginning of a new symbiotic relationship.[18]

Land reform produced a conservative countryside and a retarded rural sector sustained by agricultural subsidies and unable to adapt rapidly to demands for new crops. American interests were assured however, and Japan rapidly became the largest foreign market for US farm produce. I is important to realize that agriculture had once again been sacrificed to industrial expansion, and, as in the past, any solution to Japan's dependency and food imports had to be sought externally; in the 1970 it was to take the form of agriculture enclaves in the Third World.

Escalation of the Cold War, notably the outbreak of the Korean War in 1951, completed Japan's incorporation. Once more her economy was rapidly militarized, new armed forces (with largely pre-1945 personnel established, and Japanese troops were deployed as engineers and advisers in the Korea they had once held. The 1951 San Francisco Peace and Security Treaties formally tied Japan to American interests, and permitted her continued occupation by US troops. Between 1950 and 1955 alone the United States spent close to $2.5 billion in Japan on military goods for the Cold War effort, which, while stimulating the rationalization of industry reestablished the predominance of large-scale heavy and chemical combines. The duality of industry soon reemerged, together with the seniority and lifetime employment systems to discipline the workforce. (By 1980 the zaibatsu and konzern paid wages 30 per cent higher than small-medium companies. Productivity in the large corporations was also 60 per cent higher.) Selective development was again the dominant feature of the Japanese economy, with all the contradictions this imposed.

Such was the price Japan paid when her ruling classes accepted political and military dependence on the United States in return for a degree of economic autonomy. Oligopolistic competition between the zaibatsu remained as before. Despite US control of oil imports, Japan was able to limit foreign investment, and thereby independently promote economic growth without being forced to address the structural problems which have constantly threatened her economy. Nevertheless the weakness of consumer production, imbalances between economic sectors, reliance on Western-controlled oil, and an over-utilization of credit and turnover to finance investment and trade have created an economic fragility which continually prevents Japan from attaining the very independent role and equality she has long sought.

In many respects Japan has been fortunate. Her isolation from the major centres of capital and her proximity to a strong socialist challenge in Asia, at least permitted her a degree of independence and responsibility that postwar Germany—more easily integrated into neighbouring capitalist countries and confronted by a less vigorous revolutionary challenge—was never allowed. Japanese imperialism in Asia, therefore, revived but under the umbrella of the United States, whose initial investment and military support allowed the creation of "double colonialism" in Indochina and Korea.[19]

With the beginning of a new recession in the world economy after 1970 and the resurrection of protectionist policies, Japan found herself once more confronting the problem of market restrictions. While still politically subordinate to the United States, she reacted with an independent and aggressive trade policy which marked the beginning of a new era of intracore economic rivalry. This time no major socialist challenge existed to enforce the American community of power. Instead it was shaken by a third imperialist thrust as the major powers attempted to offset their decline in international trade by securing for themselves the benefits of Third World development. Once more Japan focused predominantly on Asia. Asian herself, and uniquely placed because of her economic role under the American umbrella, Japan possessed advantages which neither the US nor Europe could overcome. Indeed her dependence on trade for prosperity rekindled an old drive. As free trade between metropolitan powers became increasingly restricted during the late 1970s and early 1980s, Japan was faced with the same imperative she had confronted in the 1930s; to survive she had to reduce her dependence on the Western Powers and construct her own unequal economic relationships.

Notes

1. "Draft of Basin Plan for the Establishment of a Great East Asia Co-Prosperity Sphere", in Tsunoda, pp. 810-13.
2. Halliday, p. 53.
3. Morishima, p. 68.
4. Halliday, p. 101-2.
5. Ibid., p. xx.
6. See Saburo Ienaga, *Japan's Last War*, Australian National University (ANU), Canberra, 1980.
7. Halliday, pp. 69-70.
8. Morishima, pp. 103-23.

9. J.W. Dower (ed.), *Origins of the Modern Japanese State, Selected Writings of E.H. Norman*, Pantheon, New York, 1975, p. 78.

10. Ibid., *Empire and Aftermath: Yoshida Shigeru and the Japanese Experience, 1878-1954*, Council on East Asian Studies, Harvard University, Cambridge, Mass., 1979, pp. 56-61.

11. Halliday, p. 124.

12. Ibid., p. 127.

13. Ibid., pp. 128-31.

14. Ibid., pp. 132-3.

15. Ibid., pp. 141-5. Halliday presents an excellent summary of the Pacific War and the various ways it has been analysed, see pp. 141-59.

16. Dower, *Empire*, pp. 257, 289.

17. Ibid., pp. 298-9.

18. Halliday, p. 194.

19. Ibid., pp. 293-9.

7. American Hegemony

The Frontier

At the close of the Second World War the Soviet Union found herself the remaining dominant power in Europe. Having borne the brunt of war she was weak and able to do little more than secure what the Western nations had once termed the *cordon sanitaire* as her own barrier against future Western aggression. Within this wide belt of occupied East Europe Russia's ability to determine events was similarly restricted. In Finland she permitted the retention of a Western-style parliamentary system. In Poland, Hungary and Czechoslovakia strong nationalist sentiments made it necessary to reduce the Soviet presence before attempting socialist reforms. In the south, also, Rumanian and Yugoslavian nationalists wished to diminish, if not end, Soviet influence in their socialist regimes. These internal problems were not considered immediately pressing if Eastern Europe remained secure. It was not long, however, before American actions in Western Europe forced Soviet leaders to reconsider the stability of their newly-won buffer states.

The victor of the Pacific war, the United States of America, was equally determined to stabilize the war-torn West European nations. If American ambitions had been limited to restoration, conflict with the Soviet Union might have been avoided. Given their cooperation during the war years, neither perceived ideological differences as insurmountable. But the war had promoted the United States to the largest industrialized power in the world and it had suffered no internal damage or upheaval in the process. The defeat of the Axis powers, therefore, presented the United States with an opportunity to expand and to control the industrialized core nations. In pursuing an expansionist policy, America came up against the Soviet desire to retain Eastern Europe as its own sphere of influence.

American actions immediately following the Second World War have often been misunderstood, partly because of lingering Cold War propaganda, but partly also because it has become widely accepted that the United States was thrust suddenly to the fore of world politics in 1945 after a long period of isolation. These myths have served to disguise the fact that since 1776 it has pursued a policy of expansionism for purposes similar to Germany and Japan. Much of its expansion has been popularly accepted as frontier extension within the American continent, producing a concept of empire different from Britain's or Japan's.

From the time of its birth as 12 eastern states that had successfully fought for independence from Britain, expansion was regarded as essential to provide the Republic a strong economic base. The early colonists were predominantly farmers and small property owners. Their powerful beliefs in equal opportunity and social-economic mobility, which the War of Independence had done much to consolidate as the American Way of Life, became the justification for expansion into the surplus space of the vast continent. The settler drive to penetrate and develop determined the removal of all who opposed expansion, whether indigenous Indians or Mexicans. In 1822 President Monroe told Congress:

> It must be obvious to all, that the further expansion is carried, provided it be not beyond the just limit, the greater will be the freedom of action to both Governments, and the more perfect their security; and, in all other respects, the better the effect will be to the whole American people. Extent of territory . . . marks, in short the difference between a great and small power.[1]

Expansion fostered prosperity and permitted the absorption of vast numbers of immigrants fleeing from poverty and unrest in Europe. To them also, expansion offered opportunities for a better way of life. Expansion, therefore, served not only to ensure prosperity for more and more people, but it came increasingly to be seen as the only way to provide for future security. The surplus of free land, Senator Doolittle of Wisconsin declared, "will postpone for centuries, if not forever, all serious conflict between capital and labour.[2] Few politicians doubted the purpose of American imperialism. "Great as we are", argued Ignatius Donnelly of Minnesota, "we are yet in the day of small things . . . [Our] destiny is to grasp the commerce of all the seas and sway the sceptre of the world."[3]

Frontier expansion reflected the tendency of colonists to generate the colonial phenomenon themselves. Yet at the same time it created dangerous tensions within the Republic itself. Rivalry between the distinct northern and southern states for control of the new western territories eventually erupted into a bitter civil war in 1861. Historian W.A. Williams has argued that President Abraham Lincoln aimed simply to deny the incompatible economic system of the old southern plantation states the right to expand.[4] Once the secessionist Confederacy had been defeated and occupied, the North created new unequal relationships which transformed the South into a dependency whose surpluses could be used to assist northern industrial expansion.

After the civil war, therefore, expansion served also to provide the necessary base for industry. Increased penetration of the continent was accompanied by expanding immigration. America's population grew rapidly. In 1780 it had stood at only 5 million, but in 1840 it was 17 million, by 1880 63 million and by 1930 it had doubled again. By 1890 the frontier no longer offered unlimited cheap land for settlement, with the result that immigrants poured into the cities where they became cheap labour for industry. The new importance of urban communities and the growing economic power of large industrial monopolies created further conflict within the Republic, particularly with the once dominant rural population, who saw in the chaotic and often foreign conditions of industrial cities a threat to the way of life they had always held as truly American. Many of the new immigrants were derived from non-English-speaking and non-Protestant parts of Europe and presented an alien character which coincided with the new political and economic power of the metropolis. The rural community fought back, but their Populist Movement was unable to regain control of the market economy and weaken the power of industrial corporations.

As the United States was transformed into an industrial, urban, multi-ethnic society, its dominant ideology underwent radical change. Industrialization and urbanization contradicted the rural-based values of social mobility and equal opportunity: small-scale private enterprise declined, industrial monopolies restricted individual opportunities, and the wretched state of urban immigrants mocked beliefs in America as the brave new world. A new ideology, Social Darwinism, soon emerged to accommodate these contradictions and to justify the monopolization of wealth by new industrial and commercial elites. Its tenet, "survival of the fittest", relegated the poor to economic misery for reasons of personal ineptitude— they lacked industry, piety and sobreity. The wealthy, on the other hand, demonstrated natural selection in operation. Henceforth, notions of social mobility and opportunity were tied firmly to the aggressive expansion of power and wealth as represented by the new elites and not the small independent property owners.

Social Darwinism also provided a new motivation for expansion similar to Europe's civilizing mission and Japan's liberating service. It was the duty of the "fittest" races to rule in order to guarantee progress. The editor of the *Democratic Review* argued that it was America's mission

> to smite unto death the tyranny of kings, hierarchs, and oligarchs, and carry the glad tidings of peace and good will where myriads now endure an existence scarcely more enviable than the beasts of the field. [5]

Similarly, the Rev. Josiah Strong wrote in 1885,

> If I read not amiss, this powerful race will move down upon Mexico, down upon Central and South America, out upon the islands of the sea, over upon Africa and beyond . . . the precursors of a superior race. [6]

But the "divine plan", "the final competition of race", or whatever name popularly described America's mission to the world, was never simply a moral one. Salvation lay through trade and the penetration of capitalist relations. Defending the activities of religious and secular missionaries in the Middle East, the US resident consular officer declared,

> In a thousand ways they are raising the standard of morality, of intelligence, of

education . . . Directly or indirectly every phase of their work is rapidly paving the way for American commerce. . . .I know of no import better adapted to secure the future commercial supremacy of the United States. [7]

As in Europe, the popular press carried the message to the masses. Expansion sustained national economic and social well-being; the wealth obtained would trickle down to provide prosperity for all, and the patriotism generated would serve to dissolve the divisions of town and country, native and immigrant.

American imperialism intensified at the end of the nineteenth century. Like the nations of Europe, the United States experienced a sharp downturn in economic activity in the late 1880s and early 1890s and sought a solution in the control of new foreign markets. Given the intense intracore competition the new imperialism generated, the United States had not only to ensure that avenues for expansion remained open to its industry and commerce, it had also to assert itself as an equal of the major powers. These imperatives were manifested in a number of ways during the following decades, in the first instance, by war with Spain in 1898 which secured the first American colonies—Cuba, Puerto Rico, Guam and the Philippines. The Philippines also provided the United States with a foothold in Asia, the focus of her second major initiative, the declaration of an open door policy in 1899. The open door policy asserted American equality as a major imperialist power and assured it access to China, a corollary of which was the annexation of Hawaii in 1898.

President Theodore Roosevelt's declaration in 1904 that the United States would act as the policeman of the world was a logical extension of the Open Door concept. America had to ensure order in the world if an Open Door policy was to permit the expansion of trade, and for this reason he intervened in the Russo-Japanese War (1905) and in the European conflict over Morocco (1906). The policeman's role similarly justified financing Panama's revolution against Colombia in 1903 in order to secure for the United States the canal rights across the isthmus. Increasingly thereafter America interfered with greater aggressiveness in the internal affairs of Latin American nations to secure and promote her own economic interests. "Our surplus energy is beginning to look beyond our own borders", Roosevelt's successor, Taft, explained with more direct honesty, "...to find the opportunity for the profitable use of our surplus capital [and] for markets for our manufactures..." [8] Equally direct was W.H. Page, the US ambassador to Britain, who told Foreign Secretary Grey in 1913 that his country would, if necessary, shoot Mexicans "till they learn to vote and rule themselves". "Sanitary reformation" would eventually make Mexico "safe for life and investment." [9] As V.G. Kiernan observed,

Metaphors of hygiene and sickness, denoting civilization and barbarism, and of sanitary elimination of bad men and germs unfriendly to profitable investment, were to cluster thickly round the coming American hegemony. [10]

The rapid growth of American imperialism at the turn of the century reflected its new determination to provide for economic security by gain-ing control of the world's markets. Although its leaders saw no need to become embroiled in the internal affairs of Europe, they could not turn a blind eye to the effect changes in the European balance of power had on their own interests. As the American empire expanded, its well-being could be guaranteed only by seeking security from any imaginary future contingency. Hence, when President Wilson took his country into the First World War on the side of the Allies in 1917, he did so on the grounds that only by ensuring a more ordered and less competitive world could America's long-term prosperity be assured. The implications of such a grand and extensive role became clear to many Americans at the war's end; permanent entanglement in messy and intractable European affairs. In any case the boom of the 1920s and the disastrous depression in the following decade soon came to eclipse any substantial American attention to the problems of unstable Europe. For a time at least it seemed as if American interests could best be promoted by means of a less crusading and extensive foreign policy.

Nevertheless the Great Depression demonstrated that American security could not be divorced from events in Europe. As we have already seen, the world economic crisis resulted from contradictions inherent in capitalist expansion. Instead of promoting international trade, the industrialized nations increasingly resorted to trade barriers in an effort to protect themselves from damaging competition. This was not a new development but when combined with economic dislocation in the aftermath of war, the indebtedness of most European countries, and deteriorating internal economic imbalances, protectionism suppressed demand further and eventually precipitated international economic collapse. American internal contradictions also contributed. Wartime expansion rates were sustained during the 1920s by an over-zealous use of credit, which served to hide growing disparities between a depressed rural sector and a grossly inflated industrial sector. In 1929 the speculative boom faltered and crashed. Against all expectations the economy did not revive.

As consumer spending declined, businesses and banks collapsed and by 1933 over 15 million persons were unemployed, nearly one-quarter of the American labour force. The severity of the depression was without precedent and few politicians or business leaders could suggest anything other than sitting it out. Orthodox economic wisdom held that unemployment reduced wages and thereby lowered production costs. Lower costs meant cheaper commodities which would allow demand to pick up, thus regenerating investment and employment. The natural working of supply and demand would provide its own solution. All the government had to do was aid the natural process by cutting wages, lowering prices and raising taxation. But orthodox wisdom proved defective. More businesses collapsed and unemployment grew steadily worse. The years passed without sign of relief.

In the vacuum of government inactivity anything was preferable to destitution. Fascist state conscription of resources for private business offered an immediate solution in some European countries, notably

Germany and Italy, but it was one still based on the very national orientation that had fuelled the slump in the first place. The fascist solution involved regenerating economies by rearmament, a solution not popular with war-weary Britain or the United States. Reformist economists like John Maynard Keynes proposed an alternative to rearmament. Keynes argued that the central feature of the Great Depression was under-consumption If states were prepared to budget for deficits, in other words borrow money, they could restore consumption by circulating more money. Greater consumption meant restored business profitability and more employment. Turning the orthodox economic arguments on their head, Keynes argued that governments could assist recovery by cutting interest rates in order to promote investment, and by introducing massive public works schemes to absorb the unemployed and inject more money into the economy.

Keynes's proposals were frowned upon in business circles because they implied greater state control of the economy. But the core nations had little alternative. They might frown at the confidence with which the Soviet Union addressed development through state planning, but they were hardly in a position to be too critical. Indeed the rosy picture then presented of Soviet achievements combined with increasing internal unrest to make the restoration of capitalism all the more imperative, regardless of the means.

In the United States after 1932 a new Democrat Government under Franklin Delano Roosevelt triggered the Keynesian solution by accident. In seeking to alleviate social hardships and to restore business confidence (a New Deal for the nation), Roosevelt increased state expenditure through a variety of new federal institutions. Massive public works expenditure, loans and assistance to business and agricultural interest, and the implementation of welfare policies went some way to restore the American economy and lift its people out of poverty. But Roosevelt had no intention of restructuring capitalist relations or of increasing state controls beyond what was necessary to effect recovery. Once production rose, he sought to satisfy complaints of bureaucratization and corporate economic dominance by relaxing the New Deal measures and by returning to a balanced budget. The result was a new economic collapse in 1937. Two years later 17 per cent of the workforce was still unemployed. Roosevelt viewed restored international trade as the only real solution to political instability and recurrent economic collapse but given the intensely nationalistic reactions of the core countries it was not a solution which could be immediately effected. Rearmament, however, could be employed to stimulate industrial production. In fact since 1932 Roosevelt had been feeding 20 per cent of the government's tax receipts to the military.[11] Despite Congress's assertion of neutrality he stepped up naval expansion during 1938, and when war erupted in Europe in the following year, he quickly strengthened the nation's armament industries in order to cash in on increased war demands, relieved at having been presented the means to break the impasse of the previous decade.

The Cold War

The American "arsenal for democracy" brought the Keynesian solution. America's underemployed economic resources were quickly mobilized for purposes of war in a way that had never been considered morally or economically sound when social welfare had been the sole purpose. [12] Increased expenditure and deficit financing ended unemployment and restored prosperity. It also vindicated state planning as a means of reconstruction. More importantly, the United States quickly applied the lessons learned to its foreign policy. Never again should the core nations permit such a collapse by failing to cooperate in fostering international trade. Further, the Keynesian solution provided it with a new weapon against the socialist challenge which was to be applied with determination in Europe and Japan after 1945. There could no longer be any question that their welfare was essential to American security.

In 1942 the Secretary of State, Cordell Hull, had spoken of the new opportunities war presented the United States to restructure the world to its own advantage.

> Leadership towards a new system of international relations in trade and other economic affairs will devolve largely on the United States because of our great economic strength. We should assume this leadership and the responsibility that goes with it, primarily for reasons of pure national self-interest. [13]

One of the results of the US assumption of leadership was the formulation of the General Agreement on Tariffs and Trade (GATT) in 1947 which committed the core nations to reduce tariffs and promote free trade by means of multilateral bargaining rather than preferential agreement. Just as Britain had promoted free trade in the mid-19th century, now the United States, as the greatest industrial power, could only enhance its superiority by insisting that all nations open their doors to international trade. International monetary relations were also restructured with the International Monetary Fund (IMF), established to provide nations with loans to overcome balance of payments deficits. The International Bank for Reconstruction and Development (the World Bank) was also created for the purpose of encouraging private capital investment. Later it was to be used to ensure the integration of the Third World into the new world order by tying development assistance to the adoption of policies which facilitated core penetration. Both were products of the Bretton Woods (New Hampshire) financial conference in July 1944 which also proposed the convertibility of currencies and stable exchange rates in order to develop further multilateral trade. The system worked well; indeed until the mid-1960s the prosperity it engendered for the core nations made it possible to forget that it was based largely on American economic domination and continued military expenditure. When these two prerequisites could no longer be sustained, the American economic system began to collapse.

At the time, however, the new economic system was greeted with the same enthusiasm with which Europeans had embraced the new imperialism of the

Figure 7.1 : US CAPITAL EXPORT EXPANSION

One indicator of the United States' gradual economic leadership of the industrialized core by the mid-twentieth century is found in its share of world capital exports which outstrips all other major competitors (United Kingdom, France-Germany) by 1960.

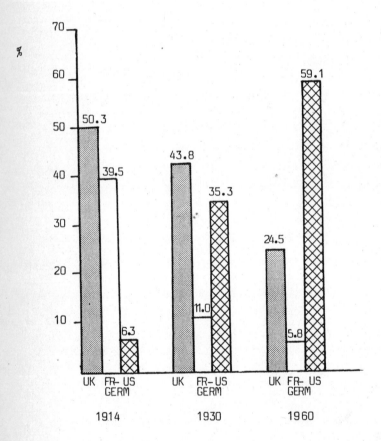

Source: Nabudere, pp 144-145

previous century. To the core nations it seemed that suddenly "the pro-blems of the prewar world had been banished to the pages of history as deplorable monuments to an earlier age of economic and political ignor-ance". [14] But the United States was concerned not only with stabilizing in-ternational trade; in the words of the National Security Council it wished also to create "a world environment in which the American system can survive and flourish". [15] By bestowing on the American dollar reserve cur-rency status, it was able to combine trade surpluses with balance of payments deficits arising out of capital exports to core countries. By in-creasing American corporate investment in the economies of these nations, the United States was able, through profit and interest repatriation, to benefit from their renewed prosperity and, to some extent, offset initial fears that such investment ran the risk of creating future rivals. In any case the American-dominated world economy demanded international coopera-tion if it was to succeed in preventing the recurrence of a 1930s-type depression.

For precisely these reasons the Marshall Plan was implemented in 1948. The war had devastated Europe and left her politically unstable. But the actual physical destruction of industrial productive facilities was less extensive than the Americans had supposed, with the result that the economies of European countries (with the exception of Britain) revived quickly and by 1947 had reached prewar levels. As Andre Gunder Frank comments, little investment was required to effect rapid production.

> [W]ith industrial and political peace assured, profitability enhanced, and prewar levels of industrial production largely reattained and surpassed . . . the United States government launch[ed] the Marshall Plan. In this way, American capital would "reconstruct" Western Europe for its own benefit and that of its then-dependent European capitalist junior partners. [16]

The Marshall Plan, which injected $22 billion into the European economies, was designed also to prevent the possibility of European nations turning socialist. The massive injection of capital to prevent unemployment, stimulate economic growth, and sustain the high levels of US production was the Keynesian solution to depression. By ensuring prosperity and by increasing the ability of people to consume, the United States hoped to make socialist alternatives less attractive to the European masses.

Russia's new position as the dominant power in Europe obviously played some part in kindling fears of Soviet domination. But Russia was hardly in a position to challenge the United States either economically or militarily. Grain production in the USSR had fallen 40 per cent during the war and in 1946 a major drought delayed plans to raise production levels. Moreover Russia faced a serious shortage of labour. War losses in excess of 20 million people had removed an entire generation. Even if the United States was not fully aware of the Soviet Union's considerable weakness, it was conscious of her potential to challenge American domination in the future. In this respect the Marshall Plan was something of an insurance policy. "We cannot go through another ten years like the last ten years at the end of the twenties and the beginning of the thirties", Dean Acheson warned in 1944, "without having the most farreaching consequences on our economic and social system."[17] What the United States feared most was the recurrence of economic depression. It knew from the bitter experience of the 1930s that this had most destabilized political institutions and caused war. With an enlarged Soviet Union on West Europe's frontiers it was not too difficult to imagine where disgruntled masses might turn for assistance from hardship. Soviet expansionism itself was not an immediate issue; the instability of Western Europe was. If the world was not to slide back into a damaging recession, a solution was desperately needed to ensure the continuance of recovery. In 1947 it was the model of 1939 which was hastily adopted—rearmament.

Rearmament, together with the Marshall Plan, would, it was hoped prevent the possibility of a new slump and the danger of social and political unrest that might arise from any "real decrease in the standard of living". In 1950 the American National Security Council made clear American postwar aims:

> Even if there was not a Soviet Union we would face the great problem . . . [that the absence of order among nations is becoming less and less tolerable.[18]

By focusing attention on the Soviet Union, the Council hoped to convince the American people of the necessity for rearmament, while at the same time permit the extension of US power. It stipulated that American policy should "foster a fundamental change in the nature of the Soviet System" and foment and support "unrest and revolt in selected strategic satellite countries" by "any means, covert or overt, violent and non violent".[19]

To sustain this new imperialist (and anti-Soviet) thrust while simultaneously stabilizing its own political and economic world order, the United States had increasingly to depend on rearmament not only to fuel industrial expansion but also to add military substance to its aggressiveness. It was a path from which it was difficult to escape, although the immediate benefits seemed at least to outweigh the risks involved. Frank comments:

> [R]earmament in the United States and profitable American investment in European cheap-labour economies fed the expansion and accumulation of American and then European and Japanese capital. Much of the success of these economies particularly of German capital, was based not on cheap labour alone—in which case low wages could not afford to buy much—but on export abroad, where wages were higher and demand was supported by American rearmament. Thus the state [which] had already intervened with political, military and economic force in the formulation of state monopoly capitalism during the depression and the war . . . [now] insured its timely salvation in the immediate postwar years.[20]

 To arouse public support for its programme of massive rearmament, the Americans simply returned to the model provided by the Second World War. Stalin, like Hitler before him, was conspiring to dominate the world. In the confusion of postwar European and Asian settlements, it was not difficult to isolate events which could support the argument. "For the sake of the free world", President Truman declared in 1947, America had no alternative but to intervene more widely in the affairs of other nations. Thus links with early American imperialism were drawn, and the "policeman of the world" prepared for a new crusade.

During the Second World War relations between the Soviet Union and the United States were strained despite their mutual desire to defeat Germany. Obviously there were historical reasons for this state of affairs, beginning initially with the Soviet rejection of capitalism in 1917. Of more immediate relevance, however, were their differing war aims. Having suffered three times from Western invasions during the twentieth century, Russia wished to ensure her future security by partitioning Germany and by creating a buffer zone of friendly East European states. American war aims, as we have already seen, were related to restoring the conditions necessary for prosperity and to ensuring that a destructive depression did not recur. As the war drew to a close, these two aims were to become more obviously contradictory, particularly as Stalin reconfirmed the Soviet intention to remain outside the capitalist world order.

During the war itself other differences served to increase tension between the two countries. The Soviet Union became suspicious of US intentions when it failed to open the promised second front in Western Europe that would relieve German pressure on the Russian front. To some extent her suspicions were justified. The Soviet Union bore the brunt of the war, 20 million deaths compared with America's 406,000. Nevertheless, both countries put aside differences long enough to defeat their common enemy and to begin planning for peace. Only when both began to implement their war aims did unity finally crumble. Poland had long caused disagreement among the Allies, particularly in respect of its future government and the apparent Soviet indifference to the German slaughter of Poles during the August 1944 Warsaw Uprising. Nevertheless Stalin proved more accommodating than Britain or the United States anticipated and at the Yalta meeting in early 1945 he promised free elections in Poland. Neither country doubted his sincerity; in fact Churchill had commented that he knew "of no government which stands to its obligations even in its own despite more solidly than the Russian Soviet Government".[21] Stalin had already sponsored free elections in Finland and Austria, left Rumania under the control of King Michael, and had granted Britain a free hand to settle the Greek Civil War which had erupted in the wake of Germany's withdrawal.

But the United States wanted more than a guarantee of free elections. If her new economic order was to prosper, international capital had to be provided free play in Eastern Europe as well. At Potsdam in July 1945 the more aggressive Harry Truman [Roosevelt had died shortly after the Yalta meeting] pressured Stalin to open the Black Sea Straits and the Danube as international waters. Stalin refused, fearing the effect of US commercial penetration on Soviet Eastern Europe. Truman, however, regarded Stalin's defensiveness as a challenge and supposed that he was planning to dominate Europe himself. By applying the logic—if you are not for us then you must be against us—Truman quickly saw sinister implications in all the difficulties of postwar settlement thereafter. Stalin was obviously a new Hitler. This time there would be no appeasement. Stalin had to be stopped, and the Americans would do it. [22] Stalin, on the other hand, was certain that the Americans now wished to renege on their wartime promises and eliminate Russian influence in East Europe and the Balkans. Playing from terrible weakness, Stalin "decided to bluff his way out by a show of calm, self-assurance, and power". [23]

Not unexpectedly, the Americans did not regard their actions as imperialist. Ever since its foundation in a war against empire, the United States had been loath to recognize what it had become. Imperialist expansion had always been couched in more acceptable terms of policing or crusades for freedom. In 1947 it was to be no different. Churchill's Iron Curtain speech in 1946 provided inspiration. He called for a new *cordon sanitaire* to isolate communism and urged retention of the wartime relationship between Britain and the United States. A speech itself, especially by a man no longer Britain's prime minister, could not generate sufficient popular support for a major American initative. Instead Truman chose bankrupt Britain's withdrawal from the Greek Civil War as the opportunity to remilitarize. Under increasing internal pressure from a rejuvenated Republican opposition, Truman bluntly told his nation in March 1947 that if the United States did not fill the vacuum left by Britain's departure the Soviet Union would.

> I believe that it must be the policy of the United States to support the free peoples who are resisting attempted subjugation by armed minorities and by outside pressure . . . If we falter in our leadership, we may endanger the peace of the world and we shall surely endanger the welfare of this nation. [24]

The civil war in Greece was never the simple matter Truman implied, but by deliberately distorting the meaning of democracy for the sake of ideological appearances, he was able to commit his country to the support of an unpopular monarchy. As Walter Lippman stated, Truman assumed that "the spread of communism could be checked by subsidizing the reactionary forces of the world". [25] America's failure to understand socialism and its refusal to acknowledge publicly its own imperialist interests, resulted in Truman's assumption being applied with disastrous results in China, Korea and Vietnam. "America was now to be the Great Surgeon, or sanitary cleanser of the globe", noted Kiernan, " 'flushing out' communists as formerly it had flushed out equally ruthless and cunning Red Indians at home." [26]

The Truman Doctrine further implied that the Greek Civil War was masterminded by the Soviets. In fact, Stalin had little interest in supporting revolutionary movements he could not control. His relations with the Guomindang in China up until the time of Mao's victory in 1949, his preference for monarchical restoration in Yugoslavia, indeed his willingness to give Britain a free hand against the Yugoslav-supported Greek ELAS partisans bore witness to his conservatism. Nevertheless, the new hostile attitude of the United States forced Stalin to reconsider Soviet relations with Eastern Europe. Certainly military withdrawal was no longer possible, given America's declared intention to penetrate the region. In fact, by continuing to occupy Eastern Europe, the Soviet Union could at least negate any threat of nuclear aggression. The United States was unlikely to obliterate those it sought to save. Stalin also ordered the strengthening of the Soviet army. Since 1945 it had been reduced from 11 million to 3 million soldiers but after 1948 it was increased to 5.5 million to stave off 'any possible threat of a nuclear attack on Russia by an implied counter-threat of a Soviet invasion of Western Europe''.[27] More importantly, the Truman Doctrine forced Stalin to discontinue those East European governments whose loyalty to the Soviet Union was questionable. Indeed, since America planned a consolidated Western order, Russia had no alternative but to establish its own socialist order. One by one the East European governments were taken over and their countries integrated into a new Council for Mutual Economic Aid (Comecon), the Soviet response to the American Organization for European Economic Cooperation (OEEC).

The United States had originally proposed that Russia and East Europe should make use of the Marshall Plan to hasten recovery. Although some East European governments were willing to accept American aid, the Russians were suspicious. In the first instance, participation was contingent on Russia revealing details of her economic resources. The Soviet economy had reached prewar levels by 1948 (it was to rise a further 50 per cent by 1953) but was still considerably weak; grain production for example was still well below 1940 levels. The last thing Stalin wished to do was undermine this strategy of bluff by admitting exhaustion and weakness. Second, the Soviets were certain that the Marshall Plan was simply a ploy to enable American domination of the East European economies; America's determination to administer the plan through the OEEC and not the UN Economic Commission for Europe seemed to confirm Soviet suspicions. Third, and perhaps of greatest concern to the Russians, was the American intention to apply the Marshall Plan to Germany.

Allied moves to combine their occupied zones with a view to creating a new Federal German Republic, together with German currency reforms in June 1948, revived Soviet fears of a strong Germany emerging so soon after the war. Only four years earlier Stalin had argued that Germany was beyond redemption.

> It would be naive to think that Germany will not attempt to restore her might and launch new aggression . . . History shows that a short period—some 20 or 30 years—is enough for Germany to recover from defeat and reestablish her might.[28]

The bitterness of the German eastern offensive was still too fresh in Russian minds for them to accept a lenient attitude towards Germany. Indeed, until the late 1950s they continued to exact heavy reparations from East Germany, the effects of which contrasted sharply with the affluence generated by American aid in the Western German sectors, particularly in Berlin, landlocked 125 miles inside East Germany. Not unnaturally Berlin became the focus for conflict between the differing policies. The issue came to a head over currency reform. Both East and West Germany had reformed their currencies in 1948, but the important question of which would predominate in the Berlin enclave remained unresolved. East Germany felt compelled to take action quickly. Given Russia' punitive policy of reparations, the continued existence of two currencies would soon undermine the value of the Eastern mark. Alternatively if they accepted the predominance of the Western mark, they would in fact be agreeing to Berlin's economic incorporation into West Germany. Stalin retaliated by blockading West Berlin, and the Western power reacted as if the Soviets were attempting to expand. But Stalin overlooked the possibility of air access to the city, with the result that the Allies began airlifting supplies to Berlin in June 1948 and thereby thwarted the Soviet attempt to delay the emergence of a revived West Germany. The Berlin blockade also provided the United States with the opportunity to commit itself publicly and firmly to the defence of Western Europe. One month before the blockade ended (May 1949) the North Atlantic Treaty Organization (NATO) was formed. Confronted by a new hostile military alliance, Russia formed her own Warsaw Pact.

America's policy of containment was like a self-fulfilling prophecy. Each unauthorized event confirmed its suspicions of a communist conspiracy. Its reactions in turn forced the Soviet Union into tightening control over its spheres of influence, or where she was not involved, drove forces deemed "hostile" into the Soviet camp. The Chinese communist victory over the Guomindang in 1949 was a case in point. The US State Department had long predicted such a victory, but against all advice Truman backed Jiang Kaishek. His inevitable defeat gave the Republican opposition a golden opportunity to accuse the Democrat government of not working hard enough to combat the spread of communism. The Chinese victory had obviously been planned by Stalin, and the Guomindang defeat was clearly a defeat of American policy.

Republican attacks and the hysteria generated by the Wisconsin senator, Joseph McCarthy, who went so far as to claim that there were communist agents in the State Department betraying the country, drove the Democrats into adopting a more inflexible American foreign policy. As the aforementioned National Security Council document illustrated, the Democrats resolved to intensify the Cold War and use military means to fight any perceived threat to its continued hegemony. When civil war broke out in Korea in June 1950, the implementation of the NSC 68 strategy was immediate.

Under the umbrella of the UN, American forces were rushed to East Asia and quickly defeated the North Korean forces that had almost succeeded in occupying the southern half of a country which had been divided temporarily by the Allies when Japanese occupation ended. The Korean war allowed America to consolidate its global hegemony. Taiwan, headquarters of the defeated Guomindang remnants, was isolated from Chinese

Figure 7.2 : THE ARMS RACE

The Cold War precipitated major expenditures on armaments, particularly by the members of the NATO Alliance, whose collective dominance of military spending remains to this day.

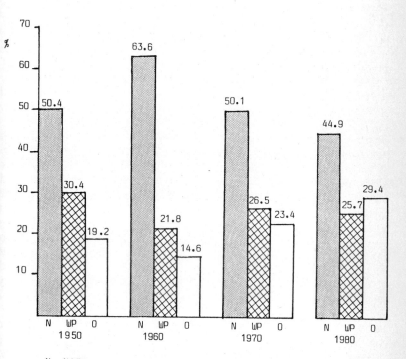

SHARES OF WORLD MILITARY SPENDING 1950-1980

N   NATO
WP WARSAW PACT
O   OTHERS

Source : D & R Smith, <u>The Economics of Militarism</u>, p.22.

attack, and the remilitarization of the Japanese economy pursued vigorously. Selective conscription was introduced into the United States to raise its armed forces to 3.5 million, an expansion paid for by a new $50 billion defence budget. Divisions and airbases in Europe were increased and new bases established in Morocco, Libya, Saudi Arabia, and Spain. Greece and Turkey were incorporated into NATO, and fresh aid given to fight communist insurgents in Indochina. American military expenditure as a proportion of GNP rose sharply as a result, from 5 per cent in 1950 to 13 per cent by 1953.[29]

America's new aggressive stance took it beyond declared objectives in Korea. In October 1950 it invaded the North and pressed towards China's frontier. With General MacArthur arguing that Korea would never be safe until the United States secured China's industrial heart, Manchuria, it was not long before China intervened and drove the American forces back to the South Korean border. Despite its obvious failure to defeat the communist forces, the Republicans—who had attained power under General Eisenhower in late 1952—argued that its policy of retaliation had been vindicated. In the future the United States would provide for her own security by meeting the socialist threat whenever and wherever it arose. During the early 1950s few Americans could doubt that this policy was not being applied internally as well. Under the Republicans McCarthyism had escalated into a purge; in the words of Paul Sweezy, "a vast and unprecedented ruthless campaign of political and ideological repression" designed to wipe out the wide popular base of the Democrat New Dealers (including workers, farmers, blacks, and ethnic minorities) which had the potential to become

> an independent political force moving more or less rapidly in an anti-capitalist direction . . . Trade unions were purged and then co-opted; radical organizing was in effect criminalized; and intellectuals were either frightened into silence or won over, by bribes and flattery, to the service of the new empire.[30]

Outside of the United States, the Republicans were also giving new meaning to the Cold War. The new Secretary of State, John Foster Dulles, declared it a moral crusade. By threatening massive nuclear retaliation, he argued, America would soon roll back the iron curtain and liberate oppressed peoples everywhere. Said Eisenhower in April 1954, the loss of any one country in Asia would destabilize the whole region, and thereby threaten American as well as European security. Massive retaliation justified nuclear · stockpiling; the "domino" theory now vindicated American intervention in Indochina.

By 1954 the United States was contributing over three-quarters of the cost of restoring French colonial rule in Indochina. When the French were defeated at Dienbienphu in May, Eisenhower decided to reject the Geneva Settlement which called for elections and the unification of Vietnam. By raising a new puppet to fight the Vietminh, Williams has argued, the United States once again assumed that "poor and demeaned peoples" would settle for promises of future equality and freedom. By associating nationalist movements in the Third World with Moscow-inspired threats, the United States demonstrated a remarkable incapacity to acknowledge that when "[f]aced with a threat to the integrity and existence of their cultures, 'inferiors' would fight rather than accept indirect destruction". [31]

The Cold War precipitated an arms race which made nonsense of traditional military concepts of victory or defeat. The only outcome of "massive nuclear retaliation" was likely to be mutual destruction. This fact only slowly dawned on the Americans. When East Europe succumbed to a wave of unrest in 1956 which toppled many of the Soviet puppets, the United States did not intervene to "liberate" their peoples. Instead it accepted the legitimacy of the Soviet sphere of influence in Europe. The last area of contention was West Berlin, which the Americans had subsidized and moulded into a shining example of the fruits of capitalism. Situated in the heart of East Germany, it remained a useful site for espionage activities. To the Soviets it represented a constant headache. Thousands of East Germans had migrated there during the 1950s, seriously depleting manpower in the East. In 1958 Russia handed over control of their sector to the Democratic Republic of Germany, which in a short time came up with a solution of sorts to the problem of West Berlin—the Berlin Wall.

By 1960 the Cold War in Europe was largely over. Questions of armament levels remained and the propaganda battles continued, but increasingly the Americans were prepared to avoid confrontation. Khrushchev's stunning attack in 1956 on Stalin's leadership—an attack which in part had precipitated the East European revolts—clearly demonstrated that, despite the claims of Dulles to the contrary, there was little unity in the socialist world. Moreover relations between China and the Soviet Union now appeared to have been strengthened only by the Korean war. When China began a second offensive in 1958 to recover her islands of Quemoy and Matsu, American brinkmanship revealed how uncommitted Russia was to her socialist ally. Hostility between the two countries increased and in 1960 the Sino-Soviet split became public.

The impact of socialist divisions was not immediate. When Democrat John Kennedy assumed the presidency in 1961 he reconfirmed the American commitment to empire. "Our frontiers today are on every continent", he declared and immediately demonstrated his willingness to repeat past errors by launching an abortive invasion against Fidel Castro's nationalist forces in Cuba in April 1961. Only the Cuban Missile crisis of late 1962 forced Kennedy to recognize "that Russia, if pushed to the wall, would fight". [32] More than any other event, it brought the United States around to accept Khrushchev's notion of "peaceful coexistence" and made possible negotiations to limit the costly arms race.

However, it did not reduce the American desire to retain its hold over the non-Soviet bloc. Unauthorized changes within the "free" world were still deemed to threaten American security. Neither Kennedy nor his successor Lyndon Johnson saw any contradiction in accepting peaceful coexistence and escalating American involvement in the Vietnamese civil war. By emphasizing peasant resettlement programmes, defoliation raids, pacification-extermination campaigns and covert war against North Vietnam, the New Frontiersmen believed that they had demonstrated the existence of a "wider choice than humiliation and all-out nuclear action"[33] in the conduct of Cold War. All non-Soviet countries fell within the American sphere of influence and any change in economic or political status not approved of by the United States was still thought to be the result of unacceptable Soviet influence. "If we don't stop the Reds in South Vietnam", Lyndon Johnson reiterated the familiar domino theory in 1965, "tomorrow they will be in Hawaii, and next week they will be in San Francisco."[34]

The cost of the Vietnam War was high, particularly after 1965 when the number of American troops stationed in South Vietnam increased to over half a million and when the conflict spread into neighbouring Cambodia (1970) and Laos (1971). Between 1965 and 1971 alone the United States pounded the small nation with over 6 million tons of bombs, three times the total tonnage dropped during the entire Second World War. "Never before has a land been so massively altered and mutilated", Senator Nelson of Wisconsin told Congress in 1972, ". . . The cold, hard, and cruel irony is that South Vietnam would have been better off losing to Hanoi than winning with us."[35] Many Americans agreed and by 1972 not even Nixon's talk of Vietnamizing the war could convince them that the United States had a moral right to remain fighting the popular Vietcong and North Vietnamese forces. Yet despite the eventual defeat of America's strategy of limited war in 1975, the United States refused to alter its perception of change in the Third World. Intervention in Iran, Chile, Nicaragua and Central America, even in small Caribbean island states like Grenada during the late 1970s and early 1980s, revealed that its imperialist thrust was far from over, and that the United States remained determined—in the words of Kissinger—to "shape events in the light of our purposes".[36]

Problems in the American World Order

By the 1970s the American world order, although no longer perceived as under threat from the Soviet Union, came under new pressure from within. Inevitably the distinction between containment of Soviet socialism and preservation of American hegemony was blurred further. Manfred Bienefeld has described the new American crisis as a disjunction between its economic strength and its global political role,[37] a disjunction, moreover, which has come about largely because of contradictions inherent in its foreign policy. By strengthening Europe and Japan to withstand socialism and buttress American hegemony, the United States reactivated the core forces most likely to challenge its dominance.

Under American leadership the core nations were remarkably successful in capturing a greater proportion of world trade—72 per cent in 1970 compared with 61 per cent in 1938—but at the expense of the United States itself. Its share of world trade declined from 21 per cent in 1950 to 12 per

cent in 1978, whereas West German trade rose from 4 to 12 per cent and
Japan's from 1 to 8 per cent. American manufacturing output in com-
parison with the combined output of ten leading industrial nations fell
from 62 per cent in 1950, to 50 per cent in 1965, and to 43 per cent
in 1976. Differing rates of productivity further emphasized American
decline. Industrial productivity increased only 4.1 per cent per annum
in the United States between 1950 and 1969, compared with 6.7 per cent
in West Europe and 13.8 per cent in Japan. Rates of profit likewise
declined, by one-third between the early 1960s and mid-1970s in Britain,
France, Italy and Japan, and by two-thirds in Germany and the United
States.[38]

The twin pressures of economic change within the core and declining
profitability forced the United States to rely more on credit to finance its
massive armaments projects and imperial crusades. In the aftermath of
the Vietnam defeats, imperial crusades and intervention in the internal
affairs of other nations could only be popularly justified by reestablishing
"Cold War as the dominant mood of international life".[39] While, to some
extent, this enabled the visible decline of American hegemony to be
obscured, it did not prevent the monetary system established in 1944 from
weakening further. In fact America's increasing use of debt to finance its
imperialist policies and to prop up its declining economy made international financial institutions and the money market more fragile.

> As long as the world economic pie had been growing moderately, the various
> capitalist interests and their states had been able to reach relatively amicable
> agreements on how to divide the pie up among themselves under the moderately
> bullying pressure of the Americans.[40]

During the 1970s, however, such cooperation began to dissolve as the
American economic order entered a new crisis.

As at the end of British hegemony before 1914, the American decline
increased competition between trading blocs and renewed internal state
and business pressures on labour to allow rates of profit to improve. The
United States responded with policies designed to bolster its
position vis-à-vis the centre nations, ending the dollar's paramountcy as international currency in 1971 and instituting new floating exchange rates
instead. Devaluation served the same purpose, making imports more expensive and increasing the competitiveness of American exports, especially
agricultural and military commodities. Its support for oil price increases
also renewed its comparative advantage. Less dependent on oil imports and
in control of the major oil companies, it was able to take advantage of
OPEC's wealth as new investors and as markets for its produce. Its early
policies, particularly of encouraging transnational investment in European
and Asian economies, likewise ensured that the new growth of European
and Asian capital was not entirely without benefit at least to American
corporate interests. But in seeking to restore economic hegemony, the
United States had encouraged the very nationalist solutions most likely
to destroy it. In addition its relative loss of competitive strength in world

trade, together with the dollar's decline as international currency, meant that the United States could no longer rely on its leadership of the imperialist system to stimulate economic growth.[41] Its era of free trade, like Britain's before, was doomed.

Despite the crisis and despite the relative decline in America's position within the core, its losses were not immediately unmanageable. More difficult to accommodate, however, was the lack of coherence increasingly visible within the core. With its hegemony waning, the United States could not simply restructure the system it had created at the end of the Second World War. Moreover, the greater international character of capital and interdependence of centre economies now made the renewed orientation towards protectionism more dangerous than in the period preceding 1945, particularly when it combined with a new and competitive imperialist thrust into the Third World which, by exploiting the latter's desire for development, sought to offset the recession's impact on core profits and industrial expansion and, thereby, in the manner of the past, resolve the core's own internal contradictions.

Notes

1. William Appleman Williams, *Empire as a Way of Life*, Oxford University Press, New York, 1980, p. 70.
2. Ibid., p. 95.
3. Ibid., p. 99.
4. W.A. Williams, "Empire as a Way of Life", *The Nation*, 2-9 August 1980, p. 107; see also V.G. Kiernan, *America: The New Imperialism, From White Settlement to World Hegemony*, Zed Press, London, 1980, pp. 55-60.
5. Williams, *Empire*, p. 88.
6. Kiernan, p. 86.
7. Williams, *Empire*, p. 125.
8. Ibid., p. 132.
9. Kiernan, p. 135.
10. Ibid., p. 144.
11. Williams, *Empire*, p. 157.
12. Galbraith, p. 221.
13. Harry Magdoff and Paul Sweezy, *The Deepening Crisis of US Capitalism*, MRP, New York, 1981, p. 186.
14. Manfred A. Bienefeld, "The International Context for National Development Strategies: Constraints and Opportunities in a Changing World", paper presented to the University of the South Pacific, October 1982, p. 22.
15. Williams, *Empire*, p. 189.
16. Andre Gunder Frank, *Crisis: In the World Economy*, Heinemann, London, 1980, pp. 25-6.
17. Barraclough, *Agadir*, p. 17.
18. National Security Council (NSC) Document 68, April 1950, quoted in Williams, *Nation*, p. 114.
19. Ibid.

20. Frank, p. 26.
21. Deutscher, p. 503.
22. Hugh Higgins, *The Cold War*, Heinemann, London, 1979, pp. 29-30.
23. Deutscher, p. 565.
24. R. Hofstadter, W. Miller, D. Aaron, *The Structure of American History*, Prentice-Hall, New Jersey, 1973, p. 361.
25. Higgins, p. 43.
26. Kiernan, p. 215.
27. Deutscher, p. 561.
28. Ibid., p. 524.
29. Higgins, p. 83; Magdoff and Sweezy, p. 18.
30. Ibid., p. 187.
31. Williams, *Nation*, p. 115.
32. Ibid., p. 116.
33. Hofstadter, p. 391.
34. Ibid., p. 405.
35. Ibid., p. 418.
36. Williams, *Nation*, p. 119.
37. Bienefeld, p. 25.
38. Frank, pp. 4, 28, 32, 34.
39. Magdoff and Sweezy, p. 189.
40. Frank, p. 48.
41. Magdoff and Sweezy, pp. 18-19.

8. The Third World

Decolonization

The attainment of independence by former colonies of the core has been among the most significant events of the post-World War Two era. One after another the colonies became sovereign nations, sixty-six in all between 1943 and 1970, the majority being in Africa and Asia. Independence was not always won easily; struggles in Indonesia, Vietnam, Malaya, Algeria, Egypt, Kenya, Angola and Mozambique bore witness to the determination of metropolitan powers to retain their colonial possessions. So too do present struggles in Namibia, New Caledonia and Palestine. In many other colonies, however, independence came more easily, not without violence but certainly without the kind of violence attempts to retain colonial status would have produced.

Associated with decolonization was the growth of a new national consciousness among the peoples of the new nations. As a means of fostering unity in the struggle against imperialism it was eminently successful; in preserving unity once the common enemy had been overcome or the goal of sovereignty attained, though, nationalism was less successful. The danger always existed that if the rulers of newly independent countries adopted the same mechanisms of rule employed by their colonial predecessors, they would similarly alienate the disaffected of their fragmented societies. In this way nationalism, as the European ruling classes had learned in the prewar era, could imperil the interests of those who were its initial promoters.

As a reaction to perceived alienation, nationalism undoubtedly has been of tremendous importance in the Third World. After all colonization meant more than the loss of sovereignty. Forced to accept an administrative system designed to preserve foreign political and economic domination, the colonized could only watch helplessly as their social systems, cultures and ideologies were eroded and remoulded to provide support for the colonial machinery.[1] Deportation, imprisonment, and even execution awaited those who dared resist the transformation. In the end, the successful penetration of missionaries, traders and industrialists left little untouched. As Simione Durutalo noted in respect of the Pacific:

> During the greater part of British rule knowledge, except that provided in carefully limited doses by the missionaries, was disdained. The people were discouraged from thinking for themselves; a thirst for knowledge was considered dangerous and subversive. Training to obey and follow and mindful of the misfortunes that befell the poor "native" who, using his and her reason, questioned however timidly the decisions of someone in authority, the people later transformed this training and fear into a conviction that one should allow one's social and economic superiors to do the thinking for the community. [2]

Deference to one's social and economic superiors also included deference to the indigenous ruling classes which had survived by collaborating with the colonial masters or had been formed to assist colonial exploitation. While reactions to colonially-induced psychological and social humiliations were used by nationalists to generate wide support, their overall importance to a movement was determined directly by the nature of the leadership. This varied considerably depending on the duration and nature of foreign political and economic domination, the extent of capitalist penetration, the mechanisms of rule employed, and upon the degree of social differentiation. Weak class structures resulted in nationalist movements being variously composed of traditional leaders, farmers, trade unionists, members of the bureaucracy and national bourgeoisie, and petty-bourgeois elements, with the latter often dominating leadership in the absence of a strong middle class. Not unnaturally bourgeois leaders invariably sought to divert expressions of discontent solely at the metropolitan power and not at their own roles in the colonial system.

Despite the challenge that independence movements initially presented to the metropolitan powers, the nature of their leadership made the task of decolonization much easier than anticipated. Local bourgeoisies were keenly aware that they ran the risk of losing their privileges if the colonial administration embarked on economic programmes which did not require their collaboration. This was particularly the case in societies where communalism increasingly appeared at odds with colonial plans for modernization. Hence, once steps towards independence were taken in the 1950s and 1960s, the colonial bourgeoisies were prepared to accept the retention of metropolitan interests in return for the retention and consolidation of their own social, political and economic roles. Not unnaturally this also suited the metropolitan nation. As Harry Magdoff comments,

> The colony could be granted formal political independence without changing anything essential and without interfering too seriously with the interests that had originally led to the conquest of the colony. [3]

After all, local bourgeoisies were part of the colonial social and economic framework, and through their leadership of independence movements they could ensure that nationalist goals would not too seriously disrupt existing social and economic relations. Self-interest was a powerful motive for stability.

Independence movements were not always led by bourgeois elements. In colonies or spheres of influence where other classes or class alliances

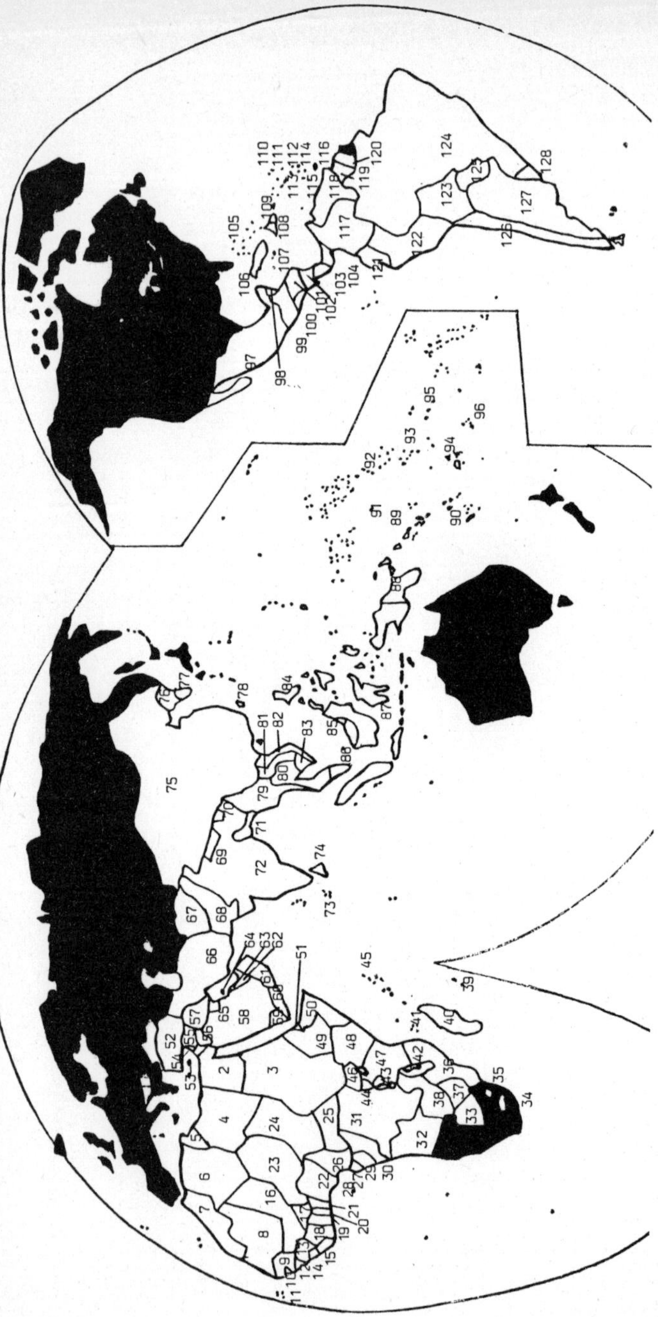

Figure 8.1   THE THIRD WORLD 1985

EAST EUROPE
1. Yugoslavia

NORTH AFRICA
2. Egypt
3. Sudan
4. Libya
5. Tunisia
6. Algeria
7. Morocco

WEST AFRICA
8. Mauritania
9. Senegal
10. Gambia
11. Cape Verde
12. Guinea Bissau
13. Guinea
14. Sierra Leone
15. Liberia
16. Mali
17. Upper Volta
18. Ivory Coast
19. Ghana
20. Togo
21. Benin
22. Nigeria
23. Niger

CENTRAL AFRICA
24. Chad
25. African Republic
26. Cameroon
27. Eq Guinea
28. Sao Tome & Principe
29. Gabon
30. Congo
31. Zaire

SOUTHERN AFRICA
32. Angola
33. Botswana
34. Lesothe
35. Swaziland
36. Mozambique
37. Zimbabwe
38. Zambia

EAST AFRICA
39. Mauritius
40. Madagascar
41. Comoros
42. Malawi
43. Burundi
44. Rwanda
45. Seychelles
46. Uganda
47. Tanzania
48. Kenya
49. Ethiopia
50. Somali
51. Djibouti

SOUTH WEST ASIA
52. Turkey
53. Cyprus
54. Lebanon
55. Syria
56. Jordan
57. Iraq
58. Saudi Arabia
59. Yemen AR
60. PDR Yemen
61. Oman
62. United Arab Emirates
63. Qatar
64. Bahrain
65. Kuwait
66. Iran
67. Afghanistan

SOUTH ASIA
68. Pakistan
69. Nepal
70. Bhutan
71. Bangladesh
72. India
73. Mauritius
74. Sri Lanka

EAST ASIA
75. China
76. North Korea
77. South Korea
78. Taiwan

SOUTH EAST ASIA
79. Burma
80. Thailand
81. Laos
82. Vietnam
83. Kampuchea
84. Philippines
85. Brunei
86. Malaysia
87. Indonesia

OCEANIA
88. Papua New Guinea
89. Solomon Is
90. Vanuatu
91. Nauru
92. Kiribati
93. Tuvalu
94. Fiji
95. W. Samoa
96. Tonga

CENTRAL AMERICA
97. Mexico
98. Belize
99. Guatemala
100. El Salvador
101. Honduras
102. Nicaragua
103. Costa Rica
104. Panama

CARIBBEAN
105. Bahamas
106. Cuba
107. Jamaica
108. Haiti
109. Dominican Rep
110. St Christopher-Nevis
111. Antiqua-Barbuda
112. Dominica
113. St Lucia
114. Barbados
115. Grenada
116. Trinidad & Tobago

SOUTH AMERICA
117. Colombia
118. Venezuela
119. Guyana
120. Suriname
121. Ecuador
122. Peru
123. Bolivia
124. Brazil
125. Paraguay
126. Chile
127. Argentina
128. Uruguay

were sufficiently strong to challenge bourgeois leadership, or where the conjunction of class discontent and foreign penetration destabilized colonial rule, well-organized classes or class fractions were able to seize control. In China, for instance, Japanese aggression during the 1930s enabled the small Communist Party to rally an increasingly exploited peasantry against the indigenous bourgeois and military leadership. In other countries, however, dissident parties were not as fortunate. The nature of colonial rule and social formation prevented successful independent action. This does not mean that we should necessarily attribute covert Machiavellian intentions to the process of decolonization. Rather we should acknowledge that in most cases it was shaped directly by the same forces which had originally established the colonial relationships and by the social formations they had produced. Decolonization, like colonialism, was a product of imperialism.

Changes in the nature of the world economy after 1945 demanded a reappraisal of the role of colonies in furthering the interests of metropolitan capital. Although colonial forms of exploitation—extraction of cheap raw materials and the incorporation of small elites as limited markets for imported manufactures—remained important, they were fast becoming inadequate as a means of extracting surplus-value. Neglect of internal infrastructural development and a reluctance to widen internal markets for fear of generating economic competition not only limited the potential for further exploitation but also bred instability within the colonies themselves, as partial transformation and the articulation of capitalist and pre-capitalist modes of production created their own contradictions and applied increasing pressure on collaborating bourgeoisies. Lacking substantial economic support and often already distanced from their societies, collaborative classes were open to challenge from disaffected elements. Most metropolitan powers had segregated colonial societies by disarticulating their economies and reintegrating their parts separately with the metropolitan economy.[4] Once nationalist movements voiced concern at the effects of disarticulation and sought allies from among those whose economic roles had been changed (and thereby gained a mass following), there was little colonial governments could do to maintain control short of investing heavily in methods of coercion.[5] This, of course, was the path taken for instance by the Dutch in Indonesia, the French in Vietnam, and the Portuguese in their African colonies. But, while it created the illusion of continued mastery (albeit at prohibitive cost), it could do little to resolve the demands of capital in a new age of multilateral imperialism. What metropolitan capital required was access to intensify exploitation of labour in the production of agricultural (and manufactured) produce and raw materials. If this could be achieved without direct political domination, so much the better.

Distorted social formations and class weaknesses, therefore, provided metropolitan capital with an avenue through which it could perpetuate core-periphery relations without the liabilities colonial government assumed. Not all imperialist leaders grasped this opportunity, especially those preoccupied with the immediate challenge nationalism and independence movements evoked. But the potential remained none the less, and once perceived provided the motivation for eventually conceding independence also to colonies like Algeria and Rhodesia with substantial minority white populations intent on perpetuating their privileges by maintaining the colonial link or by forming minority governments. As Arghiri Emmanuel suggests, by granting independence to the indigenous peoples instead, the metropolis was able "to steal a march on settlers threatening to secede", and, because of the weakness of indigenous classes, ensure the continuation of its influence and interests in the new postcolonial state.[6]

Certainly other factors influenced metropolitan attitudes towards decolonization, not the least being the potential colonies held for the continued maintenance of world power status. Often this coincided with US pressure to challenge the spread of socialism either by armed struggle against movements deemed socialist or by conceding a measure of independence to classes which would preserve and foster metropolitan interests. This has certainly been the case in the Pacific during the 1970s and 1980s where the reality of continued colonialism has been deliberately obscured by references to US "trusteeship" (the UN Trust Territories of Micronesia—the Marshalls, Marianas, and Caroline Islands) and to French "territories" or "departments" (New Caledonia, French Polynesia, and Wallis and Futuna).

According to a statement prepared in early 1985 by Fiji's Anti-Nuclear Group for submission to the UN Committee of 24 on Decolonization, colonialism in the Pacific has taken a peculiar form—that of nuclear colonialism. For this reason the forms of neocolonialism gradually being established in the US and French colonies involve even less autonomy than that granted former colonies in other parts of the world. It is worth quoting from the document at some length merely to illustrate this point.

> Many Micronesians, especially Palauans, see the US grant of "independence" to the islanders [the 1982 Compact of Free Association with the US] along with its retention of complete authority over their "defense" as a contradiction. Moreover the islands will not have the status of sovereign nations. They will have to rely on US support to gain membership to international organizations. It will be up to the US to determine whether the membership of the islands in any international negotiations threatens its "defense" rights in the islands. Clear conflicts can be envisioned over the Law of the Sea and other non-aligned efforts that threaten US freedom of movement in the world. Thus the Compact of Free Association sounds like a thinly disguised attempt to maintain on the Micronesian people US colonialism in perpetuity.[7]

The United States sees Micronesia fulfilling a vital role in securing its economic and military interests in Southeast Asia. Hence it has been prepared to misuse trusteeship to foster dependence and to abuse the notion of independence. Ultimately it has been the Micronesians themselves who have suffered.

The Micronesians have not only seen their political rights and economic

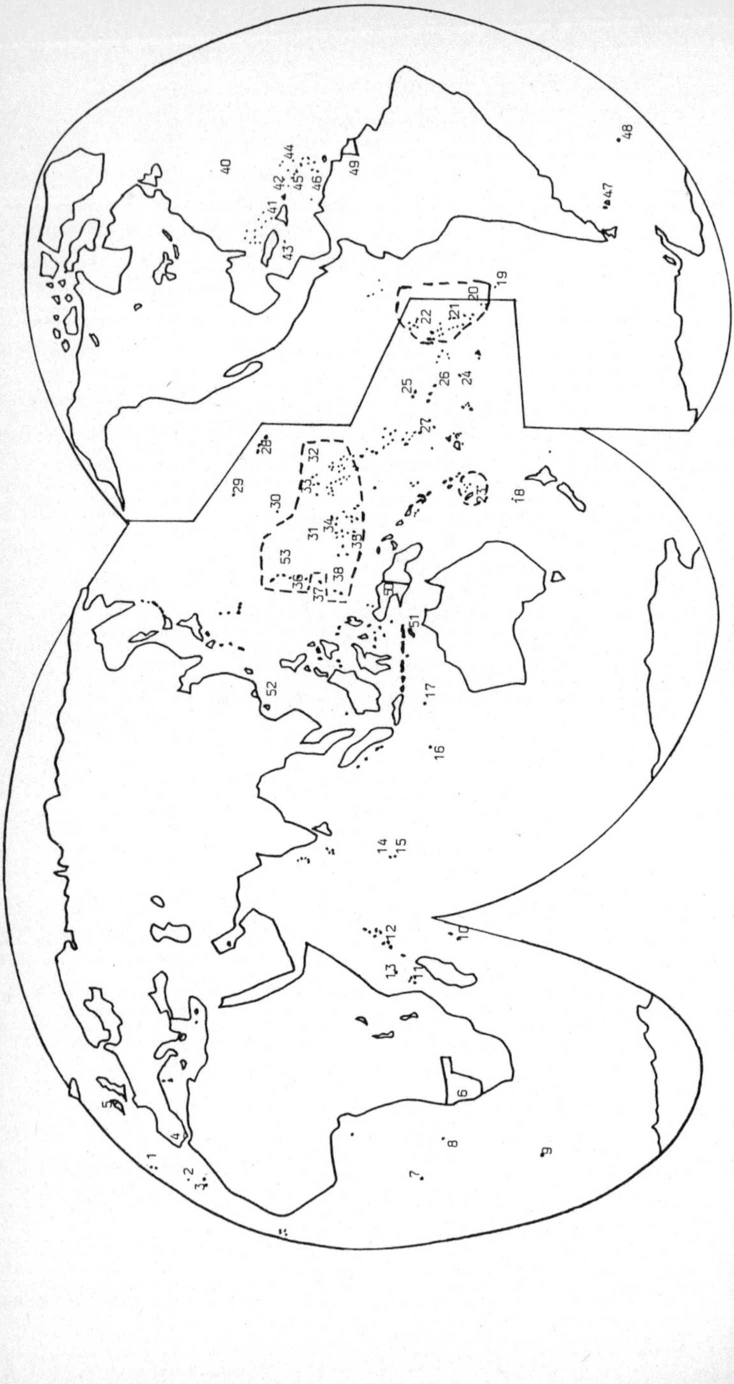

Figure 8.2   COLONIAL REMNANTS 1985

1. Azores (Port)
2. Madeira (P)
3. Canary Is (Sp)
4. Gibraltar (Br)
5. Northern Ireland (Br)
6. Namibia (South Africa)
7. Ascension Is (Br)
8. St Helena (Br)
9. Gough Is (Br)
10. Reunion (Fr)
11. Mayotte Is (Fr)
12. Amirante Is (Br)
13. Aldabra Is (Br)
14. Chagos Arch (Br)
15. Diego Garcia (US)
16. Cocos Is (Australia)
17. Christmas Is (Australia)
18. Norfolk Is (Australia)
19. Easter Is (Chile)
20. Pitcairn Is (Br)
21. Mururoa Atoll (Fr)
22. French Polynesia
23. New Caledonia and Loyalty Islands-Kanaky-(Fr)
24. Niue (NZ)
25. Tokelau (NZ)
26. E. Samoa (US)
27. Wallis and Futuna Is (Fr)
28. Hawaii (US)
29. Midway Is (US)
30. Wake Is (US)
31. UN Trust Territories of Micronesia (US)
32. Marshall Is (US)
33. Kwajalein (US)
34. Truk (US)
35. Caroline Is (US)
36. Saipan (US)
37. Guam (US)
38. Yap & Belau (US)
39. Greenland (Denmark)
40. Bermuda (Br)
41. Caicos and Turks Is (Br)
42. Puerto Rico (US)
43. Grand Cayman (Br)
44. Virgin Is (Br & US)
45. Guadeloupe (Fr)
46. St Vincent (Br)
47. Falkland Is (Br)
48. St Georgia (Be)
49. French Guiana
50. West Papua (Indonesia)
51. East Timor (Indonesia)
52. Hong Kong (Br) Macau (Port)
53. Marianas

autonomy slip from their hands but also have lost or forfeited their right to live in the land of their birth. Within the Micronesian territories placed under its trust the US has felt free to relocate people, create islands with landfills, vaporize others with nuclear weapons, and construct billions of dollars worth of buildings, military facilities and equipment. Thus after 66 nuclear tests (between 1946 and 58) on Bikini and Einwetak, 4,000 Marshallese were subjected to nuclear radio-active fallout....Micronesians have been converted into "nuclear nomads" after their ancestral home and land of birth was made uninhabitable by US nuclear weapons tests with which to defend the "Free World". Pacific peoples in the US and French colonies in Polynesia and Micronesia have died (and are dying) from radiation-related diseases like leukaemia and thyroid cancer, suffering in silence; ignorant of the cause of their malignancy and dying a slow, painful and lingering death. [8]

French Polynesia is also used as a site for nuclear testing (with similar results), while New Caledonia "with its nickel mines is the most important part of the French colonial empire in the Pacific". Recent brave attempts by Kanaks to form an independent Kanaky has forced the French govern-ment to consider revising New Caledonia's colonial status in order to accommodate nationalist feeling. The so-called Pisani Plan would permit an "independent" New Caledonia

> to join regional and international bodies, [but] France would still retain "total responsibility over the defense of the new state and public security on its ter-ritory." The proposed treaty of association . . . would also define the respon-sibilities and competence in the areas of finance, justice, international commerce and telecommunications. New Caledonia would therefore never attain the status of a sovereign nation. Pisani in his plans for "independence" is not only trying to appease the French settlers but also secure the military and economic interests of France in the Pacific region. Thus France wants to continue colonial control over New Caledonia in another guise for perpetuity. This aim has the support of the US, expressed by the US Ambassador to France who on January 13 1985 said that he favoured "the status of the continued French presence in the Pacific to avoid New Caledonia becoming a new Grenada". The French consider auth-ority over matters of defense and security as crucial in the light of their plans to continue nuclear weapons testing in French Polynesia and their opposition to the nuclear-free zone proposal supported by the South Pacific Forum countries. [9]

In general we can argue that during the thirty-odd years following World War Two, forms of neocolonialism gradually came to be regarded as more advantageous than colonialism, particularly if the metropolitan country no longer possessed the power required to sustain colonial rule. The dissolution of the British Empire provides a useful example of the interac-tion of both internal and external forces in precipitating decolonization. Probably the two most important events which stimulated reactions to imperialism were the Great Depression and World War Two. The depres-sion cut prices and demand for tropical products and made indigenous peoples aware for the first time that they were, as one British Labour MP remarked, "merely cogs in a gigantic trading machine which had suddenly collapsed and left them, their raw materials, their produce, and their living on their hands stranded and useless".[10] It also revealed just how pitiful government expenditure on social welfare, education and economic development in the colonies really was.

The Second World War also acted as a catalyst for change by damaging Britain's illusion of power and by enabling past insecurities and grievances to be aired with new aggressiveness. In some cases, for example in Ceylon, Malta, Jamaica and the Gold Coast, the stimulus war gave to local industry and to urbanization strengthened the hand of local bourgeoisies sufficiently to permit demands for concessions to be taken seriously by Britain. In colonies such as Burma where British rule had been interrupted by Japanese invasion and occupation, the emergence of strong guerilla movements made the restoration of British rule impossible. Even where no guerilla movements existed, the experience of Japanese occupation and, in some cases, of liberation by American troops, drove pent-up emotions to the fore in such a way that Britain had little choice but to accept that changes in rule were necessary. The Maasina Rule Movement (1944-1952), which attempted to unite Solomon Islanders in fraternal solidarity against the British government, is a case in point.[11]

Nevertheless, Britain had no intention of giving up her empire if she could help it. Empire enabled her to act as a major world force, but more importantly it enabled her to survive economically. In 1949 48 per cent of Britain's imports came from her empire and 57 per cent of her exports went to her far-flung colonies and dominions. The tropical regions of the empire were now beginning to assume a new importance as suppliers of vital metals (copper, tin, cobalt, gold and uranium), vegetable products (rubber and palm oil), and foods (cocoa, coffee, and groundnuts).[12] Since the beginning of the century Britain had come to rely more and more on her empire to sustain rates of industrial growth and to provide income to finance her growing balance of trade deficits. After the Second World War when Britain lost her premier trading and financial position it became all too obvious that the empire was simply a substitute for industrial rationalization and was being exploited to cushion Britain's fall in the world.[13]

Nevertheless, Britain could not easily ignore the growth of indigenous nationalist and independence movements. Colonies like India, Ceylon, Burma and Palestine could no longer be held and were granted independence or abandoned. The remainder, however, had somehow to be convinced that the retention of British rule was in their interest, that Britain really intended only to remain until their societies had been properly prepared for independence. Britain's new concept of trusteeship was not always bought by indigenous peoples, with the result that Britain had on occasion to fight to preserve her international prestige and her strategic and economic imperial interests. Cyprus (1954-59) and Egypt (1956) are but two examples. In Kenya (1952-56) many dispossessed tribes did not regard British offers of partnership with the small white community as in their interest. Similarly in Malaya (1948-57) racial and ideological divisions sparked off a major guerilla war, one of the few which Britain was actually successful in suppressing. But the effort was costly, in terms of both money and men, and Britain no longer possessed the power base necessary to sustain an extensive empire. Britain might turn to the Commonwealth as a face-saving alternative to empire, but it was no substitute. By the 1960s British capitalists were more interested in Europe and the possibilities for trade and investment within the new European Economic Community. Within a short time all the concepts of trusteeship and partnership that had evolved to lend credence to the retention of empire after 1945 were suddenly abandoned and the rush to decolonize began. Little had been done to prepare the colonies for independence, however, and Britain accepted the legitimacy of rule by local bourgeoisies in return for the maintenance of her declining investments and trade.

If the weakness and distorted character of colonial social formations proved fortuitous to imperialist interests, they did little to assist the newly independent state to attain any semblance of economic autonomy. The balance of class forces, recent in formation and often incomplete, did not permit one class alone to dominate or manipulate the state for its own purposes. Economic disarticulation further reduced the ability of capitalism to minimize non property-based structures of conflict such as it had in the core.[14] In Fiji, for instance, disarticulation and the varied reintegration of parts of her economy distorted class conflict and gave prominence instead to racial or traditional issues which served only to frustrate further goals of national development and unity. During the 1950s local white capital had attempted to shore up its weakening position by appropriating provisions granted under Britain's new policies of trusteeship and by wooing the support of Fijian bureaucrats under the pretext that increasing Indian demographic and economic growth threatened Fijian survival. While the resultant new class alliance permitted white capital to direct infrastructural developments towards its own ends and to curtail the rising power of labour, it also made Fiji more attractive to foreign capital. Hence, during the decade following independence (1970), local white capital experienced the unintended consequences of its own strategy. Its new tourist sector had all too easily been infiltrated and in turn dominated by foreign capital. Further, the state was now dominated by the Fijian bureaucrats whose support they had previously sought, but who now were intent on diverting the state's resources in order to develop their own national bourgeoisie. Such a policy required rapprochement with the Indian petty bourgeoisie and peasantry if the state's resources were not to be jeopardized, a further abandonment of white capital's earlier strategy. However, Fijian plans were themselves frustrated by the country's increasing dependence on world markets and foreign capital. Not only was the state unable to form a substantial Fijian bourgeoisie, but it had also to accept a further realignment of class forces as the uneven nature of capitalist development (both inherited and fostered by post-independence plans) and the racial basis of the electoral system exacerbated working-class and peasant discontent at the same time as the country was hit by the inflationary and recessional tendencies of the world economy.[15]

In many other Third World countries the weaknesses of class formation have produced a wide variety of often unstable class alliances as compensation and to fill the void left by the once strong metropolitan presence. Indigenous bourgeoisies have often allied with the remnants of landed classes or traditional elites in order to strengthen their position; for the same reasons they have sometimes allied with nascent working classes. [16] Such alliances have varied considerably depending on the nature of class formations and historical relationships. No single generalization is possible.

> The political behaviour of any class, group or category [writes Roxborough] is not an inherent function of the class itself, but rather a result of the interaction with other classes in the context of the overall political system. [17]

Of course any situation in which power is shared among a number of weak allied classes is not conducive to stability or the implementation of development strategies. Hence many Third World countries have experienced political intervention by their military forces designed to mediate between conflicting political alliances or to remove the threat a new class or class alliance poses for the development strategy the military identifies with.

Decolonization, then, took little account of the effects the colonial past might have on the new post-colonial nation. Naivety, blindness to the effects of distorted social formations, inflated beliefs in the superiority of Western institutions, and metropolitan desires to retain imperialist advantage shaped the character of decolonization. Given the tendency for popular justifications of imperialism to be accepted as articles of faith in themselves, it is not unexpected that distortions and injustices should have followed. But given also the war-weariness and financial exhaustion of most core nations following World War Two, it was less easy for metropolitan powers to dictate relations with the periphery as they had in the past. The rise of mass political parties in Africa and resistance movements in Asia confirmed the reduction in metropolitan power.

The new hegemony of the United States also weakened old core-periphery relationships. The United States regarded the colonial empires as anachronistic because their preferential trading arrangements conflicted with the American desire to establish multilateral trading systems around the world that would strengthen its own hegemony. Further, the American government recognized the limitations of colonial imperialism. Any system based largely on the extraction of raw materials and which did not exploit the development aspirations of local bourgeoisies was simply missing out on the potential for greater core penetration. With its huge transnational corporations, grown fat on armament expansion, the United States was in a unique position to insist on an Open Door policy similar to that originally promoted for China at the turn of the century. With a larger and more active economy, America could not help but benefit from decolonization at the expense of its weaker core partners. The United States also regarded greater core economic penetration of the Third World as essential if the spread of socialism was to be halted. To Americans socialism meant the closure of potential markets for its capital and commodities.

By 1950 East Europe, China, North Korea and parts of Indochina had already opted out of the capitalist world order, encouraging the United States to support imperialist wars against national liberation movements wherever they threatened to close the Open Door. Where doors were not closed, American interests were maintained by new economic and military mechanisms which attempted to strengthen ruling class alignments. In any case US military superiority, bolstered by a chain of bases around the globe, served as a constant reminder to would-be defectors of the dangers a challenge to American interests would provoke.

To summarize, the realignment of world power provided an international atmosphere in which movements for independence or liberation were more possible than previously. Colonial social formations had already created the internal structures necessary for nationalist movements to rally support. At the same time, however, these two circumstances made the achievement of nationalist goals illusory. Ties with old colonial rulers, pressures from the United States, and the bias of development plans towards the interests of dominant classes meant that nationalist ambitions were often frustrated. In many instances ruling classes have sought to overcome such frustrations (and weak national cohesion) by fostering new ideologies which legitimate their dominant roles and which also attempt to reduce expectations. Where ruling classes are the product of local bourgeoisie and communal leaders, as in the Pacific, such ideologies (for example the Pacific Way and Melanesian Socialism) appeal to perceived tradition and attempt—like Tennoism and Confucianism in Japan—to reduce class perceptions and channel discontent into avenues which do not erode ruling-class control.[18]

Nevertheless, weak national cohesion and the unsettling effects of economic change are not easily overcome by recourse to ideology alone. Many new Third World states have been challenged by various forms of micronationalism as communities have reacted to the erosion of their autonomy by encroaching state organs or to their failure to benefit adequately from new development plans by seeking microindependence or by withdrawing from imposed systems in order to overcome perceived deprivations through other means.[19] As in the case of the many protest movements, self-help organizations and marginal cargo cults which sprang up in Papua New Guinea (the Bougainville Napidoko Navitu, the Kabisawali Association, and the Buka Hahalis Welfare Society to name but a few), the penetration of capitalism and new state organs into relatively isolated and autonomous communal societies produced strong desires for more broadly based development through communal self-help. While such movements often challenged the state, on occasion violently, their ideological compatibility has, at the same time, facilitated their eventual assimilation, and by this means satisfied the desire of the unintegrated for equality.[20]

This brief description of decolonization—its nature and limitations—is not intended to portray the process as totally negative. Given the restraints and humiliation colonialism imposed on most peoples, its removal was generally welcomed as liberation. Indeed decolonization was seen as entirely progressive. For once the collaborating classes could feel that they were in control themselves. Regardless of the constraints they faced, they had little doubt that for the first time in decades their nations had recovered their destinies. Metropolitan powers, while still retaining considerable influence, were also aware that their relationships with the periphery were no longer the same. Access, henceforth, was dependent upon negotiation with a new state and could not be achieved simply by deals made in the core itself. [21] Further, the new leaders of the post-colonial states were determined to develop their nations in ways in which the colonial rulers had had little interest. For the first time, therefore, development became an issue for global debate and initiative, and independence was rightly regarded as the necessary precondition for national development.

Industrialization

Most newly independent nations regarded industrialization as the only way equality with the core could be achieved. Few realized that their peripheral status made autonomous economic development impossible; in any case their tendency to view economic expansion itself as a prerequisite for development soon misled them. Socialists, however, were not so easily misled. They argued that independent development was only possible after all imperialist links with the core were cut and internal social relations transformed. Understandably this was not an attractive alternative for many Third World states. Their ruling classes knew only too well who would suffer most from social reconstruction. Moreover, they were encouraged by contemporary conservative economic wisdom to believe that modernization and industrialization alone would bring rich rewards, that imperialism would decline as capitalism grew. [22]

The idea that imperialism was somehow divorced from capitalism raised problems for the Third World. After all no economy could be independent and stable if its industrial base was not founded on a strong internal market and if it was unable to control investment and sustain autonomous technological progress. Under the imperatives of capitalist development, economic independence further implied that a nation had access to the necessary resources on which growth could be based, that it possessed classes able to own, control and develop these resources independently (thereby sustaining internal capital accumulation), and that its state was both able and prepared to support the interests of its bourgeoisie. [23]

If these "prerequisites" for capitalist development were not present, if historical and contemporary factors had interceded to make them incomplete, there was little Third World countries could do to remove themselves from their colonially-induced relationship with the world economy, even if they wanted to. In Cuba, for example, not even the determination of the Castro Government after 1961 to take the socialist alternative, could substantially reduce the country's dependence on sugar exports. Radical social and agrarian reform could not overcome the scarcity of resources for independent industrialization. Even in countries with a more adequate resource base, the balance of class forces could restrict the application of development strategies. In Bolivia during the 1950s the bourgeois Movimiento Nacionalista Revolucionario came to the conclusion that if it sought economic growth outside of the capitalist world order it would only strengthen the position of rival classes. Not unnaturally it chose not to commit political suicide.

> The choice of a growth model [Roxborough notes] is not a purely economic choice, made in a vacuum; it is made in a specific political and social context and entails specific social and political consequences. [24]
> How a society moves from one stage to another will depend not only on the internal dynamics of the transition but also on how that society is inserted into the world system at a particular point in the development of that system. [25]

Unfortunately the restrictions imposed by these dual factors have not always been well understood.

In the late 1940s the United Nations' Economic Commission for Latin America (ECLA) argued that independent development could be achieved by the removal of certain internal obstacles. If Third World countries ended the political privileges of dominant elites and landed upper classes, redistributed incomes and built up a solid industrial base to service the resultant stronger market, they would reduce their dependence on manufactured imports and achieve the necessary domestic base for industrial expansion. [26] The ECLA import-substitution strategy offered a less dramatic way of cutting links with the First World than the socialist alternative, and for this reason received US support in Latin America during the 1960s in the face of the potentially destabilizing Cuban example.

However, import-substitution industrialization did not work in the way the ECLA hoped. It did not produce independent economic growth. Many consumer items previously imported were those required by the small but dominant classes and the internal manufacture of such items, while reducing consumer importation, did not broaden the base of industry sufficiently. Nor did it end dependence on imported goods; rather import-substitution industrialization necessitated increased inputs of machinery and, inevitably, foreign capital to finance growth. In the case of luxury goods, production served only to reinforce existing internal inequalities and did not offer a substantial potential for market expansion. In fact industrialization often marginalized wider sections of the community than importation had. Traditional handicraft producers, for instance, were unable to compete with cheap locally-produced manufactured goods. At the same time, the highly mechanized nature of production denied them the option of absorption into the industrial workforce. [27] Like handicraft producers in Asia and Africa during the late nineteenth century, their only escape was to return to the land. Industrialization in the Third World, therefore, tended to reduce employment and increase population pressures on the land and make agrarian transformation more difficult. The impoverishment which accompanied marginalization lowered living standards further and restricted the expansion of the internal markets on which independent industrialization depended.

This vicious cycle differentiated Third World development from that of the First. Two obstacles in particular hindered the former's development. First, in many developing nations the sources for primitive accumulation that the First World had so relied upon, had already been removed by colonization. Whereas core industries had only competed initially with internal handicraft production, Third World industry also had to compete with advanced and often more competitive products from abroad. Of course it could be argued, as the ECLA did, that tariff barriers reduced the impact of foreign competition. But if Third World countries were dependent on export earnings for capital accumulation, as indeed many were, then tariffs were liable to impede trade promotion. Certainly if loans were acquired for internal infrastructural development, especially from agencies like the World Bank, they invariably came attached with conditions preventing restrictions on foreign competition. Even if tariffs were raised successfully, transnational corporations (TNCs) were able to evade them by investing in production within the country itself. After the late 1960s in Brazil, the military government encouraged foreign investment in order to promote industrial expansion. But because this expansion again mostly concerned consumer production and was dependent on rigorous labour controls and low wages, it still did not substantially widen the market available to industry.[28] Nor did it promote the internal accumulation of capital. Indeed the predominance of foreign investment restricted its independent utilization and, not unnaturally, culminated in a net outflow of capital when foreign investors demanded their expected returns, returns moreover that were increasingly derived from the cooption of local capital which regarded foreign investment sectors as more profitable.

Second, continuing unequal exchange between the core and periphery, together with the withdrawal of accumulated surpluses described above, provided a further brake on Third World independent growth. Unequal exchange was not the result of international trade relations, as the exponents of a New International Economic Order were later to maintain, but rather the result of "production relations between the bourgeoisie and the working class across national borders as well as . . . the subjugation of the peasantry".[29] It is in this respect that TNCs have often been attacked. By moving goods internally through their international structures and by monopolizing technology and marketing, TNCs frustrated the achievement of national economic goals. Like the new national industries described earlier, their activities were capital-intensive and based on a division of labour which simply reinforced already limiting social structures. The application of inappropriate technology that did not make use of abundant labour reserves and the all too obvious inability of the domestic market to absorb the products of industry forced many Third World countries to abandon their plans for autonomous economic growth. Instead they sought to surmount domestic inadequacies by emphasizing export production, thereby reconfirming in a new way the very dependency they had initially hoped to overcome. At various times the nationalization of foreign-owned industries has been proposed as a viable way out of this dilemma. But while nationalization might satisfy immediate aspirations for autonomy, it could not overcome internal structural limitations nor of course remove TNC monopolization of markets and technology. In fact it might close markets once enjoyed by the industry under foreign ownership. Even if a sizeable internal consumer market existed, nationalization alone could not guarantee its automatic expansion. Indeed, to survive, newly nationalized industries might be forced, because of their reliance on the same consumer market, to perpetuate rather than reduce the inequalities which restricted internal growth. [30] Changing relationships with the core did not automatically reduce internal obstacles to development. Import-substitution industrialization demonstrated that the opposite was true.

The Development Debate

At the same time as Third World nations were experiencing difficulties in implementing development programmes which would stimulate independent growth, First World modernization theorists—still imbued with notions of Western infallibility—were advising that successful development could be achieved only by following the historical process established in the core. [31] In 1960, for instance, W.W. Rostow outlined a sequence of stages all countries had to pass through if their traditional societies were to modernize and a new entrepreneurial elite emerge to accumulate the necessary capital for development. The successful diffusion of capital and technology, Rostow maintained, would enable the Third World to "take-off" into self-sustained economic growth. [32] Although modernizationists accorded different emphasis to the adoption of capital and technology, Western cultural values, entrepreneurial skills or political institutions, they all regarded the West's historical experience as the only model applicable to the Third World and believed that its replication was simply a matter of removing certain traditional values and systems which inhibited diffusion. Underdevelopment or the lack of industry, therefore, could be overcome by capitalization on any terms (TNCs, the IMF, etc.) when focussed through selected industries, particularly export-oriented industries. The flow-on effects would stimulate local industry and mass consumption and lead inevitably to the Western-type mass consumption society characterized by inherent interest-group complexity and liberal (bourgeois market) democracy.

Despite the ethnocentrism and ahistorical nature of modernization theories, their acceptance by many First and Third World politicians and administrators gave them tremendous importance and influence. Core-controlled banking and development agencies have increasingly adopted modernization concepts in their dealings with the Third World, grading the latter for purposes of assistance or loans according to the degree to which core structures have been adopted and traditional restraints to diffusion removed. Ankie Hoogvelt observes:

> The World Bank and other international organizations would outline to Third World governments the appropriate socio-economic programmes to be adopted if they wished to qualify for aid flows. Western technology, Western methods of production and Western economic enterprises were all welcomed as important development agents. [33]

That Western structures might be inappropriate to Third World societies was rarely considered. That the historical experiences of the Third World made a Western-type transition to capitalism impossible was certainly never contemplated by the modernizationists. Instead they argued the impracticality of applying value judgements to the process of modernization. Hence Marius Jansen's declaration in 1961:

> . . . the important thing is *that* people read; not *what* they read, *that* they participate in the generalized functions of mass society, not whether they do so as free individuals, *that* machines operate, and not for whose benefit, and *that* things are produced, not *what* is produced. It is quite as "modern" to make guns as automobiles, and to organize concentration camps as to organize schools which teach freedom. [34]

There can be little doubt that this kind of reasoning was designed to overcome the apparent contradiction of many "modernizing" countries succumbing to military dictatorship or the rule of one party. Indeed in 1965 Samuel Huntington rationalized this growing tendency as "a precondition for sustained economic growth" and eventual democratic government. [35] Faith in the US as the ultimate model sustained any qualms over the "temporary" directions modernization might impel Third World nations. In the same decade Robert Bellah concluded that there was after all "a tendency in the modernization process which leads to the sort of society which American society is", adding also that "The whole New Frontier idea is, I think, a modern secular version of building the Holy Community on earth". [36]

Perhaps the best example of the impact of modernization theories can be found in the "green revolution" of the 1960s. Essentially the "green revolution" sought to demonstrate the ability of Western science and technology to increase agricultural output and productivity in the Third World without necessitating radical change in rural relations of production. Not unpredictably it failed. Certainly agricultural production increased as fertilizers, new strains of seeds and new methods of production were introduced. But the "green revolution" sought also to commercialize the subsistence peasant sector, to reincorporate a people whose poverty, it was feared, might precipitate revolt or revolution. In this it was not successful. Without support the peasant could not afford to participate in the "green revolution"; being so close to the poverty line few peasants dared risk innovation. Richer farmers could of course, and did. The gains they made as a result not only intensified social and economic disparities but ensured that the products of the "green revolution" remained beyond the means of the poor peasant. Invariably, as in India and Mexico,

> the effect of agrarian reform has been to give an impulse to the large, technically efficient modern sector and to retain the mass of the population as reserve labour . . . trapped on their tiny and unproductive parcels of land. [37]

Further, by failing to ensure an internal market for the new agricultural products, the "green revolution" pushed commercial agriculture into depending on export outlets in order to survive. The "green revolution", therefore, had unintended consequences.

Some of these unintended consequences only became obvious towards the end of the 1970s. The "green revolution" had pushed many Third World countries into depending on new high-yield varieties of crops which not only were more vulnerable to disease than older varieties but also required constant and costly inputs of pesticides, fertilizers and herbicides. In all cases this was a very real dependence since both seeds and agricultural inputs were monopolized by transnational agribusinesses. Herein lay another feature of the "green revolution", the relationship between Third World capital-intensive farming and TNC dominance of global commodity trade and associated production and processing mechanisms. That such a relationship should exist is not only a feature of the growing concentration of capital but also, as Susan George has revealed, indicative of the new roles of USAID and World Bank research and training programmes and infrastructural loans in promoting Third World dependence on TNCs. [38]

Third World dependence on monopolized agricultural inputs and export markets has also provided core nations a new means of pressuring states which threaten to close avenues for foreign capital penetration. The 1954 US Agriculture and Development Act (Public Law 48), which authorized the use of food as a weapon, has been recently extended by a State Department guideline (1981) to block all commercial transactions and private humanitarian dealings with countries deemed to be "enemies". Vietnam and Kampuchea have been recent targets, but the implementation of such directives has also had the effect of denying relief to drought stricken Eritrea during the Ethiopian famine in the mid-1980s. [39] Agricultural dependency has increased the scope for using food as a weapon, and this is but one effect of the whole modernization thrust which as early as 1949 the US State Department urged be used to provide a new and counter-Marxist ideology that would shape the modern world. [40]

The "green revolution" had other effects beyond the penetration of foreign capital and core abuse of agricultural dependency. Even if countries were able to achieve self-sufficiency in grain production by means of the new technology, this often had harmful effects on the foreign exchange earnings of other countries (for example, Thailand) which traditionally exported surplus grain. Further, the creation of modern agricultural sectors invariably produced new classes of wealthy farmers, which in the instance of the Punjab precipitated the development of powerful regional political movements which increasingly challenged the central authority of the Indian state.[41] Behind the veneer of communal conflict, D.K. Joshi noted in 1984, lay two decades of modernization.

> [The] prosperous Jat Sikhs, responsible for the state's "green revolution", are beginning to move this new wealth into the towns. The green revolution has run its course and staple commodities like wheat, rice, oil seeds, cotton, and sugar offer lower profits. From land the interest is shifting towards real-estate and small-scale manufacture. But the urban economic environment has been the preserve of Hindus, particularly the traders and the professionals.
>
> Even though in the past all manner of urban activity was adjustable between the communities, the challenge to old vested interests is qualitatively different this time. The Sikh farmer turned entrepreneur is blocked and is seeking political influence.[42]

Equally alarming has been the impact on ecology and the environment of the "unscientific and unplanned spread of the Green Revolution" and the hurry to reap its benefits. Chemical engineer Lawrence Surendra argued in a recent article that the large-scale use of new varieties had resulted in the loss of old plant varieties and of the animal and insect species dependent on them. India, which in 1900 had 30,000 species of rice, will have only 15 by the year 2000. Every coffee tree in Brazil is descended from a single plant. The entire soya bean industry is derived from only 6 plants found in only one place in Asia. Four varieties produce 75 per cent of Canada's wheat crop. Three-quarters of the US potato crop is dependent on four varieties. The implications of this narrowing of the genetic base on which modern agriculture is dependent are startling when one considers that, first, high-yield varieties have a limited life (5 to 15 years for cereal varieties in North America and Europe), second, new varieties can only be constantly produced by cross-breeding with older varieties, and third, the older varieties are either extinct or in danger of being lost because of deforestation, the construction of hydro dams, soil erosion, and a lack of interest on the part of many agribusinesses to collect and preserve the vital older and wild varieties.[43]

Although criticisms of the "green revolution" were prominent in the 1970s and 1980s as its effects became more widely known, the first major challenge to the whole modernization concept of development came from a rival neo-Marxist school of dependency and underdevelopment in the 1960s. Based largely on the works of Paul Baran, Andre Gunder Frank, James Petras, Frantz Fanon, Samir Amin and Walter Rodney, the dependency school addressed itself directly to the failure of development strategies to achieve their goals. The Third World, it claimed, was not a pre-modern world about to progress naturally to the level of the First. That had been a major error inherent in the concepts of modernization. Rather it was a world fashioned by imperialism, whose imposed class structures and associated unequal income distribution made self-sustained economic growth an impossible dream.[44]

Modernizationists had sought to explain underdevelopment in the Third World by reference to ahistorical notions of internal social change. The

ECLA theorists had similarly erred by equating dependency largely with external economic relationships which, they believed, could be removed by political action. Neither considered the role internal class interests might have on reproducing structures of dependency. The dependency school, however, set out to correct these past errors. First, it demonstrated that no study of Third World development could exclude an examination of the manner in which underdeveloped countries had been incorporated into the world economy. The effects of incorporation varied of course depending on the historical period under review. Second, it revealed that incorporation transformed the internal functioning of Third World societies, again in different ways depending on the nature of incorporation itself. Given the many ways such a concept of dependency could be applied, it was to be expected that differing theories would arise based on varied emphases. A.G. Frank, for instance, emphasized the effects of the extraction and transmission of surplus through a series of metropolis-satellite links that operated either globally between economic regions or internally between social classes, thereby precluding the possibility of capitalist development in the Third World. Samir Amin also argued that alliances between core and periphery bourgeoisies made autonomous capitalist development impossible. Immanuel Wallerstein used the world-system as a unit for analysis rather than the nation-state and concluded that social transition in the Third World could only take place when the world capitalist system itself collapsed. Less pessimistic have been writers like F.H. Cardoso who have suggested that development is possible in the Third World but that it would always be characterized by dependency. Many neo-Marxists, Ernesto Laclau noted, failed to apply concepts of class relations vigorously to their analyses of relations of domination and exploitation. [45] The result, according to Dan Nabudere, has been the obfuscation of class struggle. Further, the dependency school's underconsumptionist concept of unequal exchange has simply provided populist national and petty bourgeoisies an ideological tool which can be used to consolidate their own positions by deflecting all blame for national problems on an overrich and exploitative Northern centre, [46] with the clear implication that structural changes are unnecessary for development. Regardless of these points of contention, dependency theorists were united in arguing that the way underdeveloped countries had been inserted into the world economy determined a pattern of development that would be completely different from that experienced in the First World.

The major contribution of the dependency theorists, therefore, lay in their exposure of the weaknesses of previous conceptions of Third World development. Because they highlighted diversity they made no attempt to provide the kind of universalist solutions offered by the modernizationists. Instead some among them pointed to a wide variety of structural relationships which needed to be reformed if self-sustained economic growth was envisaged. Of course industrialization was possible in the Third World without substantially restructuring relationships with the world economy, and many present-day modernizationists have exploited the successes of the Newly Industrialized Countries (NICs) like Brazil, South Korea and Taiwan in order to demonstrate that the notion of dependency is wrong. If Third World countries were really restricted by relations of dependency and the expansion of their internal markets continually thwarted, how could such industrial growth as the NICs have achieved occur?

Structures of dependency, of course, are not static, and the expansion of industry in any one Third World country is no indication that the process of development has begun to proceed along lines similar to the First World. Indeed the Geneva-based International Labour Office, a United Nations affiliate, noted at the beginning of 1984 that despite impressive growth in the NICs industrialization had reemphasized existing income inequalities and forced modern urban and rural sectors to depend more heavily on exports to sustain growth.[47] In Brazil, where GNP growth rates averaged 10 per cent during the late 1960s and 1970s to the acclaim of most modernizationists, real wages actually fell 30 to 40 per cent and the major cities, particularly Sao Paulo, rapidly developed huge and expanding squatter settlements made up of the casualties of modernization development.

While modernizationists might not accept the dependency school's analysis of a dual internal-disarticulation external-articulation phenomenon, they have not been able to ignore completely these unintended consequences of economic expansion. Nor have they been able to dismiss lightly the effect of First World circumstances on the Third. As we shall see in the following chapter, the emergence of a new world recession during the 1970s pushed a number of modernization theorists (influenced also no doubt by the criticisms from the dependency school) to Keynesianism as a solution to the obvious differences in development between the First and Third Worlds. The First World, they now argued, should provide higher and more stable prices for Third World commodities and agree to a massive relocation of industry and finance to foster a New International Economic Order (NIEO) (see Chapter 9) more conducive to development. While appearing to concede the importance of external relations in shaping the nature of Third World development, the new bourgeois-liberal orthodoxy in fact drew little from any analysis of Third World social formation, nor indeed did it demonstrate any understanding of the complex interaction of internal and external factors that had made the dependency approaches so valuable. Rather its new position was derived from once more examining the experiences of the First World. In the late 1940s the Marshall Plan had restored prosperity to a war-devastated Europe. Surely a similar extensive application of investment could do the same for the periphery. Modernization theorists, it seemed, had failed to overcome their Eurocentric bias.

The Nature of Third World Development

One of the premises behind the NIEO, in part of the whole North-South dialogue concept, was the belief that it was still possible for the Third World to replicate the processes of development that had been so beneficial to the First World. If the latter was prepared to redistribute its surplus, it might enable the Third World to overcome problems of underconsumption and generate a new mass demand that would be of benefit to both Worlds. Bourgeois-liberal theory, derived largely from Western experiences of the Great Depression and postwar European recovery, simply reasserted the idea that "The country that is more developed industrially only shows to the less developed, the image of its future".[48]

Throughout this book we have used the terms core and periphery to indicate a relationship between metropolitan and Third World countries that was not based on equality. In fact the periphery was a creation of the core, functional to the expansion of its capital. European, American and later Japanese bourgeoisies had incorporated various parts of the world into their economies in order to sustain profitability and expansion. In doing so they had of necessity to transform the societies and economies they encountered. After insertion into the world economy, therefore, Third World societies evolved in ways markedly different from the First. Imperialism distorted social formations, disarticulated economies, and created forms of development that reinforced their imposed roles in the world economy. None of these effects of imperialism vanished with the attainment of independence, as the leaders of the post-colonial states were soon to discover. Their ability to adopt a particular development strategy was limited by the very nature of their colonial inheritance.

Changes in the core itself, due largely to the restoration of prosperity under American hegemony, demonstrated also that the core still regarded the Third World as functional to its welfare. Although the emphasis of foreign investment in the Third World has shifted from raw material extraction and commercial agriculture to industrial consumer production, there has been no marked reduction in Third World dependency.[49] Many countries in the Third World have industrialized and established modern sectors utilizing the latest technology, but their method of development has served only to emphasize their subservience to the demands of core capital. In fact, changes in technology and communications, and in the organization of capital, have allowed the core to make greater use of the periphery than before. Infrastructural developments in the Third World have likewise permitted greater exploitation. Capital exports from the core to establish new industries and loans to cover balance of trade deficits have integrated the Third World into the world economy more thoroughly than ever for the purpose of surplus-value extraction. Penetration has also been fostered by TNC monopolization of markets and technology, by international aid programmes, by the wholesale adoption of Western institutions and methods of production, and by the purchase of military weaponry to suppress internal unrest and to assist the core in its struggle against socialism.

The dependent role of the Third World in the world economy is not sustained only by pressure or influence from the core. It has also been shaped by those classes within the Third World which have a vested interest in dependent development. In countries where the modern sector does not depend on internal demand, there is little incentive for the national or foreign bourgeoisie to redirect development inwards, particularly when overseas markets are plentiful. One of the basic contradictions of capitalist development that we already noted is that the very necessary continuous production of surplus is dependent upon a mass demand that can only be created by redistributing the surplus beyond its narrow class ownership. In the Third World that mass demand is external to the countries in which the commodities are produced. Thus industrial profitability and competitiveness are maintained by utilizing the Third World not as an expanding market for commodity consumption but as a source of cheap labour. Hence the demands of capital to maximize profits and retain its class foundation ensures that the surplus is withdrawn from internal mass consumption and that the kind of income distribution necessary to permit integrated economic expansion and development does not occur. [50] Further, in both the Third and First Worlds, Nabudere asserts,

> When state intervention goes beyond its function as a coercive arm of the bourgeoisie and directly helps the profitability of enterprises as well as furthering the concentration and centralization of capital . . . it creates new crises . . . In this way state expenditure on arms production, bureaucracy and "unproductive" areas gives fuel to the inflationary process already inherent in the economy and acts as a weapon against the gains the workers have made as well as reducing the money value of accumulated debts . . . [This] constitutes the real central crisis of bourgeois economic ideology. [51]

The manner of insertion into the world economy and the vested interests of capital, together with state-support policies, have therefore made it extremely difficult for Third World countries to break free from imperialism and the dependency it implies.

Let us consider two broad examples. First, the role of mineral and plantation enclaves in the Third World. Enclave production did not of course end when colonies attained independence; in fact many post-colonial governments came to rely heavily on the taxation derived from this activity to finance their own budgets. But the development or extension of enclaves did little to assist the formation of a balanced economy due to its dependence on markets external to the country itself. Further, the post-colonial state could not guarantee that the enclave's owners, whether foreign or local, would spend their surpluses in the interests of national development. There existed a further danger of high interest rates in the enclave sector attracting local capital away from national investments. Both problems have arisen in the case of oil-producing Third World countries where, despite the huge reserves available as a result of oil price increases, little self-generating economic development has occurred. Oil owners have preferred to export their capital for more profitable investment in the First World.

Free trade or export zones have similar implications, all the more tragic perhaps because many Third World leaders have deluded themselves into thinking that this form of enclave production will stimulate employment and investment, generate foreign currency reserves, and promote the transfer of technology and skills. Free trade zones, like mineral or plantation enclaves, are dependent upon external markets and bear little or no relationship to internal demand. They cannot, because of their very nature, promote self-sustained economic growth or internal economic integration. [52] If anything the continuance and recent expansion of enclave forms of production demonstrate the Third World's inability to transcend its peripheral status, especially during the present economic crisis when falling profitability has driven capital to utilize Third World labour in order to reduce production costs.

The disarticulation of Third World economies and the integration of their separate parts with the world economy, have created internal structural fragmentation, even in countries with industrialization policies specifically designed to promote independent development, our second example. [53] In a study of India, Argentina, Brazil and Mexico, Fernando Henrique Cardoso found that the industrial sector survived only by creating a kind of internal colonial relationship with the backward sectors of its economy. Such duality, he maintained,

> results directly . . . . from capitalist expansion and is functional to that expansion in so far as it helps keep wages at a low level and diminishes political pressures inside the modern sector . . .

Although internal markets are important for industrial expansion, particularly in the case of Argentina and Brazil, and although foreign capital investment is often lower than indigenous investment, the ability of the industrial sector to maximize its opportunities for expansion is hampered by the continued flow of capital to the core (because of the core's technological monopoly and use of indigenous capital) and by the very limiting duality of the economy on which industry depends for profitability. [54]

Cardoso's notion of a dual economy forms part of a long and complicated debate over the articulation of modes of production within the Third World. Can precapitalist modes of production survive alongside the implanted capitalist mode? If so, are they subordinated and functional to it? Or do precapitalist modes themselves survive by utilizing the capitalist market? There is no space to elaborate properly on this debate, except to reproduce H. Wolfe's argument that the persistence of precapitalist enterprises, particularly in rural communities, is indicative of the

> effect of the struggle of agents organized under differentiated relations and forces of production. The relations of articulation are themselves relations of struggle and may have the consequence of disintegrating rather than maintaining the precapitalist modes.

In the countryside merchant capital exercises increasing control over the labour process of peasants, and, as we noted earlier, international capital had monopolized the instruments of production and the means to dispose of produce. [55]

However, this does not indicate that precapitalist relations are being gradually transformed into capitalist relations. The "green revolution" demonstrated international capital's need for a new class of capitalist farmers, but it did not eliminate subsistence agriculture. Anibal Quijano Obregón, in a manner similar to Cardoso's treatment of the urban workforce, has argued that capitalist penetration of rural relations depresses and modifies the precapitalist sector. Hence, a growing contingent of manpower (increased by the very high rates of demographic growth in the precapitalist sector compared with others) is forced to remain outside the labour market of the dominant levels of the rural economy. Because even the new intermediate levels are not extensive enough to absorb it, the contingent is forced to migrate geographically or to seek refuge in a new rural "marginal pole" constituted by what was previously called the subsistence economy and by the complex of commercial and service activities of the lowest level with limited productive resources and on a precarious level of organization. [56] These changes obviously sharpen uneven development and social conflict, but they do not herald the development of autonomous economic growth. Rather, as Cardoso suggests, such forms of dependent development are an important component of contemporary imperialism. Functioning within a new international division of labour, Third World industrialization has not been marked by increased capital flows from the core or by a greater share of international trade. (The Third World's share of international trade declined from 32 per cent in 1948 to 21 per cent by 1968.) Instead the new form of imperialism continues to generate the very dependency which has distinguished Third World development since colonialism first transformed their societies.

The development of a new international division of labour, of which we shall say more in the following chapter, is related to a series of transformations within the world capitalist system. Changes in terms of trade, declining profitability, the development of new technology, and restrictions on multilateral trade have placed new pressures on capital and forced it to restructure its relations with the various parts that make up the world economy. Such a progress of restructuring is not new and we have already examined its impact on the world in the late nineteenth century when Germany and Japan began to demand equality with the core nations, and in the 1930s when declining opportunities for international trade combined with overproduction to precipitate a long recession. Problems of competition have always bedevilled intracore relations and whenever "the tenants of privilege" have coopted opposing groups by giving them a share of the spoils of exploitation, they succeed in eliminating competitors only in the short run. In the long run, of course, they merely raise the stakes for the next opposition movement created in the next crisis of the world economy. [57] Thus Australia and Canada, for instance, rose economically by acting as sub-imperialists. Their cooption, however, did not mean that they would always continue to act in the interests of foreign capital. If anything the ability of the dominions to integrate production

Figure 8.3 : WORLD TRADE

The following graph reveals not only First World dominance of global trade, but also the role export production plays in the economies of the Third World. (See also Figure 9.1).

WORLD TRADE SHARES 1938-76

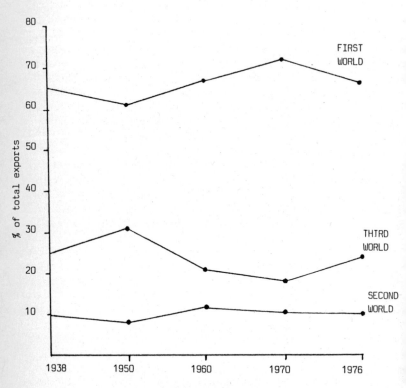

Source : Frank, <u>Crisis in the World Economy</u>, p.4.

into an autocentric industrial structure posed dangers for the future. [58] One way of preventing coopted groups from challenging dominant core interests was to restrict their activities by means of foreign investment or regional strategies. Thus the Pacific Rim Strategy (see Chapter 9) has been seen as a way of ensuring Canadian or Australian subservience to American and Japanese capital and enabling the latter to make greater use of Third World labour in their quest for maximum economic advantage. The dynamics of capital, therefore, should make us wary of assigning to Third World industrialization the beginnings of self-sustained economic growth. The Third World's all too obvious internal structural fragmentation and reliance on external markets serves only to emphasize continued dependence.

The development of the Third World is a history of the development of capitalism on a global scale; confusing accounts of its progress owe more to the perspectives and expectations of its reviewers than to the process itself. Indeed many Third World leaders like India's Jawaharlal Nehru believed that it was possible to take a third path of development by using the state to develop a unique economy that was neither capitalist nor socialist. Not unexpectedly nonalignment has proved impossible. By continuing to operate within the world economy, and by failing to establish an egalitarian society based on social ownership, India succeeded in expanding her productive forces only by means of a new powerful state sector. But the pattern of development begun by colonialism remained, marked in the countryside by the appearance of a new modern agricultural sector which grew at the expense of the mass of peasant poor, whose continued inability to consume acted as a brake on industrial development. Lacking sufficient capital and viable internal markets, both private and state industries in India have been forced more and more to concentrate on export markets and on the relatively small urban Indian middle classes. Without a change in the mode of production, India's state has been unable to reduce the impact of her integration into the world economy and to alleviate the poverty of the people it claims to represent. [59] Instead it has produced a form of "counterfeit socialism" (to use Tom Kemp's expression) and precipitated a "partial and lopsided form of industrialization which only sharpens regional and class disparities and social contradictions"— in other words "growth without development". [60]

Whether state-directed or not, economic and social development is governed by the imperatives of capitalism. Governments may well choose to ignore the realities of internal inequalities and focus instead on achieving higher rates of economic growth in the belief that the benefits of expansion will trickle down, but students of the contemporary era cannot afford to be so naive as to expect that capitalist development can take place without the contradictions inherent in capitalism. Given the dictates of class interests and of capital's need to sustain profitability, it.is not sufficient to explain the nature of Third World development by reference to the small size of their markets or to the limitations imposed by their internal structures. These are features not causes of underdevelopment, and as such reveal the Third World's failure to escape the patterns imposed and perpetuated by the structures of imperialism.

Three Worlds or One?

Third World development was constrained by the manner of the periphery's insertion into the world economy. Its ability to restructure that mode of articulation was likewise constrained by the nature of class forces within its own societies. At any given point in time, there existed complex relationships between various internal classes and developments within the world economy that determined what reforms were politically and economically possible. Imperialism dictated that particular forms of economic activity predominated within any one Third World country and that the class formations which arose were not such that would permit autocentric development. Classes were not always distinct; production for the core meant that there were often strong social and economic links between landowners and bourgeoisie. Working classes also have been affected by dependent development. Isolated in enclave production or in large foreign enterprises, their ability to act as an independent class has been continually restrained by the presence of a numerically strong peasantry increasingly marginalized by commercial agriculture. In the absence of any one strong class capable of hegemony, Third World countries have experienced a number of different class alignments which have sought to stabilize class relations to their advantage. Given the Third World's continued dependency and the economic cleavages it has produced, such stability has been unattainable. Instead class alliances have constantly changed as relationships with the core have altered the balance of class forces and presented ruling class fractions new opportunities for maintaining control.

In Bolivia, as we earlier noted, the dominance of the foreign tin mining companies and landed hacendado class was weakened by the depressed state of world markets in the 1930s and broken in 1952 by a revolutionary alliance of discontented middle and working classes which nationalized the mines and distributed land to the peasantry. But the alliance could not hold, unless the middle classes were prepared to surrender power to an increasingly radical working class. The choice they faced was simple. Either they gave in to popular demands for greater income distribution and risked political suicide or they suppressed working-class discontent and attempted to consolidate bourgeois control of the state. Given the general backwardness of the Bolivian economy, the latter aim was not possible without foreign support. In confronting working class political independence, the Bolivian bourgeoisie and middle classes chose dependence on the very world economy from which they had tried to escape eleven years earlier.[61]

Throughout the remainder of South America similar shifts in alliances occurred as the bourgeoisie sought to take advantage of the decline in export-oriented economies and to ally with new urban middle and working classes against the once dominant landed classes. But their ability to achieve any semblance of hegemony was always frustrated by the economic structures inherited, by the self-interest of coopted and allied classes, and by changes in core-periphery relations. In the Third World the bourgeoisie lacked the autonomy their First World counterparts had achieved. Their accomplishments were always partial and rarely carried through: import substitution succumbed to a new form of dependency directed by TNCs; democracy gave way to political and military repression. As import substitution industrialization collapsed in Brazil, a military coup (1964) took place to maintain the status quo and restore industrial profitability. But the "economic miracle" of the military regime added a new partner to the ruling classes. Foreign capital, already heavily involved in Brazil due to the country's high debts, now oriented the manufacture of commodities towards export, without resolving the problems that had created the crisis in the first instance. "In the historical development of the Third World", observed Ian Roxborough, "each form of incompleteness fe[d] on and intensifie[d] the other." [62] In at least one case—Chile—the ruling elite now acts solely on its own behalf and on the behalf of foreign capital. The consolidation of this ruling elite has been accompanied by the depoliticization of Chilean society and by attempts to destroy the economic position of the middle class with its nationalist susceptibility. As one colleague recently remarked, Chile may well now be an example of a fully "recolonized" periphery, where the indigenous middle class has been severely repressed both politically and economically by a military regime which increasingly resembles a US garrison.

In India, by way of contrast, the colonially-generated weakness of the bourgeoisie encouraged the state to take a dominant role in initiating development in the name of "socialism". Nehru believed that an independent state would be able to promote production in a way that did not accumulate wealth and power in the hands of any one class. Accordingly, during the 1950s and 1960s the state nationalized large-scale basic industries and directed the development of artisan and small-scale industry. While these measures were relatively successful in containing bourgeois development, they were unable—in the absence of changes in ownership patterns—to reduce disparities in income and wealth, with the result that state socialism did not end peasant marginalization or strengthen internal markets. [63] India has demonstrated that even where state functionaries act independently of any class, there can be no automatic reduction in dependency without changes in the mode of production and in a country's mode of articulation with the world economy.

Second World countries have also found development constrained by the legacies of imperialism. In constructing socialist economic systems the choices open to communist parties have been inhibited by the level of their nation's material-technical base, the nature of prevailing cultural traditions and values, international economic and political relations (the extent of political or economic dependence), the presence or absence of charismatic political leadership, and, importantly, the methods used to achieve political power and the duration of revolutionary conflict. [64] Such factors have been largely responsible for the differences in socialist practices in eastern Europe, China, Cuba, Vietnam, Ethiopia, Afghanistan, Korea, Kampuchea, Laos, Mongolia, and the Soviet Union. Revolution may have enabled an elite committed to economic growth to reduce the impact of private vested interests and to alter the correlation of class forces, but it could not automatically overcome all obstacles to development. [65] Nor of course did the removal of bourgeois relations automatically produce socialism. These points were made forcibly by Mao Zedong in China after the mid-1950s.

> Marxism [he argued] can develop only through struggle, and not only is this true of the past and present, but it is necessarily true of the future as well.

This he claimed was "the law of development".

> All the socialist countries have a very long way to go before differences between ownership by the whole people and collective ownership, between workers and peasants, between town and country, between mental and manual labourers are eliminated; before all classes and class differences are abolished and a communist society with its principle "from each according to his ability, to each according to his needs" is realized. [66]

For Mao development was a process which reflected class struggle and the contradictions of economic growth. In this respect the Second World was no different from the Third.

Concerned that the Soviet model of socialist construction created excessive centralization and promoted wasteful and often irresponsible bureaucratization, Mao sought to direct China away from policies that might increase elitism and inequalities, and thereby remove all possibility of an independent self-reliant future. But as each challenge (the Great Leap Forward, the Socialist Education Movement, and the Cultural Revolution) took him closer to isolating those within the Communist Party whom he regarded as protagonists of the "capitalist road", he was unable to prevent the development of contradictory and ultimately self-defeating tendencies: his movement's collapse into dogma and unsatisfactory behavioural notions of class, its generation of factionalism and opportunism, and its challenge of the one organ necessary to implement the Mass Line—the Communist Party. Reliance on the Red Guards and the Army was not enough and, in any case, soon revealed its own dangers. Further, much of the impetus for the Cultural Revolution lay in China's political isolation, its loss of Soviet aid, and its concern with American imperialism in Southeast Asia. By the mid-1970s China's external relations had begun to change, and the leadership of the Revolution had passed to a small disadvantaged group which all too easily fell victim to its own inadequacies, not to mention Party intrigue. Nevertheless, despite its failure, Mao's Cultural Revolution was the most dramatic example of a nation groping for a development strategy that would break completely the shackles of its past and set a new pattern of balanced development where industry catered for local needs and drew on local resources and abundant labour.

One of the features of the contemporary era has been the growth of faith in the ability of people or classes to transcend history. The British in the late nineteenth century, the Germans and Japanese in the first half of the twentieth century, and the Americans after World War Two all believed they had moved into a new era in which past injustices would be removed to make way for an age of equality, justice and freedom. The same hope inspired revolutionaries in Soviet Russia and the People's Republic of China, as indeed it did in the decolonized Third World during and after the 1950s. In every instance, however, there has been no transcending new era. Nations have had to accommodate themselves to the realities of continuous and contradictory change. Nationalism and patriotism, politics and ideology may have ruled on the surface, but beneath "the imperative necessities of the capitalist mode of production" continue to exercise the determining role.[67] This is true of the whole world, regardless of whatever hierarchical divisions we may construct on the basis of ideological or economic differences. There is but one world and one world economy. For that reason nations have been unable to "develop into societies bearing any resemblance, except in their ideology, to the ideal . . . they seek".[68] The contradictions of development in the world shape our contemporary era, disturbing though they may be. Yet within them lie the possibilities for change, which, if seized, can enable people to begin the process of removing the shackles in which history has bound them.[69]

Notes

1. Thomas Hodgkin, "African and Third World Theories of Imperialism", in Owen and Sutcliffe, pp. 98-9.
2 . Simione Durutalo, "The Liberation of the Pacific Island Intellectual", *Review*, 10 (September, 1983), pp. 10, 14.
3. Magdoff, "Imperialism without Colonies", p. 164.
4. Roxborough, p. 68.
5. Robinson, p. 138.
6. Emmanuel, pp. 93-4.
7. Simione Durutalo, Fiji Anti-Nuclear Group's (FANG) Statement to the UN Committee of 24 on Decolonization, 4-6 March 1985, Port Moresby, Papua, New Guinea, p. 2.
8. Ibid.
9. Ibid., p. 3.
10. Porter, p. 281.
11. Hugh Larcey, *Pacific Protest, The Maasina Rule Movement, Solomon Islands, 1944-1952*, Institute of Pacific Studies, University of the South Pacific, Suva, 1983.
12. Porter, pp. 320-1.
13. Ibid., p. 353.
14. Roxborough, p. 73; see also pp. 73-5 for a description of Third World class

formations.
15. W. Sutherland, "The State and Capitalist Development in Fiji", Parts 3 and 4 passim.
16. Prabhat Patnaik, "Imperialism and the Growth of Industrial Capitalism", in Owen and Sutcliffe, pp. 228-9; Sen, pp. 180-93.
17. Roxborough, p. 87.
18. For further discussion of attempts to impose an orthodoxy by selective use of tradition see M.C. Howard, "Vanuatu: The Myth of Melanesian Socialism", *Labour Capital and Society*, 16:2 (November 1983), pp. 176-203; and Halliday, pp. 263-5; and, Morishima, pp. 194-201.
19. Samir Amin, "The Disarticulation of Economy within 'Developing Societies'", in Alavi and Shanin, p. 207.
20. R.J. May, "Micronationalism: What, when and why?" in R.J. May (ed.), *Micronationalist Movements in Papua New Guinea*, ANU, Canberra, 1982, pp. 422-448.
21. Hamza Alavi, "State and Class under Peripheral Capitalism", in Alavi and Shanin, pp. 302-3.
22. See Bill Warren, "Imperialism and Capitalist Industry", *New Left Review*, 81, (1973).
23. Bob Sutcliffe, "Imperialism and Industrialization in the Third World", in Owen and Sutcliffe, pp. 174-7; and Michael Barratt Brown, "Developing Societies as a part of an International Political Economy", in Alavi and Shanin, p. 170.
24. Roxborough, p. 39.
25. Ibid., p. 25.
26. Henry Bernstein, "Industrialization, Development, and Dependence", in Alavi and Shanin, p. 221.
27. Paul Sweezy, *The Theory of Capitalist Development*, MRP, New York, 1956, p. 326; and Paul Prebisch, "Roots of Crisis: What went wrong in Latin America", *South*, 35 (September 1983), pp. 67-8.
28. Roxborough, pp. 36-9.
29. Nabudere, pp. 235-6.
30. Sutcliffe, pp. 187-90.
31. Richard Higgott, "Competing Theoretical Perspectives on Development and Underdevelopment: A recent intellectual history", *Politics*, XIII (May 1978), pp. 29-31.
32. W.W. Rostow, *The Stages of Economic Growth*, Cambridge University Press, 1960. For summaries of the modernization school see A.M.M. Hoogvelt, *The Third World in Global Development*, Macmillan, London, 1982; A.A. Mazrui, *World Politics*, 21:1 (1968), pp. 69-83; and Roxborough, pp. 13-26.
33. Hoogvelt, p. 118.
34. Dower, *Origins*, p. 48.
35. S. Huntington, *Political Order in Changing Societies*, Yale University Press, 1968.
36. Dower, *Origins*, p. 36.
37. Roxborough, p. 103.
38. S. George, *Corporate Control of Food in the Third World*, Australian Freedom from Hunger Campaign, 1980, pp. 18-20; see also S. George, *Feeding the Few, Corporate Control of Food*, IPS, Washington, 1979.
39. *South*, December 1984, pp. 56-7.
40. Dower, *Origins*, p. 44.
41. Lawrence Surendra, "Seeds of disaster, germs of hope", *Far Eastern Economic Review (FEER)*, 22, March 1984, pp. 64-5.

42. *Fiji Times*, 30 April 1984, p. 6.
43. Surendra, pp. 64-5.
44. The main dependency debates centre around Paul Baran's *The Political Economy of Growth* (MRP, New York, 1967) and A.G. Frank's *Capitalism and Underdevelopment in Latin America* (MRP, New York, 1967). Colin Ley's "Underdevelopment and Development: Critical Notes" (*Journal of Contemporary Asia*, 7: 1, 1977, pp. 82-115) is an excellent critical review of the dependency debate.
45. Roxborough, pp. 45-53, provides a useful summary of the main issues arising from the Frank-Laclau debate.
46. Nabudere, pp. 223-4, 238, 268-79.
47. *World Labour Report*, cited in *FEER*, 23 February 1984, pp. 63-4.
48. Roxborough, p. 43.
49. Fernando Henrique Cardoso, "Dependency and Development in Latin America", in Alavi and Shanin, p. 116.
50. Ibid., Immanuel Wallerstein, "The Rise and Future Demise of the World Capitalist System: Concepts for Comparative Analysis", p. 50.
51. Nabudere, pp. 171-2.
52. Barratt Brown, pp. 157-9.
53. Amin, p. 208.
54. Cardoso, p. 119.
55. H. Wolfe, "Introduction", in H. Wolfe (ed.), *The Articulation of Modes of Production, Essays from Economy and Society*, Routledge and Kegan Paul, London, 1980, pp. 40-1.
56. Ibid., A.Q. Obregón, "The Marginal Pole of the Economy and the Marginalized Labour Force", pp. 273-86.
57. Wallerstein, p. 50.
58. Amin, p. 208.
59. Sen, p. 217.
60. T. Kemp, *Industrialization in the Non-Western World*, pp. 88, 93, 98.
61. Roxborough, pp. 148-51.
62. Ibid., pp. 146-7.
63. Sen, pp. 101-4.
64. Breth and Ward, pp. 25-6.
65. Roxborough, p. 140.
66. *Resolution on CPC History*, p. 23; and "On Khruschev's Phoney Communism and its Historical Lessons for the World", *Peking Review*, 17 July 1964.
67. Tom Kemp, "The Marxist Theory of Imperialism", in Owen and Sutcliffe, p. 26.
68. Barratt Brown, p. 170.
69. Alavi and Shanin, p. 8.

9. Crisis Revisited

Crisis

By 1971 the world faced a new crisis. The economic order created under American leadership following the Second World War was no longer sustainable despite American efforts to shore up its mechanisms of control. The director of the National Security Council suggested in May 1983 that it had been gravely weakened by a growing disjunction between political and economic power. "The economic centre of gravity of the world is rapidly shifting to the Pacific Basin", he concluded, but "the political and military centre of gravity is still in the northern hemisphere."[1] While motivated by concern to strengthen relations with America's strongest Asian ally, Japan, the director was acknowledging a remarkable change which had occurred within the core and the periphery during the 1970s. Its origins lay in part in the huge balance of trade deficits, occasioned by the rising cost of military expansion and economic aid, experienced by the United States at the beginning of that decade. As we saw earlier, the tremendous outlays demanded by the Vietnam War combined with falling rates of productivity to weaken the US position vis-á-vis other core nations, in particular Western Europe (which after the 1957 Treaty of Rome had united economically in a European Common Market) and Japan, while European and Japanese economic expansion during the 1960s resulted in new competing trade and currency blocs which increasingly restricted American hegemonic policies. At the same time, however, rivalry contradicted the growing interdependence of their economies and made coherent responses to the crisis more difficult.

This inability to act coherently was sharpened by the core's continued persistence in regarding itself as all-important. US National Security Adviser, Henry Kissinger, told Chilean Foreign Minister Gabriel Valdes in 1969:

> The axis of history starts in Moscow, goes to Bonn, crosses over to Washington and then goes to Tokyo. What happens in the South is of no importance.[2]

In the decade which followed, however, the Third World demonstrated that it was no longer simply of peripheral importance to the world economy.

The actions of OPEC and the expansion of the NICs provided their own confirmation.

These twin intracore and periphery challenges combined in the 1970s and 1980s with a crisis in confidence, generated by a deepening recession, to weaken further the postwar order. This process is described by Ankie Hoogvelt in her recent and masterly account of contemporary global development.

> The turn of the decade [1969-70] saw an end to the long period of post-war economic boom. Economic recession began to hit the industrial countries, sending its reverberations throughout the developing world. The post-war economic boom which had trebled the world's industrial product had succeeded in doing so only by rapacious use of the world's natural resources, including oil. After all their colonial past had bestowed upon many countries of the Western world access to cheap supplies of Third World minerals. The terms of trade with which the Third World countries traditionally exchange their precious resources for the West's industrial produces were deteriorating and this contributed to a widening . . . gap between the First and Third Worlds. OPEC's decision to quadruple the price of oil in 1973 was a first instance of concerted political defiance on the part of the Third World. It furthermore deepened the economic recession and made double-digit inflation a permanent feature of the world economy. The economic stagnation, moreover, coupled with adverse weather conditions which brought disastrous crop failures in several parts of the world, pushed a delicate but so far positive balance between the world's food supplies and the world's population to a negative one, and whipped up new Malthusian fears of over-population. The leading sector of world industrial growth in the post-war boom had been the armaments sector, and various localised struggles (Vietnam and the Middle East) acted as reminders of the potential for total destruction of which the super-powers were now capable. And, finally, the combined effects of in-dustrialisation, urbanisation, and technological revolutions in agriculture on the environment erupted into a series of well-publicised ecological imbalances. [3]

Disillusionment followed rapidly as, like the late Victorians before them, the contemporaries of the 1970s saw their hopes for everlasting upward progress swiftly vanishing. And, as had been the case during the immediate pre-First World War years, advocates of direct action implied a way out of the impasse which simultaneously diverted popular attention from otherwise intractable problems. This time the rewards were higher, but so too were the risks, and the core's manoeuvrability was precariously reduced. It is to this crisis and the transformations it effected that the final chapter is addressed.

In Chapter 5 we noted Marx's comment that the contradictions generated by the process of development result in conflict and the eventual collapse of existing relations of production as a new mode of production gains ascendancy. When feudal relations of production were no longer compatible with expanding bourgeois productive forces, Marx argued, they were "burst asunder". [4] The transition to capitalism, however, did not transcend history; rather it set in train a process of change which merely extended and intensified its own contradictory nature. The spread of industrialization during the nineteenth century, for instance, did not enable capitalists to sustain profitability in the face of declining productivity. The embourgeoisement of the proletariat, the application of new scientific discoveries to production, the aggressive search for new avenues for investment and profit, and the union of financial and industrial capital enabled capitalists to escape the crisis, but at the same time raised the stakes in such a way as to ensure greater competition and greater vulnerability. Crises were a warning to restructure, but the process was painful and not always certain of success. Under such circumstances it is not surprising that the early twentieth century witnessed a devastating depression sandwiched between two world wars.

The establishment of American hegemony after 1945 reflected a major shift in the balance of power within the core rather than a change in the system itself since the same conflict between the need to increase consumption while reducing costs of production remained. Although the application of new technology, rising core standards of living, and the regulation of loans and investment on an internationally controlled basis served to reduce the impact of this conflict for a time, it could not remove it. Indeed the mechanisms of free trade, so essential for guaranteeing American access to world markets, merely established a new framework in which international rivalry could continue, especially once Europe and Japan recovered from the devastation of war and the new Third World began pressing for equal development. The result once more was reduced profitability, overproduction, declining productivity and expansionary investment which served to destabilize relationships between output and employment and force new efforts to rationalize industry (to increase competitiveness) or raise new national and regional barriers.[5] The crisis generated by this intensified international rivalry has affected both the core and the periphery and reasserted the logic of capitalist transformation.

The Core

For the United States the sudden and unprecedented balance of trade deficit in 1971 and the following devaluation of the dollar, the establishment of wage and price controls, the introduction of a new surcharge on imports, and the suspension of the dollar's convertibility into gold two years later marked the beginning of a new downturn in the economy. When combined with defeats in US foreign policy, growing dependence on imported oil, inflation and unemployment, it appeared as if the United States was declining rapidly. Yet the decline was far from absolute. The US dollar remained the main international currency because it was less susceptible to weakening as a result of the recession. (Trade accounted for only 10 per cent of the US GNP compared for example with 29 per cent of the German GNP.) Further, the recession was not spread evenly among the capitalist nations. This more than anything else created intracore rivalry and added to the impression of drastic American decline. Western Europe's combined GNP equalled America's, a factor which undoubtedly made the former's automatic subordination to US consumer and political values less acceptable. Japan's GNP also rose from 10 per cent of the US GNP in 1965 to 40 per cent by 1980. During the 1970s a new mood of cultural and economic assertion swept Europe and Japan as the assumptions which had previously subordinated them to the superior United States were gradually eroded.[6]

Although increased trade and currency tensions are unlikely to precipitate a major intracore conflict, as has happened in the past, they do highlight the continuing impact of external and internal contradictions on international relations as America's partners renew their struggle for comparative advantage within the core by claiming a right to protect internal markets from foreign competition while at the same time insisting upon access to those of their rivals.

The European economies, for example, expanded rapidly after the 1950s due to their incorporation into a regional economic bloc (the EEC). While the wider base offered by such a grouping allowed industry to escape the constraints of size and internal fragmentation which had earlier been a feature of their national economies, it could not reduce the impact of declining profitability and increased competition within the wider world economy. Nor of course has the recent incorporation of Greece into the EEC, and nor has the inclusion of Spain and Portugal. Instead, Europe has resorted to various regional protectionist measures to offset American and Japanese competition. Trade barriers, while contrary to the post war order's emphasis on free trade, have been increasingly erected to limit the impact of imported goods, especially high technology commodities from Asia, and American and Australasian agricultural products. Defensive moves alone have proved inadequate and European states have gradually realized that technological leadership requires greater state investment in research and development, and a more aggressive effort to establish new markets. The restructuring caused by this adaptation to greater competition has also drawn the EEC to reconsider its relations with the Third World, for the latter is now seen as a means to overcome many of the internal problems restructuring has produced. The recently proposed Kervyn-Laure scheme for mutual aid demonstrates this new approach. The scheme calls for a European loan of $US10 billion annually for five years to the Third World to finance imports from the EEC. Such a loan, it is suggested, would promote a one per cent growth rate within the EEC and thereby alleviate its chronic unemployment problems, while also serving to promote much needed development in the Third World.[7]

Competition and the imperatives of expansion and profitability have produced similar responses in Japan. Smaller in size and lacking the large internal resource and market base of the EEC, Japan is more vulnerable to trade fluctuations than her European counterparts. Further, her internal structures are less flexible. With poor welfare facilities, the Japanese ruling classes are only too aware of the conflict an increase in unemployment would generate. Accordingly they have been prepared to sacrifice agricultural and retail sector efficiency in order to create a safety valve for those who would otherwise be unemployed. To reform these sectors would jeopardize political and social harmony.[8] Nevertheless, by fostering free trade in order to secure economic expansion Japan is increasingly exposing these internal structures to the kind of change it wishes to avoid.

So far Japan has been fortunate in being able to manage this potentially disruptive contradiction. Her trade surplus with the EEC alone rose from $US300 million in 1970 to $10 billion in 1981. By 1982 her total world trade surplus stood at $20 billion and her invisible deficits had been substantially reduced. Although productivity slumped to 3.4 per cent in 1983, Japan has retained a growth rate consistently higher than both the EEC and the United States. This, together with trade surpluses, has enabled her to emerge in the 1980s as a major creditor nation.

Japan's "success" since the 1960s has been built on the same responses as Europe; her internal market has been widened, investments have increased and new external markets obtained. Contemporary analysts who glorify the application of Confucianism to capitalism often miss this point. The electronics industry provides an example. First, Japan has coordinated and expanded investment in new technology. In 1976 the Japanese government launched a five-year programme for strategic planning and invested $350 million into large-scale integrated circuitry research. By 1981 total Japanese research and development expenditure grossed $25 billion, four times more than a decade earlier, and the equivalent of 2.4 per cent of her GNP. Much of this new investment has been in fifth generation computers.[9]

Second, access to American (and later European) markets, achieved largely by exploiting internal US corporate rivalry, provided further dividends. American electronics manufacturers had long refused to supply mass merchandisers whose pricing policies they could not control. The Japanese, however, were more than keen to supply the merchandisers. When the American manufacturers responded during the 1960s by shifting their production to cheaper East Asia, the Japanese simply began automating production, a move that was only possible because of the development of integrated circuitry. When, under pressure from its manufacturers, the United States government began to meet this new threat by restricting imports, the Japanese shifted production to the United States itself.[10] Offshore production might not provide a long-term solution to Japan's need to expand, however. Already the EEC is moving to tax Japanese commodities produced internally and the United States might well react similarly to the proposed production of Japanese cars within the United States that do not fall under its car import quota system.

Japan's promotion of free trade leaves her open to criticism of her own protective barriers. The United States, in particular, has sought to reduce the impact of declining markets by prompting Japan to lift restrictions on agricultural produce. Japan currently buys $7 billion of agricultural goods (1982) from the United States, three-quarters of which are livestock feed and fertilizer. Already she has been forced (1978) to extend imports of beef, oranges and grapefruit, and the Americans have demanded further access, obtaining in 1984 for example an increase in beef sales much to the chagrin of major suppliers like Australia. $9 billion of food imports also enter Japan from her own projects in Asia and Latin America. Free trade, therefore, while beneficial for Japan's own export drive, could be disastrous if applied to herself. Her heavily subsidized agricultural sector, for instance, would be placed under greater strain if it had to compete internationally; already its 4½ million farming families are forced to obtain 80 per cent of their incomes from non-farming sources. [11]

The Japanese response has been to suggest a new international division of labour similar in principle to its Co-Prosperity Sphere of the 1930s. Hikaru Kerns has argued that:

> The success of Asean and the durability of the European Economic Community has enhanced the possibility that unless Japan finds its niche in a bloc of nations, the country will be left behind increasingly to negotiate economic and political arrangements on its own, confronting unified regional interests. [12]

To reduce that possibility Japan has invested heavily in Asia, raising direct investment from $US166 million in 1970 to over $9 billion in 1981. Direct and indirect returns from investments and loans, while guaranteeing Japan's continued healthy surpluses and credit, do little to offset the new competition investments create. To limit that competition and to restrict its internal impact, Japan has urged the formal creation of a new and stable international division of labour.

Known as the Pacific Rim Strategy, the new order would consist of four tiers, with Japan (and the United States) at the top providing capital, technology and planning. Canada, Australia and New Zealand would form a second tier as the suppliers of minerals, energy and food. Below them, the Third World of Asia and Latin America would satisfy demand for cheap resources and labour. [13] A fourth tier, the socialist countries of Asia (notably China), has also been suggested. Although exploitation of this tier may be similar to that of the third's, the exact manner of its insertion and the impact of its economic size still remain unknown factors to be accommodated aside from ideological considerations.

The Strategy has so far received little official recognition in the Pacific Basin, but has gained informal ratification from private interests (those represented in the 1967 Pacific Basin Economic Council), from a series of study groups and seminars (the 1979-80 Japanese study group, the 1980 Canberra Seminar, the 1980 Japanese Special Committee on Pacific Cooperation), and at various meetings in Bangkok and Bali during 1982 and 1983. Indeed it could be argued that while formal ratification of such a strategy would be premature, many of its features are already evident in the restructuring that we shall examine presently. Japanese foreign aid works deliberately to shape this policy, although it remains restricted by Japan's small foreign assistance in relation to GNP compared with other core nations. [14] Core rivalry obviously prevents formal recognition (recently the Japanese Government shunned all references to a Pacific Economic Community or even a Pacific Community and spoke instead of less formal cooperation, ostensibly because it wished to avoid antagonizing a sensitive Asean)[15] and the United States sees closer ties with Japan as one way to avert effective Japanese Pacific Basin hegemony. For the moment Japan has acquiesced, but the country's greater competitiveness, knowledge of, and access to Asian markets, and flexibility in investments and penetration will work to her advantage.

The Asean countries of South East Asia have therefore emerged as Japan's major economic grouping during the 1970s, with offshore facilities being established for Japanese capital—iron and steel foundries in Malaysia, South Korea and Taiwan; aluminium smelters in Indonesia; and petro-chemical industries in Singapore and South Korea. While these have served to sustain Japanese competitiveness and allow her to restructure her own industries by focusing more, for instance, on special alloy production (requiring fewer raw materials and producing a higher added value), offshore production has also generated new centres of competition and raised Asean demands which go beyond the aims of Japanese development assistance. In 1982 Japan halted the transfer of iron and steel technology to East Asia to reduce competition with her own industries. Such actions have however proved counterproductive, for they have strengthened Asean's resolve to form a more independent grouping, which even China has endorsed.[16]

Unity within the Pacific Basin might not be entirely to Japan's liking. Plans can after all be reshuffled. Relations with the second tier have also substantially improved [by 1984 Japan accounted for nearly one-third of all Australian exports], although conflict exists between the trading interests of the US and Australasia in the Japanese market. Tension therefore is multiplex. Nevertheless, Saburo Okita's *Japan in the Year 2000* forecasts a bright future. Japan's current 10 per cent share of the world economy (up from 8 per cent in 1978) is expected to rise to 12 per cent before the end of the century. Perhaps more significantly for the core, her share of the Organization for Economic Cooperation and Development's (OECD) GNP is expected to rise from 16 per cent to 21 per cent.[17]

The core's restructuring has also been affected by the reemergence of many socialist countries as active participants in the world economic order. If we accept the Maoist interpretation of development quoted at the end of the last chapter, such events need not be cynically analysed. As Hamza Alavi and Teodor Shanin have stated,

> Things said about the cruelty of choices within "developing societies" shape also the nature of the alternative regimes and not only of the defenders of the status quo.[18]

While socialist participation has not followed similar paths, their increased share of global manufacturing production has undoubtedly surpassed any achievement in the Third World, rising from 18.1 per cent in 1960 to 27 per cent in 1975. In fact the core has become increasingly dependent on trade with the "East" or Second World, a factor which not unnaturally has conflicted with US attempts to reassert its hegemony. European

Figure 9.1 : THE ROLE OF EXPORTS IN INCUSTRIALIZATION

Despite increasing trade links between the First and Second Worlds, export production remains more functional to the success of First World industrial strategies than to those of the Second World.

INDUSTRIAL OUTPUT AND TRADE, 1938-1970

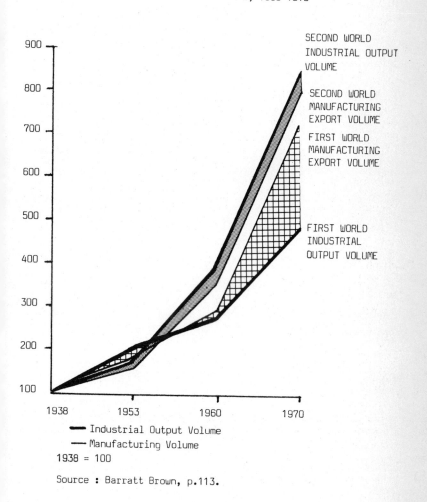

Source : Barratt Brown, p.113.

and American corporate reluctance to ensure a full embargo on grain and high technology sales to Russia after the latter's invasion of Afghanistan in late 1979, for instance, demonstrated the new interdependence. The United States had much less to lose by pressuring the Soviet Union, although grain sales during the 1970s not only overcame the effects of declining Japanese and European purchases but also reduced reserves so as to permit higher grain prices. Nevertheless, its exports to Comecon in 1980 (mostly foods) amounted to $4 billion compared with Europe's $23 billion.[19] Also both France and Germany anticipate receiving nearly one-third of their natural gas needs from the Siberian Hamburg pipeline in the next decade. Russia might require Western grain to offset agricultural inefficiency and crop failures, but the core is becoming equally dependent also on Russian raw materials, and the Americans have regarded such developments as a threat to their own monopoly position in Europe. Nevertheless interdependence works both ways, as for example in the case of East European countries which have reoriented production to satisfy Western markets and sought financial assistance from the IMF and World Bank. When the Polish economy collapsed in 1980, there were fears that the Polish Government might default on its $US28 billion debt to core lending institutions which had been directing the Polish economy during the previous years without success.

In China, too, increased private management has effected a new division of labour to reduce the proportion of population directly dependent on agriculture and to seek new (internal and external) markets which will finance further development. While this radical departure in economic policy is often portrayed as a betrayal of Maoist principles, it should be remembered that export production, while expanded, still forms a small part of China's GNP and that the major thrust of development remains, as before, internal integration. Undoubtedly the rise of market or capitalist relations has the potential for creating social conflicts; for the moment, however, they enable greater productivity by providing a wider consumer base to act as an incentive for agricultural capital accumulation.

One of the important tasks of the responsibility system, for example, is to divert excess labour from agricultural production into specialized occupations associated with agriculture or into brigade enterprises, in order to provide new sources of investment finance to plough into rural production and enable a much needed alternative focus for surplus population to the large cities. By 1984 small town industries had grown to such an extent that they accounted for 28.3 per cent of the total national industrial output value. Professor Fei Xiaotong notes:

> One important aspect is a determination not to move rural people wholesale to cities, there to undergo a "baptism" of modernization, but instead to develop industry in the countryside. Mechanized agriculture and industrial production will gradually bring the amenities of modern life to the rural areas, creating great changes in the people's material and cultural life.[20]

China's development is not dependent on export production and its emphasis remains the creation of a strong and integrated internal base. Mao Zedong's policy of communal self-sufficiency and decentralized industrialization has been superseded by the new formation in the 1980s of new regional cooperation policies which establish a new division of labour by focusing industrial production in the cities and small towns, and by connecting backward regions to urban and internal demands. Whether this results in the marginalization of less developed regions as Mao feared or will indeed result in greater internal economic integration, has yet to be seen. Its aim, nevertheless, remains one of making China less dependent on foreign revenue and raw materials in order to fuel growth and to promote her independence in the world order. [21]

The successful emergence of competitive socialist economies and rising intracore competition frustrated American initiatives to sustain US hegemony. The effects of recession within the United States, particularly when combined with the crisis of authority generated by the Watergate scandal, caused further alarm. So too did the dramatic speeding up of a general shift in employment patterns which emphasized the nation's decline in productivity. Between 1950 and 1978 an 18 per cent decline in private goods sector employment was matched by a corresponding increase in private and government service employment. While this shift reflected the new importance of sales and distribution in realizing surplus value and of the growing power of finance capital over all other economic sectors, it also demonstrated the impact of inflation in pushing employment into the service industry and in driving women into the workforce to cope with increases in the cost of living. Between 1976 and 1980 real wages fell 10 per cent in the United States. [22] As we shall see later, some employment sectors were more threatened by recession than others, and by the end of the 1970s large numbers of blue-collar workers (most visibly steel and car manufacturing workers) faced redundancy as a result of Japanese and NIC imports. Ironically their vulnerability made them susceptible to the new jingoistic nationalism of the likewise threatened bourgeoisie whose anti-inflationary policies in reality further assaulted the working classes.

While these changes increased internal tensions and were used to justify demonstrations of hegemonic intent, they did not reflect the overall state of the US economy. The United States still led the world in space technology, exploration, and military weaponry. A new export drive, particularly in agricultural products, enabled the US to increase her access to core markets and to produce a healthy trade surplus with the EEC by the 1980s. While OPEC's actions, and a growing dependence on imported oil, inflamed American public opinion, they disguised the extent to which US companies profited from oil price rises (profits rose 200 per cent between 1971 and 1979) and were able to diversify into new energy activities. Also hidden were the substantial steps the government took to reduce US dependence on OPEC oil. Similarly, the impact of the NICs was not entirely negative and the US certainly benefited from their increased demands for consumer, raw material and military products. Indeed by 1981 40 per cent of all US manufactured exports went to the Third World.

Balance of payments difficulties also revealed only one side of the picture. During the 1970s there was a tremendous flow of capital into the US from its own overseas investments and from overseas investors seeking higher rates of return and political stability in the US capital market. Between 1966 and 1978 US foreign investments of $50 billion generated an income of $203 billion, of which $132 billion was repatriated. Banks also established new branches overseas, to such an extent that overseas earnings for the top 13 US banks rose from 18.8 per cent of their total earnings in 1970 to 49.6 per cent by 1976.[23] Foreign capital likewise moved into the US at a faster rate than previously. By 1980 one-quarter of the loans made in the US were by foreign banks. Twenty-eight per cent of all West German foreign investment went to the US, and 23 per cent of Japanese investment.[24]

The US economy, therefore, was far from moribund, but its dominance was being eroded. Indeed the inflow of money during the 1970s inflated the value of the dollar by over thirty per cent, creating difficulties for exporters and import-competing industries. By 1984 the US merchandise trade deficit had risen to a new high of $125 billion and its current account deficit to $100 billion. Since US savings are now insufficient to finance both the huge federal government deficit and private sector investment, the US is forced to borrow upwards of $80 billion each year. Not only does the US dollar face the possibility of collapse if overseas investors lose confidence and pull out, but, as *South* magazine reported, there is a very real possibility of the whole US surplus on overseas services (historically used to offset its deficit on merchandise trade) also being wiped out.[25]

If the growing debt crisis and the successes of OPEC during the 1970s seemed to confirm US decline in the public mind, so too did the dramatic examples of the failure of US initiative in the Third World. During the 1970s a new wave of revolutions occurred which in most cases represented the last of the old struggles against colonial domination or pre-capitalist monarchies. In 1974 a revolution toppled Haile Selassie's Ethiopian government. In the same year another revolution in Portugal precipitated revolts in her remaining colonies (Angola 1975, Mozambique 1975, Guinea-Bissau 1974, Cape Verde 1975, and Sao Tome 1975). The new regimes these changes created strengthened pressure on white-ruled South Africa and were important in securing the formation of Zimbabwe in 1980 and in uniting opposition to the CIA-South African involvement in Namibia. In 1975 also the pro-American regimes in Indochina finally collapsed, and revolutions also occurred in Afghanistan (1978) and in Iran (1979). In Latin America in 1979 the Sandinista Movement swept into power in Nicaragua as did the New Jewel Movement in Grenada.[26]

The loss of Vietnam was the most serious for the United States, not only because of her investments in Indochina, but also because of its effects on American prestige. Iran, Nicaragua, Ethiopia and Angola had been strategically important to the US, and the eventual use of Cuban troops and Soviet aid in the last two to strengthen their new governments gave fresh impetus to notions of US decline and the spread of Soviet Russia. Indeed it was a major reason for America's move away from detente with the USSR at the end of the 1970s and its determination to gain a new margin of military superiority. Soviet-bloc military expenditures were only half of those of the US and its allies, but its decision in the 1960s to seek parity with the US had certainly narrowed America's superiority. As in trade with the core, the US felt the need to restore its earlier undisputed hegemony.

Soviet influence in the Third World was also much reduced and she had never recovered from her loss of China and Egypt as allies. Nor did Russia present the same appeal to the Third World she had twenty or thirty years before. Consumer shortages, agricultural problems, the lack of any real increase in political liberty, growing political tensions in East Europe, and the Soviet tendency to replicate her own political structures in the Third World,

> demoralized those who aspire[d] to a socialist alternative and . . . emboldened those [in the US] who want[ed] to roll back the revolutions of this century by advocating a capitalist restoration in the East. [27]

Russia's invasion of Afghanistan in December 1979 to bolster her unstable socialist ally, and America's inability to free her hostages in Iran demonstrated that the "days when it could unilaterally enforce its will were past". [28] The Suez Crisis in 1956 had demonstrated that fact to Britain but the United States has still to acknowledge its own changed position. "You see", Kissinger once remarked, "when one wields power, and when one has it for a long time, one ends up thinking one has a right to it." [29]

This attitude has particularly affected US relations with her southern neighbours, where the combined effects of recession and indigenous industrialization have resulted in the United States losing 28 per cent of its Latin American market. The US trade representative at the OECD ministerial meeting in Paris in May 1983 saw the maintenance of southern links as imperative. "You can't have solid recovery in the US", he claimed, "if you lose that much of your external market." [30] Socialist threats therefore were taken seriously because of their potential for closing the door to American interests. Such a perception, when combined with a long history of military intervention in Latin America, has made change in the South extremely difficult. It has also meant that events in Cuba, Vietnam, Angola, Mozambique, Iran, Nicaragua, Grenada and El Salvador during the 1970s and 1980s are now seen as indications that methods of indirect control are no longer viable. A recent Institute of Social Studies (the Hague) Workshop on Latin America has argued:

> With such a syndrome, the traditional norms of rational foreign policy are suspended and political discourse acquires pathological characteristics. Under these circumstances, the social roots of the conflict which are crucial to defining a solution and a new accommodation with the United States, vanish from the field of vision of the US administration. Instead . . . conflict . . . is seen entirely in terms of the international balance of power and any change is seen as a threat to the global balance of power. [31]

Thus Nicaragua, dependent on the West for 43 per cent of its aid, is increasingly seen as a socialist threat which must be exterminated. To quote Kissinger again:

> If we cannot manage Central America it will be impossible to convince threatened nations in the Gulf and other places that we know how to manage the global equilibrium. [32]

For precisely the same reasons Kissinger had escalated the Vietnam war into Kampuchea and had facilitated the military coup in Chile. Ten years later the same imperative remained, but increasingly at the risk of tragic parody and farce.

The Periphery

The difficulties experienced by the United States in retaining an initiative it had long regarded as its right were not due solely to an expansion in the perimeters of the world economy or to renewed intracore rivalry. The emergence of a Third World as an effective entity in its own right, particularly within the United Nations Organization, also provided a substantial challenge during the 1970s. The origins of that challenge lay in two separate Third World movements which, in the bleak circumstances of deepening recession, joined forces to demand that the core reappraise its attitude towards the periphery.

The first source of the challenge lay in the Non-Aligned Movement. Formed at the 1955 Bandung Conference of Africa and Asia, it established the notion of a third force in the world and during the late 1950s and 1960s focused on the largely political issues of decolonization and Third World solidarity. From the time of its 1970 Lusaka meeting, however, it rapidly shifted its orientation to economic concerns, stressing self-reliance as a necessary concept for development and the continuance of political independence. By the time of the 1973 Algiers Conference the transformation was complete. Moreover, the Movement now argued that self-reliance was only possible if world economic relations were altered to allow for a New International Economic Order (NIEO). Aware that the Third World's majority in the United Nations provided a more effective forum than its own conferences, the Movement decided to press the UN General Assembly to accept a declaration of intention to establish a NIEO.

The second source of the challenge was Latin American in origin. Because of its failure to direct independent industrialization, the ECLA came to accept the desirability of creating an economic organization that could challenge the core's OECD and promote Third World solidarity. Accordingly, in 1964 the United Nations Conference on Trade and Development (UNCTAD) met for the first time and established a caucus known as the Group of 77 to direct solidarity in matters of trade and development. Subsequent meetings in New Delhi (1968) and in Santiago (1972) were instrumental in establishing the 1976 Generalized System of

Preferences (GSPs) which facilitated the entry of Third World products into the core. Of greater importance, however, was UNCTAD's reaction to the 1971 monetary crisis. In demanding greater Third World decision-making and participatory powers in international monetary organizations, UNCTAD became more politicized. Like the Non-Aligned Movement, it lacked bargaining power and turned to the United Nations General Assembly for assistance, requesting that it adopt a Charter of Economic Rights and Duties of States to secure for Third World states greater powers in their relations with TNCs and monetary institutions. The adoption of the Charter by the General Assembly in November 1974 provided the NIEO with the principles on which it could be based. The two movements were now unified in purpose. [33]

Boosted by the success of OPEC in raising oil export prices, Third World representatives exerted increased pressure on the core between 1974 and 1976. Meeting in Lima in 1974, the Group of 77 called for increased industrialization and greater access for Third World products. At Dacca (1975) developing nations urged the establishment of raw material producer associations similar to OPEC and the creation of a solidarity fund to finance buffer stock. UNCTAD IV in Nairobi (1976) went further and introduced a plan to stabilize Third World commodity prices. During 1976 demands were also pressed for a greater say in the affairs of the IMF. Since the first rumblings of currency crisis in 1969, Special Drawing Rights (SDRs) had been issued to IMF members in direct ratio to their subscription or quota to the Fund. Since voting rights were tied to subscriptions, the Third World was disadvantaged. Although they accounted for 81 per cent of IMF membership, they possessed only 36 per cent of the vote. At an IMF conference in Kingston they demanded voting reform, an increased allocation of SDRs, and a linking of the latter to development finance. [34]

The demand for a NIEO was the single most important challenge from the ruling classes of the Third World since decolonization. But it was a demand only, for it placed the onus on the core itself to redress unequal economic structures. Given that the core was less dependent on the Third World than vice-versa this was unlikely to happen, and increasingly the Third World relied upon OPEC to throw its weight behind the NIEO, a willingness that the core exploited during the remainder of the decade by recycling OPEC petrodollars to the Third World. Once OPEC capital dried up in the early 1980s, the façade of core cooperation became all too apparent. The vagueness of the NIEO demands also allowed exploitation. Beyond calling for increased opportunities for more of the same, the NIEO demands presented no new development strategy. It was all too easy therefore for the core to buy off key Third World countries and break their solidarity. The attack came first from Henry Kissinger at the Seventh Special Session of the UN in 1975. By watering down NIEO resolutions, by fragmenting its programmes, and by offering participation on steering committees the United States succeeded in separating the more developed Third World from the remainder [35] in a move reminiscent of the way in which the nineteenth century core ruling classes had

divided its working classes. In the late 1970s the process of embourgeoisement was applied increasingly to give selected Third World countries a
stake in preserving the old order and to blunt the NIEO demands.

Failure to retain the initiative was disastrous for the Third World. The
Lomé Convention in 1975 provided a further example. Instigated in part
by Caribbean leaders after Britain's entry into the EEC, it provided for
the stabilization of raw material prices for a new Africa-Caribbean-Pacific
(ACP) Third World grouping. Its main achievement lay principally in
regulating and guaranteeing sugar production, but again the onus for its
success or otherwise lay with the EEC. By perpetuating colonial commercial
relationships in a new form and by renewing ACP dependence on that relationship, the possibility of long-term solutions to developmental problems
were effectively postponed.

In this respect the first Association of South East Asian Nations (Asean)
Summit in Bali (1976) was more promising, as success was not dependent
upon the willingness of the core to cooperate. (Its members are Thailand,
Malaysia, Singapore, Indonesia, the Philippines, and Brunei.) Although
Asean had suffered from fragmentation since its inception in 1967, the
invasion of Kampuchea by Vietnam and increasing dissatisfaction with
Japanese and American aid and investment gave cooperation a new vital
meaning. The 1983 Asean Industrial Joint Ventures Scheme which increases
preferential tariff treatment within the region is perhaps the most promising
breakthrough in this respect, though the motivation for Asean will probably
remain more political than economic for some time. As American influence
in the region declines further by the end of the century and as China
reemerges as the predominant Asian power, Asean is likely to form closer
ties with Indochina. For Vietnam such a move would be an acceptable alternative to Russian influence; for Asean also it would strengthen the region
against both Japanese and future Chinese dominance and enable a more
viable regional economic bloc to emerge.

The growth of the Southern African Development Coordination
Conference (SADCC) and the more recent Eastern-Southern Preferential
Trade Area (ESAPTA) offer opportunities similar to Asean's to reduce
colonially-derived forms of dependence and to foster linkages between the
separate African states. Given the history of the West African Economic
Community (ECOWAS) this will be no easy task, particularly also since
much of the finance sought for the industrial base of such cooperation
remains external to the regions themselves. Many of the neocolonial trade
and economic cooperation agreements that have arisen since the call for
a NIEO have, therefore, failed whenever unequal relationships were simply
perpetuated. Like the South Pacific island countries' SPARTECA (the
South Pacific Regional Trade and Economic Cooperation Agreement
between Australia and New Zealand and the Forum island countries was
signed in Tarawa, Kiribati in 1980), the "onus for giving force and credibility" to agreements has often been mistakenly placed with core nations.[36]
Nabudere has argued that responsibility for such failures must also lie with
the dependency theoreticians. Because neo-Marxists neglected the political

preconditions for development, they provided Third World bourgeoisies a "ready-made ideology" with which to win more concessions from their core counterparts. [37] Commodity trade and price negotiations do not represent a challenge to the system itself, only the emergence of increased intraclass tension within the core-periphery dialectic.

The Rise and Fall of International Keynesianism

Nevertheless, the call for a NIEO was well timed. Already the core's optimism concerning future progress had been severely shaken by inflation and unemployment as the recession deepened at the beginning of the 1970s. In fact the First World's future looked bleak. Its insatiable drive for greater levels of production and consumption promised only pollution and resource depletion. In 1972 the Club of Rome released a report, whose gloomy outline of the physical, demographic, and economic growth limits facing the world, seemed to justify a growing crisis in confidence. [38] The Third World's demand for NIEO merely deepened that gloom, bringing, as Ankie Hoogvelt recorded, an awesome insight:

> the advanced world might never recover [from the recession] unless at least part of the underdeveloped world [was] . . . brought up to a standard of life where people and nations play a decent role as economic consumers. [39]

Without realizing it the Third World had given the core a much needed shot in the arm, and the result was to be a NIEO for the First World rather than the periphery.

The Club of Rome's second report provided some indication of what a NIEO shaped by the core might entail. Published in 1976 as *Mankind at the Turning Point*, [40] it stressed the interdependence of the world and the need for global rather than national strategies. Even if the Third World was to industrialize it would remain dependent on the core; indeed anticipated food shortages demanded that the Third World accelerate its trade of raw materials. Jan Tinbergen's third Club of Rome report was more explicit. [41] The periphery must abandon all ideas of ever catching up with the core. Maldistribution of resources, and the potential it created for wars of retribution, could only be avoided by creating a new international division of labour based on the very "laws" of comparative advantage the NIEO originators had sought to avoid. Further, while Third World nations would have to accept greater responsibility for domestic basic needs and income redistribution, global development strategies would in future focus more on the individual than on the nation-state. These ahistorical scenarios all failed to detail how the process of change was to be effected. But one thing was clear, they reflected the growing acceptability of a Keynesian solution to the world recession. This the Brandt Report in 1980 also belatedly reflected. [42]

The Brandt Report was a popular version of the liberal rethinking generated by the experiences of the 1970s. It called for a Keynesian redistribution of wealth on a global scale and for a new international division of labour that would necessitate restructuring in the core (North) and the periphery (South). Like Tinbergen, Chairman Brandt urged the Third World to become more self-reliant but without damaging existing trade arrangements. Greater internal resourcefulness and the adoption of small-scale industry and agrarian reform would give Third World governments a stronger base from which to bargain with the core. Third World strategists, however, found little in the Report to satisfy their aspirations, yet they offered no alternatives themselves. The Argentinian Bariloche Foundation in 1976 had urged the adoption of more egalitarian systems to provide for basic needs, and of new defensive Third World trading blocs. [43] But beyond calling for a greater transfer of resources from the core, it seemed as if the Third World, in abdicating the centre stage, in delegating initiative to the First World, had succumbed to inertia.

Third World solidarity in the 1970s, then, was achieved at a cost. By arguing that internal social inequalities were the result of unequal external relationships, the Third World's representatives failed to draw the connection with the logic of capitalist relations while at the same time underestimating capitalism's ability to transform itself without altering those social inequalities. They failed, therefore, to appreciate that the basis of core-periphery differences lay with social formations. The core had expanded capitalist relations, first, by proletarianization—creating a new division of labour based on property relations and wage dependency— and second, by embourgeoisement—aligning the interests of a group within the discontented working classes to those of the bourgeoisie by changing the organization of production, by raising wages and introducing welfare programmes. Social formations in the periphery, however, never followed the same path. Their own ruling classes were the products of colonial collaboration, and proletarianization had been restricted in part by perpetuating and distorting precapitalist systems of production. Traditional systems of support allowed wages to remain lower than in the core, but at the same time their retention reduced the need for stabilizing but expensive embourgeoisement.

Third World social formations and their disarticulated modes of production, therefore, formed the basis for unequal relationships and slow development. Their patterns have and do vary widely; these differences are reflected in the resource-based economies of Indonesia and Bolivia; in the labour-intensive industries of the Asian NICs, and in the domestic and export industries of Mexico, Argentina and Brazil. [44] The point is that no matter how often the Third World called for additional aid, the redistribution of industry or for greater transfers of technology, it would never overcome inequalities until it first transformed both the internal and external relationships that begat dependency. Since the NIEO this has not occurred.

The core awoke to the potential threat a united Third World presented, particularly in the aftermath of OPEC's triumph, and responded by accepting the NIEO demand for greater direct investment in the Third

World. [45] (In 1960 the Third World received approximately half of total overseas direct investment. By 1974 its share had fallen to one-quarter. By 1981 it had risen again to one-third.) But it did so without increasing core-derived investment itself. The increase in oil prices provided a new source of funds which were quickly recycled to satisfy Third World demands. Its spread was not even. Given that two-thirds of all investment remained in the core itself and given also the reluctance of investors to invest where profits might not be substantial, the additional investments went largely to a small group of favoured countries, predominantly the NICs and after 1979 China. By the end of the 1970s even this additional investment was in jeopardy. As the availability of petrodollars declined, the core increasingly pushed the Third World away from its major lending institutions. Indeed by 1981 the availability of investment funds for the Third World had declined so much that upwards of one-third of all investment was being financed by the reinvestment of profits, not by the injection of fresh capital.

The export of capital continues to be the major means by which the core extracts itself from crises and seeks to restore profitability. In fact, as in the late nineteenth century, the income this generates is being withdrawn from the Third World to accommodate deficits in the core. The returns from periphery investment are unknown but a recent report indicated that the United States generated $32 billion from its overseas investments in 1981. Of this $13 billion was reinvested and the remainder remitted to the United States. Further, capital exceeding the value of new investments by $4 billion was also withdrawn. [46] As we noted in Chapter 3, Arghiri Emmanuel has suggested that this outflow of capital indicates that investment imperialism is little more than a myth. In percentage terms American investments in 1970 were substantially lower than Britain's when she was still a major power in 1914 (9.1 per cent of national income compared with Britain's 200 per cent). In the late nineteenth century, as today, recession and structural crises resulted not in a massive export of capital from the core but among other things in the search for new outlets for goods. Hence, Emmanuel argues, the underdeveloped world does not face a flood of restrictive and binding capital imports, but rather a dearth of investment made worse by internal structures and limited markets which restrict both the flow of capital and its use. [47] While this latter statement is undoubtedly true, it is necessary to remember that the Third World's dependence on core finance capital is at the root of the problem, a condition initiated and fostered by imperialism and no less governed by capitalism's continued subservience to profit.

During the 1970s the First World increasingly resorted to debt to prevent stagnation. Debt became a new source of profit as high inflation rates allowed repayment with cheaper dollars. The inflationary environment and the absence of attractive investment opportunities drove capitalists to speculation (in stock options, foreign currencies and trading commodities, financial and currency futures) in order to increase profits. [48] By 1982 the value of spot trading in currencies was over 15 times the value of world

Figure 9.2.   THE NATURE OF FOREIGN INVESTMENT TO THE THIRD WORLD

1.   WHERE DOES IT COME FROM?

OECD DIRECT INVESTMENT IN DEVELOPING COUNTRIES 1970 AND 1981.
Total OECD Direct Investments   1970 US$ 42,712 billion
(excluding support for private enterprises) 1981 US$131,252 billion

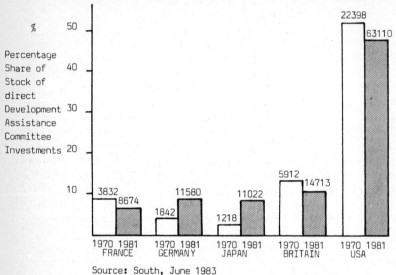

Source: <u>South</u>, June 1983

2.   PROPORTIONS   OF   DEVELOPMENT   ASSISTANCE   COMMITTEE
PRIVATE AND OFFICIAL INVESTMENT

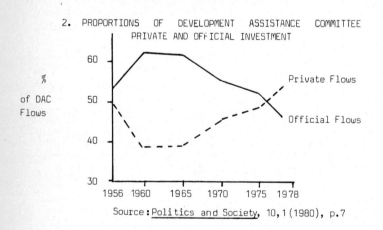

Source: <u>Politics and Society</u>, 10,1(1980), p.7

.rade. These huge sums of quickly movable private international liquidity not only overwhelmed official liquidity (global official reserves fell 23 per cent during 1980-1983) but also destabilized Third World exchange rates. [49] With recession and protectionism intensifying, speculative capital movements increasing, the Third World experienced greater balance of payments difficulties. By 1982 33 countries were in payment arrears and nearly 50 were engaged in debt-rescheduling discussions.

Between 1978 and 1980 the non-oil-producing Third World's deficit account with the World Bank rose from $26 billion to $70 billion. Further, as OPEC surpluses receded, the United States and other OECD nations sought to reduce the funds already available through international organizations. The European Bank for International Settlements slashed its loans in the first quarter of 1983 to $500 million, down from $9.8 billion in the corresponding period of 1982. [50] Similarly the International Development Agency (IDA), the World Bank's soft loan institution most important for the more underdeveloped Third World, which had earlier raised its loans from $4 billion in 1979 to $15 billion in 1981, suddenly cut its programme in 1982 and followed the IMF decree "of the lender of the last resort".

Because of rising deficits, Third World countries have had to turn more to private sources, at twice the cost, just to service their debts and cover deficits. Accordingly their share of the world's short-term debt rose from 41 per cent in 1981 to 66 per cent in 1982, [51] reinforcing the trend remarked upon earlier, that the interest and principal payments of developing countries are increasingly financing new core assistance. Given that the logical conclusion of such a trend is that countries will eventually pay out more than they earn for debts and servicing, it was not unexpected that the spectre of default should have been recently raised, most notably in the case of Mexico in 1982 and the Philippines in 1983-84. The Third World reaction was one of despondency. Gone were all the hopes for a NIEO. When the Non-Aligned Movement met in New Delhi in March 1983 it could only propose fresh talks with core countries to resolve the periphery's problems. Not many members even bothered to attend when these were eventually held in New York. UNCTAD's Secretary-General, Gamani Corea, told delegates at Belgrade in May 1983 that because of the world's "interdependence" there could be no prospects of improvement until recovery had first been effected in the core. [52] With short-lived Keynesian solutions to global problems already abandoned by both the core and periphery, there remained no liberal alternative to austerity.

The World Order Transformed

The deflection of NIEO demands did not automatically doom the Third World to continued dependency any more than colonialism once had. The spread of capitalism, Samir Amin noted, has continually created forces it cannot control. Since the Second World War these forces, most notably Third World rebellions, have assumed the initiative for change. The rise

181

Figure 9.3
EXTERNAL DEBT OUTSTANDING IN THE THIRD WORLD 1979-1984

	US$ billion		
	1979	1982	1984
ALL DEVELOPING COUNTRIES	472	724.8	812.4
Non-oil Developing Countries	395.3	633.3	710.9
Short Term Debt	59.1	125.1	88.1
Long Term Debt	336.2	508.2	622.8
Official Creditors (Government and International Institutions)	133.4	189.3	235.0
Private Creditors	202.8	318.9	387.8
Major Exporters of Manufacturers	154	249.9	274.8
Low Income Countries	62.7	81.8	94.8
Africa (excluding S. Africa)	45.3	62.5	70.7
Asia	92.8	152.6	179.3
Europe	55	73.3	76.6
Middle East	32.0	45.6	56.2
W. Hemisphere	157.8	283.1	310.5

Source : FEER, 27 September 1984.

f national liberation movements forced the core to decolonize. Revolu-
onary struggles in Asia, Africa and Latin America provoked fresh
sponses from the core, [53] while the OPEC revolt and NIEO demands in
e 1970s similarly demonstrated that change has been increasingly dic-
ted by forces generated outside the core. As capitalist industrialization
panded, first in its various colonial and later neocolonial forms, it fostered
w social interest groups whose raised expectations and incorporation
erely generated new contradictions which themselves produced tensions
d conflict. The diversity and growth of capitalist relations, therefore,
as served only to increase the scope for independent initiative and ac-
on. [54] Cooption and embourgeoisement are after all only short-term solu-
ons; they do not themselves remove the causes of revolt nor prevent its
currence.

When the Third World presented its demand for a NIEO, the core reacted
ensure that it did not further threaten economic stability. The First World
cepted in part the need to relocate industry and increase raw material
ices but only for the benefit of a small proportion of the Third World.
y creating a new international division of labour based on the export of
eap manufactures from the periphery, the core was thus able to break
hird World solidarity but at the cost of creating new and potentially
reatening contradictions; for a new international division of labour
ecessitated marginalizing working and sometimes middle classes within
th the First and Third Worlds. [55] The Brandt Report in particular had
ddressed itself to this problem, singling out those who in the future would
ose the greatest threat to the new world order—the core working classes
fected by industrial relocation, the marginalized and exploited classes
f the industrializing periphery, and the Third World nations which would
fectively become a Fourth World.

The new international division of labour, writes Hoogvelt, is based on
Triple Alliance of selected Third World bourgeoisies, whose states have
een granted increased participation in the world economy, and interna-
onal industrial and financial capital whose new strength will ensure that,
espite core state reluctance, redistribution will continue to benefit their
ew Third World partners.

It does not require a theory of conspiracy to believe . . . that even if the initiative for the OPEC price increases came from the oil-producing peripheral
countries* . . . the fact that OPEC has been permitted to get away with it, is
entirely due to the positive economic and financial consequences of the OPEC
action for international capital. And just as it was, at that time (1976), the interest of international capital which influenced and moderated the North's reaction to both OPEC and the NIEO, it will now again be the interest of international

t has been argued that the US encouraged OPEC to increase oil prices as a way of reduc-
g the impact of European and Japanese rivalry. Their economies were more dependent
 oil imports than the American economy.

Figure 9.4 : THE DISTRIBUTION OF FOREIGN
INVESTMENT IN THE THIRD WORLD

Net Receipts of Foreign Direct Investment from Main
OECD Countries, 1981.

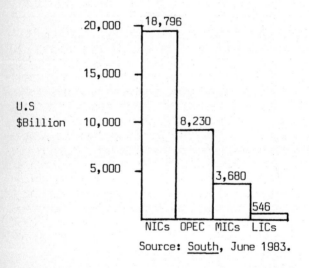

Source: <u>South</u>, June 1983.

capital that will bring recalcitrant Northern governments to . . . support their bankers' overseas adventures with massive injections of aid and public lending to those areas where international capital is most at risk. [56]

The interest of international capital, therefore, demanded that all notions of independent industrialization be squashed. It was as necessary to readjust the NIEO demands as it was to suppress self-reliant initiatives in Iran, Indonesia, Guatemala, Brazil and Chile during the 1970s. The use of a triple alliance to promote export strategies rapidly became the core's long-term alternative to periphery initiative that might frustrate core leadership and worsen intracore rivalry, and must be viewed as involving a similar kind of transformation as occurred during the so-called "second industrial revolution" in the late nineteenth century. Low profit rates, inflation and increased environmental restraints in the core, the availability of cheap labour in the Third World and the creation of new transportation, communications, and production technology have made transformation possible. [57] In the Third World it has been implemented through the NICs and Special Export Zones (SEZs).

The success of the NICs (principally South Korea, Singapore, Taiwan and Hong Kong in Asia, and Mexico and Brazil in Latin America) in sustaining high growth rates (8.2 per cent during the 1970s and 4.6 per cent in the early 1980s), in substantially increasing their share of exports as a proportion of GNP, and in raising domestic investment has become representative of the real NIEO. But it is a success subject to increasing constraints, not the least being the growth of protective barriers in the core to reduce the internal impact of the new international division of labour. Japan, as we noted earlier, restricted imports of cheap South Korean steel to protect her own steel industry, already overstaffed and working at only 63 per cent capacity. (NIC imports into the US have reduced domestic shipbuilding and textile production. Steel production has fallen 58 per cent.) South Korea's competitiveness is due largely to low wages. Whereas wages as a share of total steel costs amount to 24 per cent in the United States and 18 per cent in Japan, in South Korea they contribute only 5 per cent. [58]

Herein lies the NICs' major contradiction. Their export strategies depend on low wages, but low wages inhibit their ability to expand domestic consumption and aggravate internal social tensions, especially when state policies marginalize peasantry and even middle classes. One of the most dramatic examples of this second contradiction occurred in South Korea's Kwangju city in May 1980. Poor living standards and low wages among workers in the export-oriented electronics industry sparked off a major demonstration which was brutally suppressed. In response the city rose up in revolt, thereby precipitating a major military offensive costing some 2,000 lives, and new repressive civil legislation. [59] Hence Manfred Bienefeld's comment that the NICs illustrate the "disturbing possibility that . . . the competitive process is beginning to [indicate] that the most 'efficient' form of social organization of production" may be one more centralized and corporative than before. [60] Military and political repression enable greater competitiveness but, as Ted Wheelwright has commented, unlike the fascism of previous crises (in Germany and Italy) which were oriented toward internally-based national economic development, the NICs remain dependent on the metropolitan powers. [61]

Industrial expansion in the NICs is reliant upon continuing core assistance, particularly in the provision of markets for export products and in the encouragement of investment and technology flows. Seventy per cent of all direct foreign investment in the Third World goes predominantly to the NICs; this together with market access has most contributed to their industrialization. But it has not produced the kind of independence the NIEO anticipated and in fact has simply made the NICs the most debt ridden of Third World nations. Brazil for instance owes the core $US99 billion and has to meet $8-9 billion a year in debt service payments. These high costs and balance of payment difficulties have worsened the prospect for global economic recovery. In the Philippines the instability of a credit backed economy dependent on confidence became all too obvious in the political crisis generated by the murder of Opposition leader Benigno Aquino in August 1983. Within weeks investors withdrew over $1 billion dollars from the country, forcing the government to restrict planned development and to enact further austerity moves. Noting among other things the increased resort to "monetarist mumbo-jumbo" to offset problems generated by a credit-inflated world recession, one British economist warned, "We have been here before; we are back in the intellectual confusion of the 1930s". [62]

The SEZs (special export or free trade zones) are also part of the new division of labour and suffer similar problems. Under conditions of greater competition caused by recession, governments promoting investment in export zones are forced to offer greater and greater incentives in order to attract foreign investors, to the extent that their outlays often exceed the benefits gained. A recent ILO report on SEZs noted that they rarely contribute to domestic employment because raw materials used in the zone are largely imported. [63] If governments seek to overcome these problems by imposing stricter conditions, investors pull out or refuse to come, as China discovered in the case of its Shenzen zone. Low wages, poor job security and conditions of employment, the non-transference of technology and increased internal shortages and inflation have typified SEZs and made them the poor man's version of the NICs. Neither have resulted in the creation of a strong internal market on which to base viable economic development.

The promotion of NICs and SEZs have strengthened the kind of circular economic thinking that has become notorious during the 1980s. Faced with increasing balance of payments difficulties, Third World countries are urged to export more in order to pay for imports needed to foster growth and employment in export manufacturing sectors. The kind of restructuring this necessitates, they are told, "will need a longer recession". [64] It is not a problem of course which faces the Third World alone; it affects OECD nations as well, particularly those lower in the pecking order. In removing import controls with Australia under the CER agreement, New Zealand has been forced to rationalize industrial production. Invariably this has meant, first, increased unemployment as industries have shifted production to the larger and more profitable Australian market, and second, the marginalization of its South Island to the status of an agricultural zone.[65] Only when the cost of living falls dramatically in New Zealand will it again become attractive to core investors, by which time it will have become yet another off-shore production facility. Under conditions of free trade, capitalism's "law" of comparative advantage can be devastating in its effects. Recession merely intensifies the process. "When the economic cake stops growing", wrote Frank in 1982, "the music stops playing and everyone is obliged to scramble for another musical chair at the dinner table of austerity."[66]

Prospects

The embourgeoisement of the NICs (and OPEC), and the promotion of export strategies broke the Third World challenge of the 1970s. Their incorporation effectively tied Third World development to the retention and welfare of the old order. Having succeeded in weakening Third World solidarity, the core set about in the early 1980s to ensure that the new international division of labour did not weaken its own leadership of the world economy. For the United States in particular the promotion of the NICs served the same purpose as its earlier support of OPEC: to offset the challenge presented to its hegemony by the expanding EEC and Japanese blocs. Hence its preparedness to grant preferential access to the American market. By the 1980s, however, such access was beginning to have a damaging effect even on the American economy. The NICs were becoming too successful. Accordingly in 1983 the Trilateral Commission, celebrating its tenth birthday as the core's private strategist, informed the NICs that their trading privileges must end within two years. Commodity price stabilization, in particular the IMF's Compensatory Financing Facility (CFF)—which had been used to offset close to 60 per cent of the slump in commodity prices between 1979 and 1982—will be abandoned for greater trade liberalization. GATT will be extended to include the NICs, possibly also covering for the first time service investment and high technology flows.[67] Also the General System of Preferences (GSP), which granted duty-free status to Third World and particularly NIC imports, will be gradually reduced. Greater core penetration of and advantage over the periphery will thereby be assured.

In case the UNCTAD VI organizers still retained hopes for a NIEO, the US State Department warned in April 1983 that it would support only "evolutionary change" in the economic system "but with a concern to preserve the system's fundamentals". It was a warning, however, that was not addressed solely to the NICs.

> Experience has shown that development is achieved when sound, market-oriented domestic policies are pursued in a climate where private investment is encouraged and in a political atmosphere that fosters practical solutions to problems. If LDCs [Less Developed Countries] pursue such policies, they can benefit from increased international trade and investment. [68]

For the less developed Third World the core's application of free trade policies will be more disastrous. With the viability of SEZs undermined, commodity prices falling, and protectionism rising despite free trade pressures, the Third World has little to look forward to under the new division of labour. Even its own international organizations have failed to respond positively. UNCTAD's "dynamics of new interdependence" simply promises more of the same.

With the withdrawal of petrodollars as a major source of international loans and the core's preference for investment in the NICs, the LDCs have seen even their traditional sources of deficit financing dwindling during the 1980s. In 1983 the IMF faced liquidity problems when the United States refused to increase its quota share, thereby placing both its soft loan agencies for LDCs—the IDA and Enlarged Access Policy—in jeopardy. Less able to diversify exports because of raised competition and sluggish demand, and suffering from reductions in internal economic activity, the LDCs suffer most from the reduction in assistance. Containing over half the world's population and the greatest number of absolute poor (80 per cent of those below the poverty line), their poverty and lack of exploitable resources merely increase their vulnerability. [69] For them the core's export recovery strategy, and its declaration that the Third World must wait for the effects of recovery to trickle down, offers no hope. They will have little to lose, therefore, if in the adoption of policies of self-reliance or in the transformation of class relations they challenge the core's manipulation of the world economy. Indeed it would be entirely consistent with what we have discovered in our examination of the contemporary era. The development and spread of capitalism has continually raised contradictions to provide a dialectic of social and economic change within which the struggle for equality remains the most pervasive force of the contemporary era.

The transformations of the last decade are part of that dialectic and as such can form the basis for general comments concerning future world prospects. This is not an exercise in crystal-gazing, nor an affirmation of predestination. Rather as students of the contemporary era we must recognize that there is a pattern shaping the lives of our peoples which, while on occasions it has offered opportunities beyond the aspirations of our predecessors, has also imposed severe limitations from which it has become increasingly difficult to escape. What was true for the late Victorians, fed on visions of a brave new world and bolstered by a system of alliances that also—it was claimed—represented the march of civilization, may well come to pass for the generation born in the twilight of American hegemony. 1914 and 1939 were not quirks of fate, the descent of satanic forces upon an unsuspecting world. As Geoffrey Barraclough argued:

The risk of a world conflagration arises not so much when a state deliberately provokes a general war—that is hardly ever the case—as when the great powers' willingness to compromise and find peaceful solutions has been eroded by a growing sense of crisis and the sudden emergence of problems to which the traditional solutions provide no answer. [70]

That was the situation in the years immediately prior to 1914 when fears of recession and growing internal tensions drove the European nations to war. The spread of industrialization had generated intense intracore rivalry which made more difficult attempts to contain the contradictions of capitalist development and maintain the existing social system. War did not resolve those contradictions, nor of course did it prevent social change. In the depressed economic conditions of the decades which followed, the same imperatives remained. It is not difficult to comprehend why these should have been translated into new aggressive ideologies by the three countries which had most to lose by the emergence of the huge Soviet and American blocs and by growing internal class conflict, namely Germany, Italy and Japan. Nor is it difficult to understand why, having succeeded in establishing hegemony at the close of World War Two, the United States should be most reluctant to accept the waning of its predominance some 25 years later. At stake are not only the rights that leadership endows, but the whole economic and social structure built around it. To permit a decline in world status would be tantamount to opening its ruling classes to radical transformation, a choice plainly not acceptable to the ruling classes themselves.

The challenge to US hegemony was clearly at its strongest within the core, but it also found visible expression during the 1970s in the unevenness of recession, in the new assertiveness of Third World organizations, and more dramatically in the US foreign policy reversals experienced in Indochina. Certainly the American leadership responded quickly by applying new trade and currency measures to weaken the core challenge and consolidate a new international division of labour that both deflected Third World criticism and tied their development more firmly to the needs of US capital. Not unexpectedly these measures were only partially successful. US economic assertiveness antagonized its core partners and weakened its arguments for trade liberalization. Similarly, the renewed emphasis on export strategies, while drawing some Third World countries deeper into the US fold, simultaneously, intensified internal tensions which threatened to have an opposite effect. The marginalization of the LDCs, in part an outcome of this transformation of international relations, likewise promoted instability in the Third World and demonstrated the inadequacies of the new international division of labour. The achievement of new socialist gains in this quarter further frustrated US goals in the mid-1970s. Each reaction then has tended to produce a contradictory effect. Indeed, by tying Third World aid more firmly to immediate US foreign policy objectives, by refusing to sanction new international cooperation agreements (for example the Law of the Sea Treaty and the World Bank's energy lending facility), and by maintaining a high exchange rate as a symbol of US strength, the United States has contradicted the very multilateral basis of its hegemony. Cooperation has been gradually replaced by belligerent, self-centred, "go-it-alone" policies, multilateral trade by increasing resort to protectionism. "The irony of the US heavy-handed policies", Jeffrey Garten observed in 1985, is that they can only rebound on the US itself.

> After all, 50 per cent of the US budget is financed from abroad, the top nine US banks have loans to the Third World of more than 200 per cent of their primary capital base, 70 per cent of American production is exposed to international trade and 50 per cent of the growth in US population is attributable to immigration. An inward-looking economic policy which damages the US' trading partners will soon boomerang against Washington. [71]

If the logic of change was lost on the American leadership, the visible contradictions it aroused were not. Inevitably perhaps, wider and more drastic action was called for to overcome these. To defend a more aggressive US response, a new climate of urgency had to be fostered, a new Cold War. By abandoning detente, and the policy of linkage with the Soviet Union which had been pursued since the 1960s, the United States hoped to regain more effectively her declining hegemony. Not only would a renewed Cold War enable the US to obtain a margin of global strategic superiority (which it now recognized had most promoted US interests in the late 1940s and 1950s) but it would also provide it with a new lever to pressure rival core nations to bow to US leadership. Cold War would justify a reduction in European-Soviet trade links, thus promoting greater dependency on the United States, and would necessitate greater core expenditures on armaments which could also have possible beneficial flow-over effects for US manufacturing interests. The development of further conventional military capabilities, which a new war mood would similarly foster, might likewise enable future Third World revolutions and reversals in US foreign policy to be contained or prevented. [72]

For many people America's new aggressiveness was symbolized by the election of Ronald Reagan at the end of 1980. On attaining office in 1981 his first Secretary of State, General Haig, declared that the new administration's task was "the restoration of US economic and military strength". [73] Reagan undoubtedly subordinated US foreign policy to this objective more thoroughly than his immediate predecessors, but he too was succumbing to a momentum which by the 1980s would have been difficult for any president to reverse. The loss of Vietnam in 1975 and the new wave of revolutions in the Third World which followed, quickly developed into potent symbols of US decay. Similarly the Soviet policy of pursuing military parity with the United States now merged with the Russian and Cuban presence in many of the new revolutionary areas to drive numerous US politicians to demand a renewed margin of military superiority over the Soviet Union. As during the late 1940s, the vast increase in military expenditure such a policy required, could only be justified to the American people by maintaining that Third World revolutions were part of a renewed

Soviet attempt at world domination.

Undoubtedly changes in the US political climate facilitated the making of a second Cold War, as Fred Halliday has argued. But their significance lay in the implications they held for the established order, and it is in this respect that they are similar to those which confronted Europe's ruling classes before 1914 and 1939. The new demographic importance of the conservative south and west, the impact of the recession on purchasing power and more visibly of Japan and the NICs on traditionally important industrial sectors (iron and steel, textiles, ship building, cars) as well as on the much praised new technology sectors, combined with the disillusionment which followed Vietnam's loss to push America's ruling classes to demand a rebirth, [74] a way out of the crisis that would demonstrate renewed vitality and leadership to those affected by economic dislocation, and above all reverse the changes that had so obviously weakened America's economic and political standing in the world. Monetarist policies which took some of the pressure off capital and enabled further concentration were increasingly applied to a wide range of economic problems, along with the slashing of welfare provisions and liberal measures for abortion, gun controls and equal rights, the latter now being regarded as epitomizing American decay. The revival of militarism, therefore, was an all too natural banner for a "reborn" United States to display. It enabled "a demonstration at home and abroad" of America's regeneration and of its new hegemonic intent. [75]

The transition to a new aggressive assertion of US power began under President Carter in the late 1970s amid the publicity generated by the Iranian hostage crisis and the presence of Soviet bloc troops in Angola, Ethiopia and Afghanistan. US military expenditure was increased, the Diego Garcia base in the Indian Ocean expanded, a new task force established at Key West to facilitate intervention in the Caribbean, the commitment to withdraw troops from South Korea abandoned, and in 1980 the use of conventional and nuclear deployments in the Persian Gulf was authorized in the event of future threats to US interests. Increased pressure was also applied to the Soviet Union and this assumed both ideological (the plight of dissidents, Soviet "involvement" in the attempted assassination of the Pope, exaggerations of Soviet arms production) and economic (grain sanctions, forcing new military burdens on the Soviet Union to weaken her stagnant economy) dimensions. Pressure was also placed on her allies. The long process of reconciliation with Vietnam was abandoned with the result that she was forced to rely more heavily on a reluctant Russia for aid. In 1978 Vietnam joined Comecon and signed a 20-year friendship treaty with the USSR. "Let them stew in their Soviet juice", a US official remarked at the end of 1981. "Hanoi hasn't paid its dues; we aid those countries which we defeat, not those countries which defeat us." [76] In 1927 a Japanese official had made much the same comment about Manchuria. "The past history of Japan has always been that we punish those who behave impolitely towards us." [77] In the late 1970s the United States was experiencing the same need to secure its future as Japan had done during the 1930s.

The election of Ronald Reagan in late 1980 promised a more forthright expression of American intent than even Carter's substantial concessions. A stronger programme of economic warfare was introduced, designed in the instance of sanctions against Poland (December 1981) to aggravate the economic problems of the Soviet bloc so as to reduce its military capabilities and undermine its social system.[78] Reagan also increased US military expenditure by 13 per cent in 1982, raised the CIA's budget by one-quarter in 1983, boosted sales to client Third World states, and developed plans to increase the US nuclear arsenal by 70 per cent to some 40,000 operational warheads. Plans were also laid for the eventual use of the neutron bomb by NATO, for the development of new chemical warfare weaponry, and for space weaponry research. Half the space shuttle loads during 1982-84 belonged to the military.

The new US strategy to reassert its power, to confront socialism, to increase its presence in the Third World, to "roll back the iron curtain," and dominate its rival core partners has not been as easy to implement in the 1980s as it was after the Second World War. Not only is there no strong socialist threat, but its core partners no longer see their interests as subordinate to America's. Indeed it is their new strength which has in part precipitated the American response. That strength also enables them to take advantage of the new climate of bellicosity and intervention with increasing radical resort to the use of outright power as in the conflicts involving Argentina, Angola, Mozambique and Lebanon.

At the same time the wide publicity given Third World problems in recent years has made assertions of Soviet interventionism less acceptable as an explanation for Third World unrest. The invasion of Grenada in 1983 may have been symbolic of US intent, but the application of such determination to troubled allies in South Korea or the Philippines has awakened many Americans to the dangers a Cold War momentum could present. Vietnam has not been forgotten. Nor of course have the implications of nuclear war, particularly as many US military personnel have argued that by following a "counter-force" strategy, the US could win a nuclear exchange with the Soviet Union.[79]

Weapons exist for the purpose of winning wars, but their employment—as we have noted throughout these pages—is rarely the result of casual or irrational choice. The basis for all conflict is generated in specific economic and political conditions.

No one in his right mind supposes that unrest in the Third World is fabricated in Moscow, though the Russians might cautiously (but so far not very successfully) seek to profit from it. The neurotic fear of the Soviet Union and of communist subversion which appeared to inspire American policy under Reagan and Haig, the belief, real or pretended, that it has a finger in every pie, stirring up disaffection in Africa, Latin America and the Middle East, corresponds less to political reality than to a growing sense of frustration as the US watches a world built in the American image falling apart about its ears.[80]

The climate of bellicosity and confusion that has come to infect the 1980s is a reflection of the growing disjunction between economic and military power that we commented on at the beginning of this chapter, and of capital's inability to resolve its own contradictory tendencies without resort to militarism and economic nationalism. In the case of the United States, militarism and increasingly self-centred economic policies have been projected as solutions to the effects of inequalities within the Third World and between the Third and First Worlds. They are also symptomatic of the revival of competition within the First World itself as capitalism's restructuring has altered relations between core nations and between their bourgeoisies. "What we are witnessing," to quote Barraclough again, "as people were witnessing in 1911, is the crumbling of a system, the crisis of a society in the throes of irresistible change."[81]

Since capitalism began its historic task of uniting the world's peoples, it has been unable to withstand the pressures that have resulted from the unevenness of the process. It is perhaps too easy to regard the major preoccupations of the late twentieth century as reflecting choices between capitalism and socialism or the undeniable potential for self-destruction that a renewed Cold War offers. But popular preoccupations have a habit of confusing causes and responses. To illustrate this point we need only to recall our examination of capitalism's crises earlier in the century. The German and Japanese attempts at empire building were responses to the internationalization of capital and its unevenness, not in the first instance the cause of capitalism's problems. The same must also be said of contemporary preoccupations lest we are tempted to believe that the solution to all problems can be found in forthright actions that break the supposed impasse. That was the way of 1914 and 1939. As the century draws to a close it has become even more imperative that such distinctions be firmly grasped and that capitalism's role be accorded the primacy it deserves. Ever since its emergence in Western Europe and its incorporation of most parts of the world, capitalism has been gradually raising and socializing the productive forces of humankind. Never before has it been more possible to create a world system based on abundance rather than scarcity, and yet capitalism's very success has simultaneously widened the gap between those who possess that ability and those who do not or who are disadvantaged by capitalism's relations of production. Indeed herein lie the roots of tension and conflict within the world system and the source of people's inability to act as free agents and transcend history. From this contradiction also comes the dialectic of social and economic transformation that has been the focus of our introductory history, the product of the irreversible processes of change that have gripped the world in the last two centuries and the forces they have woken but cannot suppress.

Notes

1. R. Nations, "Pax Pacifica: The Reagasone Prosperity Plan", *FEER*, 14 July 1983, pp. 55-56.
2. Seymour M. Hersh, *Kissinger: The Price of Power*, Faber and Faber, London, 1983; *South*, September 1983, p. 28.
3. Hoogvelt, pp. 121-2.
4. See above chapter 5, p. 105.
5. Bienefeld, p. 33.
6. Fred Halliday, *The Making of the Second Cold War*, Verso, London, 1983, pp. 176-8, 259.
7. Henri-Claude de Bettignies, "Can Europe Survive the Pacific Century?" *Euro-Asia Business Review (EABR)*, 1 (October 1982), pp. 10-14.
8. Ibid., Jean-Pierre Lehman, "Japan and the World Economy: International accountability vs national interests", pp. 26-31.
9. Makoto Kikuchi, *Japanese Electronics: A Worm's Eye View of its Evolution*, Simal Press, Tokyo, 1983; Marcel Barang, "Vaulting into the Fifth Generation: Japan goes for No. 1", *South*, September 1983, p. 21.
10. Gene Gregory, "Asia's Electronics Revolution", *EABR*, 1 (October 1982), p. 45.
11. Mark Tharp, "The Stalemate Lingers", *FEER*, 22 September 1983, pp. 85-6.
12. Ibid., "Aiming to mate Asean with the Pacific Basin", 11 June 1982, p. 71.
13. C.J. Crough and E.L. Wheelwright, *Transnational Corporations and the Pacific*, Working paper 12, TNC Research Project, University of Sydney, 1982, pp. 44-6.
14. "Shift into overdrive", *South*, September 1983, p. 21.
15. *FEER*, 31 January 1985, pp. 28-31.
16. Jin Fuyao, *Guoji Wenti Yanjiu*, Beijing Institute of International Studies, 1983, also quoted in *FEER*, 14 July 1983, p. 62.
17. "Echoes of the Future", *South*, September 1983, p. 23.
18. Alavi and Shanin, p. 8.
19. F. Halliday, p. 184.
20. Fei Xiaotong, "New Path Way for Modernization," *China Reconstructs*, January 1985, p. 14.
21. Teresa Ma, "The Canton Connection", *FEER*, 28 July 1983, pp. 48-9.
22. Magdoff and Sweezy, pp. 122-3, 165.
23. Ibid.
24. F. Halliday, p. 183.
25. M. Westlake, "Where will the Buck Stop?" *South*, December 1984, p. 76.
26. F. Halliday, pp. 81-103.
27. Ibid., p. 145.
28. Short, p. 467.
29. *FEER*, 10 November 1983, p. 89.
30. *UNCTAD Bulletin*, 193 (May 1983), p. 14.
31. *South*, September 1983, p. 16.
32. Ibid., p. 13.
33. Hoogvelt, pp. 74-80, provides an excellent description of the origins of the NIEO which greatly influenced this presentation.
34. Ibid., pp. 80-4.
35. Ibid., pp. 86-95.
36. William Sutherland, "SPARTECA and Continued Problems of Dependence", *Review* 9 (November 1982), pp. 4-11; see also "Ballet Shoe and Cry", *Islands Business*, February 1985, pp. 47-8 on metropolitan quota and export

promotion restrictions which undermine the usefulness of SPARTECA.
37. Nabudere, p. 238.
38. D. Meadows, et. al., *The Limits of Growth*, Universe Books, New York, 1972.
39. Hoogvelt, p. 138.
40. M. Mesarovic and E. Pestel, *Mankind at the Turning Point*, North American Library, New York, 1976.
41. Jan Tinbergen and A. Dolman (eds.), *Reshaping the International Order*, Dutton, New York, 1976.
42. *North-South: A Programme for Survival*, Report of the Independent Commission on International Development Issues under the Chairmanship of Willy Brandt, Pan, London, 1980.
43. Hoogvelt, pp. 144-5.
44. Ibid., pp. 174-184; Ernesto Laclau, "Feudalism and Capitalism in Latin America", *New Left Review*, 67, 1971; I. Wallerstein, *The Capitalist World Economy*, Cambridge University Press, 1980, p. 19.
45. Hoogvelt, p. 60; *South*, June 1983, pp. 55-7.
46. Ibid.
47. Emmanuel, pp. 100-3.
48. Magdoff and Sweezy, pp. 10-11.
49. D. Avromovic, "Why the war on debts must be global", *FEER*, 5 April 1984, pp. 80-3.
50. Robert Manning, "Reagan: sights on a new order", *South*, September 1983, pp. 9-10.
51. *FEER*, 17 September 1982, p. 72.
52. *UNCTAD Bulletin*, 193 (May 1983), pp. 1-3.
53. Samir Amin, *Class and Nation; historically and in the current crisis*, Heinemann, London, 1980, pp. 189-94.
54. Hoogvelt, pp. 185-7.
55. Amin, *Class and Nation*, pp. 175-8.
56. Hoogvelt, p. 211.
57. Bienefeld, p. 44; Crough and Wheelwright, p. 7.
58. Mark Tharp, "Steel: Japan is NICked", *FEER*, 17 November 1983, p. 68.
59. Rob Stevens, "Death at Kwangju", *New Zealand Monthly Review (NZMR)*, XXV (November 1983), pp. 17-8.
60. Bienefeld, p. 48.
61. Crough and Wheelwright, pp. 48-9.
62. Sir Alec Cairncross, *FEER*, 23 June 1983, p. 83.
63. ILO Report, "Employment and Multinationals in Asian Export Processing Zones", Bangkok, 1983, quoted in *FEER*, 15 September 1983, pp. 88-91.
64. Ibid., 16 August 1983, pp. 39-45.
65. Wolfgang Rosenberg, "CER and the Labour Party", *NZMR*, op. cit., p. 12; see also W. Rosenberg, CER, Sanity or Sell-out? *NZMR*, Christchurch, 1982.
66. A.G. Frank, "The Old Order Changes Not", *FEER*, 3 September 1983, pp. 58-60.
67. Ibid., Trilateral Commission Report, 8 September 1983, pp. 58-60.
68. *UNCTAD Bulletin*, 193 (May 1983), p. 14.
69. Hoogvelt, p. 214.
70. Barraclough, *Agadir*, p. 168.
71. J.E. Garten, "In a self-destructive ideological warp", *FEER*, 21 February 1985, pp. 64-5.
72. F. Halliday, p. 102. The following interpretation owes much to Halliday's incisive analysis of recent events.

73. Ibid., p. 11-12.
74. Ibid., pp. 16-17.
75. Ibid., p. 130.
76. *FEER*, 25 December 1981.
77. Dower, *Empire*, p. 74.
78. F. Halliday, pp. 200, 241-7.
79. Ibid., pp. 52-53.
80. Barraclough, *Agadir*, p. 170.
81. Ibid., p. 168.

Further Reading

Chapter 1

a) Interpretation

G. Barraclough, *An Introduction to Contemporary History*, Penguin, Harmondsworth, 1969.

A. Bullock, "A Promethean Age", in A. Bullock (ed.), *The Twentieth Century*, Thames and Hudson, London, 1971, pp. 25-7.

E.J. Hobsbawm, "From Social History to the History of Society", in F. Gilbert and S.R. Graudbard (eds.), *Historical Studies Today*, W.W. Norton, New York, 1972, pp. 1-26.

F. Stern (ed.), *The Varieties of History, from Voltaire to the Present*, Macmillan, London, 1976.

D. Thomson, *The Aims of History, Values of the Historical Attitude*, Thames and Hudson, London, 1974.

b) General Histories

M.D. Biddis, *The Age of the Masses, Ideas and Society in Europe since 1870*, Penguin, Harmondsworth, 1977.

J. Foreman-Peck, *A History of the World Economy, International Economic Relations since 1850*, Harvester, Brighton, 1983.

J. Joll, *Europe since 1870, An International History*, Penguin, Harmondsworth, 1976.

D. Nabudere, *The Political Economy of Imperialism, Its theoretical and polemical treatment from mercantilist to multilateral imperialism*, Zed, London, 1978.

J.E. Spero, *The Politics of International Economic Relations*, Allen and Unwin, London, 1982.

H. Thomas, *An Unfinished History of the World*, Pan, London, 1981.

c) Nationalism

E. Kamenka (ed.), *Nationalism, The Nature and Evolution of an Idea*, ANU, Canberra, 1975.

T. Nairn, "The Modern Janus", in T. Nairn, *The Break-up of Britain, Crisis and Neo-Nationalism*, Verso, London, 1981, pp. 329-63.

A.D. Smith, *Nationalism in the Twentieth Century*, Martin Robertson, Oxford, 1979.

Chapter 2

C.M. Cipolla, *Before the Industrial Revolution, European Society and Economy, 1000-1700*, Methuen, London, 1981.

P. Deane, *The First Industrial Revolution*, Cambridge University Press, 1965.

E.J. Howsbawm, *Industry and Empire*, Penguin, Harmondsworth, 1969.

T. Kemp, *Industrialization in Nineteenth Century Europe*, Longman, London, 1969.

————, *Historical Patterns of Industrialization*, Longman, London, 1978.

E. Mandel, *Introduction to Marxism*, Ink Links, London, 1979.

K. Marx and F. Engels, *The Communist Manifesto*, Nentori, Tirana, 1981.

P. Mathias, *The First Industrial Nation, An Economic History of Britain, 1800-1914*, Methuen, London, 1983.

M. Morishima, *Why has Japan 'Succeeded'? Western Technology and the Japanese Ethos*, Cambridge University Press, 1982.

D. Nabudere, *The Political Economy of Imperialism*, Zed, London, 1978.

E.H. Norman, *Japan's Emergence as a Modern State*, Institute of Pacific Relations, Washington, 1940.

J.K.J. Thomson, "British Industrialization and the External World: A Unique Experience on an Archetypal Model?" in M. Bienefeld and M. Godfrey (eds.), *The Struggle for Development: National Strategies in an International Context*, Wiley and Sons, Chichester, 1982, pp. 65-92.

Chapter 3

a)   General

M. Barratt Brown, *The Economics of Imperialism*, Penguin, Harmondsworth, 1974.

A. Brewer, *Marxist Theories of Imperialism, A Critical Survey*, Routledge and Kegan Paul, London, 1980.

M. Edelstein, *Overseas Investment in the Age of High Imperialism, The United Kingdom, 1850-1913*, Methuen, London, 1982.

A. Emmanuel, "White-Settler Colonialism and the Myth of Investment Imperialsim", in H. Alavi and T. Shanin (eds.), *The Sociology of "Developing Societies"*, Macmillan, London, 1982, pp. 88-105.

L.K. Hunt, "Theories of Imperialism: The Writings of Hobson, Luxemburg and Lenin", in L.K. Hunt, *The History of Economic Thought, A Critical Perspective*, Wadsworth, California, 1979.

V.G. Kiernan, *Marxism and Imperialism*, Edward Arnold, London, 1974.

————, *European Empires from Conquest to Collapse, 1815-1960*, Leicester University Press, 1982.

V.I. Lenin, *Imperialism, The Highest Stage of Capitalism*, Foreign Languages Press, Beijing, 1975.

H. Magdoff, *The Age of Imperialism, The Economics of US Foreign Policy*, Monthly Review Press (MRP), New York, 1969.

————, *Imperialism: From the Colonial Age to the Present*, MRP, New York, 1978.

D. Nabudere, *A Political Economy of Imperialism*, Zed, London, 1978.

R. Owen and B. Sutcliffe (eds.), *Studies in the Theory of Imperialism*, Longman, London, 1972.

B. Porter, *The Lion's Share: A Short History of British Imperialism, 1850-1970*, Longman, London, 1975.

Area Studies

. Charlesworth, *British Rule and the Indian Economy, 1800-1914*, Macmillan, London, 1982.

Chesneaux, M. Bastid, M.C. Bergère, *China from the Opium Wars to the 1911 Revolution*, Pantheon, New York, 1976.

. Davidson, *African History, Themes and Outlines*, Paladin, Herts, 1974.

.C. Howard, N. Plange, S. Durutalo and R. Witton, *The Political Economy of the South Pacific*, James Cook University, Townsville, 1983.

C.Y. Hsu, *The Rise of Modern China*, Oxford University Press, 1983.

C.C. Huang (ed.), *The Development of Underdevelopment in China, A Symposium*, Sharpe, New York, 1978.

Narayan, *The Political Economy of Fiji*, South Pacific Review Press, Suva, 1984.

. Sen, *The State, Industrialization and Class Formations in India, A neo-Marxist perspective on colonialism, underdevelopment, and development*, Routledge and Kegan Paul, London, 1982.

. de Schweinitz Jnr., *The Rise and Fall of British India, Imperialism as Inequality*, Methuen, London, 1983.

. Shouyi, *An Outline History of China*, Foreign Languages Press, Beijing, 1982.

√. Sutherland, "The State and Capitalist Development in Fiji", PhD. Thesis, University of Canterbury, 1984.

Chapter 4

. Barraclough, *From Agadir to Armageddon, Anatomy of a Crisis*, Weidenfeld and Nicholson, London, 1982.

. Bullock, *Hitler, a Study in Tyranny*, Penguin, Harmondsworth, 1962.

Halliday, *A Political History of Japanese Capitalism*, MRP, New York, 1975.

Joll, *Europe since 1970*, Penguin, Harmondsworth, 1976.

.W. Koch (ed.), *The Origins of the First World War, Great Power Rivalry and German War Aims*, Macmillan, London, 1972.

√.F. Mandle, *Fascism*, Heinemann, Auckland, 1968.

. Nabudere, *The Political Economy of Imperialism*, Zed, London, 1978.

.M. Robertson (ed.), *The Origins of the Second World War, Historical Interpretations*, Macmillan, London, 1971.

.J.P. Taylor, *The Origins of the Second World War*, Penguin, Harmondsworth, 1963.

————, *The Course of German History*, Methuen, London, 1961.

Chapter 5

. Breth and I. Ward, *Socialism, the Options*, Hargeen, Melbourne, 1982.

.H. Carr, *The Russian Revolution from Lenin to Stalin, 1917-1929*, Macmillan, London, 1979.

Deutscher, *Stalin, A Political Biography*, Penguin, Harmondsworth, 1960.

————, *The Unfinished Revolution, Russia 1917-1967*, Oxford University Press, 1967.

. Kerblay, *Modern Soviet Society*, Methuen, London, 1983.

. Mandel, *Introduction to Marxism*, Ink Links, London, 1979.

. Marx and F. Engels, *The Communist Manifesto*, Nentori, Tirana, 1981.

D. McLellan, *Marxism after Marx, An Introduction*, Macmillan, London, 1980.
————, *The Thought of Karl Marx*, Macmillan, London, 1980.
A. Nove, *Political Economy and Soviet Socialism*, Allen and Unwin, London, 1979.
————, *An Economic History of the USSR*, Penguin, Harmondsworth, 1982.
————, *Stalinism and After*, Allen and Unwin, London, 1975.
A. Szymanski, *Is the Red Flag Flying: The Political Economy of the Soviet Union*, Zed, London, 1979.
E.P. Thomson, *The Making of the English Working Class*, Penguin, Harmondsworth, 1970.

Chapter 6

M. Bronfenbrenner, "The Japanese Model Re-examined: Why Concern Ourselve with Japan", in M. Bienefeld and M. Godfrey, *The Struggle for Development* Wiley and Sons, Chichester, 1982.
J.W. Dower, "E.H. Norman, Japan and the Uses of History", in Dower (ed.), *Origin of the Modern Japanese State, Selected Writings of E.H. Norman*, Pantheon New York, 1975, pp. 3-101.
————, *Empire and Aftermath: Yoshida Shigeru and the Japanese Experience 1878-1954*, Harvard University Press, 1979.
J. Halliday, *A Political History of Japanese Capitalism*, MRP, New York, 1975.
S. Kamata, *Japan in the Passing Lane, An Insiders Account of Life in a Japanes Auto-Factory*, Allen and Unwin, London, 1983.
J. Livingston, J. Moore, and F. Oldfather (eds.), *The Japan Reader, Volume One Imperial Japan: 1800-1945*, and *Volume Two: Post War Japan: 1945 to th Present*, Pantheon, New York, 1973.
M. Morishima, *Why has Japan 'Succeeded'?* Cambridge University Press, 1982.

Chapter 7

S. Ambrose, *Rise to Globalism: American Foreign Policy, 1938-1980, since 1938* Penguin, Harmondsworth, 1980.
C. Archer, *International Organizations*, Allen and Unwin, London, 1983.
E. Bradbury and H. Temperley (ed.), *Introduction to American Studies*, Longman 1981.
N. Chomsky, "The US: From Greece to El Salvador", in N. Chomsky, J. Steel and J. Gittings, *Superpowers in Collision: The New Cold War*, Penguin Harmondsworth, 1982, pp. 20-42
D.F. Fleming, *The Cold War and its Origins*, Allen and Unwin, London, 1961
H. Higgins, *The Cold War*, Heinemann, London, 1979.
D. Horowitz, *From Yalta to Vietnam*, Penguin, Harmondsworth, 1967.
V.G. Kiernan, *America: The New Imperialism, From White Settlement to Worl Hegemony*, Zed, London, 1980.
H. Magdoff and P. Sweezy, *The Deepening Crisis of US Capitalism*, MRP, Ne York, 1981.
D. Nabudere, *The Political Economy of Imperialism*, Zed, London, 1978.
J.E. Spero, *The Politics of International Economic Relations*, Allen and Unwin London, 1982.

W.A. Williams, *Empire as a Way of Life*, Oxford University Press, 1980.

Chapter 8

a) General
H. Alavi and T. Shanin (eds), *The Sociology of 'Developing Societies'*, Macmillan, London, 1982.

G. Kitching, *Development and Underdevelopment in Historical Perspective*, Methuen, London, 1982.

D. Nabudere, *The Political Economy of Imperialism*, Zed, London, 1978.

R.I. Rhodes (ed.), *Imperialism and Underdevelopment: a reader*, MRP, New York, 1970.

I. Roxborough, *Theories of Underdevelopment*, Macmillan, London, 1979.

J.E. Spero, *The Politics of International Economic Relations*, Allen and Unwin, London, 1982.

b) Area Studies
C. Ake, *Revolutionary Pressures in Africa*, Zed, London, 1978.

B. Brugger, *China: Liberation and Transformation, 1942-1962*, Croom Helm, London, 1981.

————, *China: Radicalism to Revisionalism, 1962-1979*, Croom Helm, London, 1981.

J. Chesneaux, *The People's Republic, 1949-1976*, Harvester, Brighton, 1979.

J.G. Gurley, *China's Economy and the Maoist Strategy*, MRP, New York, 1976.

P.C.W. Gutkind and P. Waterman (eds.), *African Social Studies, A Radical Reader*, Heinemann, London, 1977.

J. Jeffrey, *Asia—the Winning of Independence*, Macmillan, London, 1981.

P.S. Jha, *India, A Political Economy of Stagnation*, Oxford University Press, 1980.

G. Pendle, *A History of Latin America*, Penguin, Harmondsworth, 1976.

J.F. Petras, *Class, State and Power in the Third World, with case studies on class conflict in Latin America*, Zed, London, 1981.

W. Tordoff, *Government and Politics in Africa*, Macmillan, London, 1984.

c) The Development Debate
S. Amin, *Unequal Development*, Harvester, Brighton, 1978.

F.H. Cardoso, *Dependency and Development in Latin America*, University of California Press, 1979.

A.G. Frank, *Capitalism and Underdevelopment in Latin America, Historical Studies in Latin America*, MRP, New York, 1967.

R. Higgott, "Competing Theoretical Perspectives on Development and Underdevelopment: A Recent Intellectual History", *Politics*, XIII (May 1978), pp. 26-41.

A. Hoogvelt, *The Sociology of Developing Societies*, Macmillan, London, 1976.

. Huntington, *Political Order in Changing Societies*, Yale University Press, 1968.

C.Leys, "Underdevelopment and Development: Critical Notes", *Journal of Contemporary Asia*, 7,(1, 1979), pp. 82-115.

P.J. O'Brien, "A Critique of Latin America Theories of Dependency", in I. Oxaal, T. Barrett, and D. Booth (eds), *Beyond the Sociology of Development*, Routledge and Kegan Paul, London, 1975, pp. 7-27.

. Petras and K. Trachte, "Liberal, Structural and Radical Approaches to Political

Economy: An assessment and an alternative", *Contemporary Crises*, 3(1979) pp. 109-47.

W.W. Rostow, *The Stages of Economic Growth, A non-Communist Manifesto* Cambridge University Press, 1960.

P. Sweezy, *The Theory of Capitalist Development*, MRP, New York, 1969.

d) The Third World

N. Ball, "The Military in Politics: Who Benefits and How?" *World Development* 9, (6, 1981), pp. 569-82.

P. Baran, *The Political Economy of Growth*, MRP, New York, 1967.

S. de Brunhoff, *State, Capital, and Economic Policy*, Pluto, London, 1978.

A. Emmanuel, *Unequal Exchange, A Study of the Imperialism of Trade*, MRP New York, 1972.

S. George, *Feeding the Few: Corporate Control of Food*, IPS, Washington, 1979

D. Goodman and M. Redclift, *From Peasant to Proletariat, Capitalist Development and Agrarian Transitions*, Blackwell, Oxford, 1981.

A. Hoogvelt, *The Third World in Global Development*, Macmillan, London, 1980

A. Klieman, "Confined to the Barracks: Emergencies and the Military in Developing Societies", *Comparative Politics*, January 1980, pp. 143-63.

C. Leys, "The 'Overdeveloped' Post-Colonial State—A Reevaluation", *Review of African Political Economy*, 5 (January-April 1976), pp. 39-48.

H. Wolfe (ed.), *The Articulation of Modes of Production, Essays from Economy and Society*, Routledge and Kegan Paul, London, 1980.

W. Ziemann and M. Lanzendorfer, "The State in Peripheral Societies," in R. Miliband and J. Saville (eds), *The Socialist Register 1977*, Merlin, London, 1977 pp. 143-177.

Chapter 9

S. Amin, *Class and Nation: Historically and in the Current Crisis*, Heinemann London, 1980.

C. Archer, *International Organizations*, Allen and Unwin, London, 1983.

G. Barraclough, *From Agadir to Armageddon*, Weidenfeld and Nicholson, London, 1982.

M.A. Bienefeld, "The International Context for National Development Strategies Constraints and Opportunities in a Changing World," in M. Beinefeld and M. Godfrey (eds), *The Struggle for Development*, Wiley and Sons, Chichester, 1982 pp. 25-64.

R. Breth and I. Ward, *Socialism, the Options*, Hargren, Melbourne, 1982.

N. Chomsky, J. Steele, and J. Gittings, *Superpowers in Collision*, Penguin Harmondsworth, 1982.

C.J. Crough and E.L. Wheelwright, *Transnational Corporations and the Pacific* TNC Research Project, University of Sydney, 1982.

A.G. Frank, *Crisis: in the World Economy*, Heinemann, London, 1980.

————, *Crisis: in the Third World*, Heinemann, London, 1981.

F. Halliday, *Threat from the East? Soviet Policy from Afghanistan and Iran to the Horn of Africa*, Penguin, Harmondsworth, 1982.

————, *The Making of the Second Cold War*, Verso, London, 1983.

J. Halliday and G. McCormack, *Japanese Imperialism Today: Co-prosperity in Greater East Asia*, Penguin, Harmondsworth, 1973.

T. Hayter, *The Creation of World Poverty, An Alternative View to the Brandt*

Report, Pluto, 1983, London.

A. Hoogvelt, *The Third World in Global Development*, Macmillan, London, 1980.

T. Kemp, *Industrialization in the Non-Western World*, Longman, London, 1983.

H. Magdoff and P. Sweezy, *The Deepening Crisis of US Capitalism*, MRP, New York, 1981.

North-South: A Programme for Survival; The Report of the Independent Commission on International Development Issues under the Chairmanship of Willy Brandt, Pan, London, 1980.

M. Selden and V. Lippit (ed.), *The Transition to Socialism in China*, Croom Helm, London, 1982.

D. Smith and R. Smith, *The Economics of Militarism*, Pluto, London, 1983.

C. Tugendhat, *The Multinationals*, Pelican, London, 1973.

I. Wallerstein, *The Capitalist World Economy*, Cambridge University Press, 1979.

B. Warren, *Imperialism, Pioneer of Capitalism*, New Left Books, London, 1980.

G. Yu (ed.), *China's Socialist Modernization*, Foreign Languages Press, Beijing, 1984.

Index